California Counties

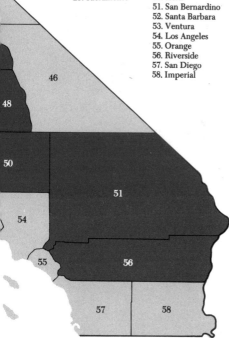

The Connoisseurs' Handbook
of California Wines

The wine ratings and descriptions in this book are based substantially on evaluations that appear in *Connoisseurs' Guide to California Wine*, the leading publication covering the California wine scene. The symbols and their meanings are as follows:

❀❀❀ An exceptional wine, worth a special search.

❀❀ A distinctive wine, likely to be memorable.

❀ A fine example of a given type or style.

♛ A wine of average quality. The accompanying tasting note provides further description.

δ Below average. A wine to avoid.

↯ A wine regarded as a "best buy," based on price and quality.

The Connoisseurs' Handbook
of California Wines
Second edition, revised

by Charles E. Olken and Earl G. Singer

Editors of *Connoisseurs' Guide to California Wine*

and Norman S. Roby

ALFRED A. KNOPF   NEW YORK

1982

Library of Congress Cataloging in Publication Data
Olken, Charles E.
The connoisseurs' handbook of California wines.

1. Wine and wine making—California.
2. Wine and wine making—United States.
I. Singer, Earl G., II. Roby, Norman, S. III. Title.
TP557.O43 1982   641.2′22′09794   81-48103
ISBN 0-394-71005-3   AACR2

Manufactured in the United States of America
Published November 17, 1980
Reprinted twice
Fourth printing, November 1981
Second edition, revised and expanded, September 1982

A NOTE ABOUT THE AUTHORS

Charles E. Olken and Earl G. Singer publish *Connoisseurs'
Guide to California Wine,* the foremost newsletter covering
the California wine scene. Norman S. Roby is
a well-known wine writer.
All three men live in the San Francisco area.

Composition by The Haddon Craftsmen, Inc.,
Scranton, Pennsylvania
Printing and binding by Kingsport Press, Inc.,
Kingsport, Tennessee
Maps by Jean-Paul Tremblay
End paper chart by James Paul Faris
Design by Lazin and Katalan with Betty Anderson

Contents

California Wine Regions

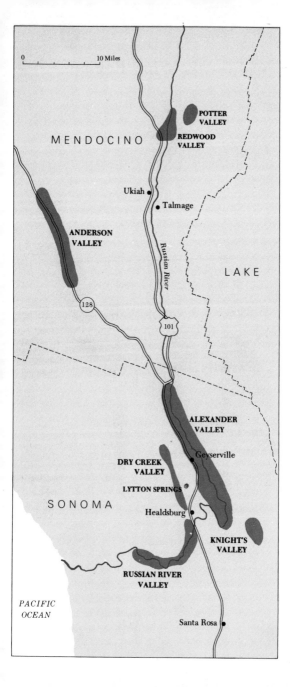

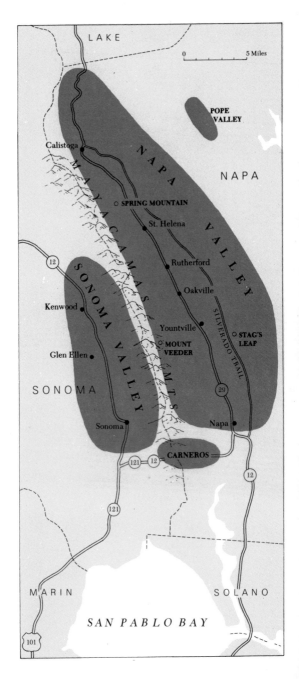

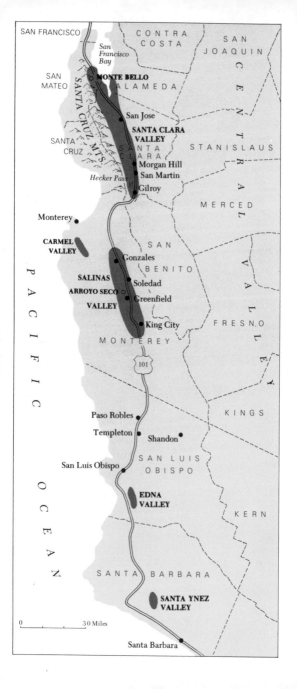

Introduction

In the early 1970s Baron Philippe de Rothschild, proprietor of Château Mouton-Rothschild, was quoted as saying: "California wines are like Coca-Cola—they all taste the same." By 1980 the Baron, like so many of his fellow Europeans, had apparently changed his mind. He came to America to announce a partnership with winery owner Robert Mondavi to produce wine in the Napa Valley.

The Baron is not the first Frenchman—and presumably not the last—to eat crow with his California Cabernet Sauvignon. California now stands center stage in the world theater of wine. Along with highly deserved recognition has come incredible growth—in vineyard acreage, in the amount of wine produced, in the number of wineries and places where grapes are grown. Where once the California wine scene was tranquil and relatively uncomplicated, there is now a veritable maze of names and styles, of "who's" and "where's" as difficult to sort out as anything Europe has to offer—and yet as rewarding.

Connoisseurs' Handbook of California Wines goes straight to the heart of the problem posed by this growth, presenting a comprehensive, concise, and authoritative survey of the wine scene as it exists today. Here are the grape and wine types, the regions large and small, the wineries and their wines, the terms used by winemakers and winelovers. Each producer, each area, each variety receives its own entry and is discussed in depth. A quick cross-check from winery to wine type to vintage can thus yield a complete picture of almost every important wine produced in California. Readers seeking specific buying guidelines are urged to view the vintage commentary and wine reviews in tandem.

Though California remains preeminent today for its sheer size and quality record, grape growing and winemaking are becoming increasingly important in other parts of the country as well. These local wine industries contribute to expanding wine awareness but they also merit serious attention for many of their wines. Therefore, substantial protions of this book are devoted to wineries and wines of the Pacific Northwest, the Midwest, the Northeast, and the Southeast of the United States. A few major wineries in Canada are also included.

An American wine is usually identified by either the name of the primary grape type (such as Chenin Blanc) used in making it, or by a more generalized name (such as red table wine) if it is a blend. The first section of the *Connoisseurs' Handbook* deals with the 101 most popular grape and wine types whose names appear on labels in America. GRAPE AND WINE VARIETIES includes virtually all the wine names and grapes likely to appear on labels, omitting only the grape varieties grown experimentally, those used for blending, and those not used to make wine. Included are everything from the leading varietals of California (Cabernet Sauvignon, Chardonnay, Zinfandel) to the most prominent varietals of the East (Seyval Blanc, Baco Noir), to generic names for blends (burgundy, white table wine) and specific wine types (champagne, rosé). In general, any name that turns up on more than one U.S. wine label will be found here.

The name on the label is only the beginning, however, when it comes to understanding the wine. Especially for the better wines, it is important to find out about the quality of the fruit from which the wine is made—and this quality is frequently dependent on weather during a particular growing season. No winery ever made exciting wine from poor-quality grapes. The second section, entitled CALIFORNIA VINTAGES, contains a detailed analysis of the year-by-year differences in grape and wine quality caused by annual variations in climatic conditions. It focuses on the five wines most amenable to this sort of critical analysis in California: Cabernet Sauvignon, Chardonnay, Pinot Noir, North Coast Zinfandel, and Amador County Zinfandel. These are the wines whose aging characteristics and general quality levels vary the most according to vintage and can be most reasonably described on a vintage basis. The judgments expressed here necessarily apply more directly to wines from Napa, Sonoma, and Mendocino counties than to wines from the Central Coast or from other still-developing areas where annual data on success or failure is still insufficient to identify distinct vintage patterns. Nevertheless, it is fair to say that the vast majority of wines produced in America that benefit from aging are covered by this discussion of California vintages. The information in this chapter is summarized in a convenient chart form inside the back cover.

The third section is WINE GEOGRAPHY. In compiling the information for it we were reminded of the old real-estate adage that the three most important determinants of success are "location, location, and location." In addition to a good grape variety and good weather, a good location is essential if one is to have a chance at making a fine wine. Unfortunately the helter-skelter growth of the California wine industry during the past decade has frequently led to the planting of high-priced varietals in the wrong places. This comprehensive guide to the areas where grapes are grown spells out in detail the characteristics and quality of the resulting wines. Regions as large as the Willamette Valley or Sonoma County are defined and discussed; so are smaller concentrations, such as Rutherford in the Napa Valley. This section also covers the main locations of California wineries.

Section Four, WINERIES AND WINES IN CALIFORNIA, in many ways represents the heart of the *Connoisseurs' Handbook*. Contained here is a comprehensive listing of California wineries and the wines they make, plus entries on trademarks and secondary labels—more than 400 in all. Each principal entry offers information about the history of the winery, its production and capacity, quality performance, special strengths and interests. Wines representative of its ability and achievement are described using specific tasting terms and given a quality rating. Where appropriate, general price levels are indicated, and wines we consider to be *Best Buys* are specially noted.

In Section Five, WINERIES AND WINES OUTSIDE CALIFORNIA, the *Connoisseurs' Handbook* covers the hundreds of producers in the Pacific Northwest and the rest of the country who are dedicated to making quality wines. Given the often less hospitable climatic conditions they face, producers in these states deserve recognition for both effort and performance, particularly for their table wines and champagnes. Thus, they are accorded the same treatment given California wines in Section Four.

The sixth section, WINE LANGUAGE, is a compendium of wine terminology and descriptions. Included here are terms and phrases appearing on labels, along with clear explanations of their customary usage and true meanings—for example the difference between "produced and bottled by" (a legally controlled expression meaning what it says) and "vinted by" (an uncontrolled phrase totally lacking in definition). This chapter also provides for the sensory terms most often used in describing the appearance, smell, taste, and feel of wine, lending consistency to their use in the wine discussions in Sections Four and Five. We have done this with care but also with the humble awareness that in matters of taste no judgment is final. One person's "complex, elegant, mouth-filling dinner wine" may well be someone else's "unassuming little Zinfandel."

TOURING, the final section, is dedicated to the proposition that nothing beats a first-hand visit to the vineyard and winery. This is a personal, opinionated chapter and probably does a better job of explaining our love affair with California wine than anything else in the book.

Our intention throughout the *Connoisseurs' Handbook* is to provide useful information in a crisp cross-reference format. Each section approaches the California—or American—wine scene from a different angle; yet employed in combination they become a complete guide to wines of the United States, making sense out of the sometimes dizzying array of wines, wineries, places, and words. We hope this book leads to a greater understanding of American wines—and even more, to the greater enjoyment of them.

Since the first edition appeared, the California wine industry has continued growing at a mind-boggling rate and, though less frenetically, winemaking in other states is also expanding. This second edition takes all of the recent changes into consideration and expands the coverage to include more than 125 new wineries and brands from California and another two dozen producers from elsewhere in the country. Earlier entries have been updated and revised. Not only have we added many more specific wine reviews, but also we have upgraded the wines from numerous producers, downgrading others whose quality has, alas, slipped. To keep abreast, travel was required and as a result, our touring section has also been greatly enlarged.

Much of the material in this book is based upon research and tastings conducted by *Connoisseurs' Guide to California Wine*, edited and published six times a year by Charles Olken and Earl Singer and distributed only by subscription. A one-year subscription is $25. The *Guide* reviews up to 1,500 wines, mostly vintage-dated varietals, each year. Readers of the *Handbook* interested in subscribing to *Connoisseurs' Guide* may receive a free copy of the latest issue by writing to *Connoisseurs' Guide to California Wine*, P.O. Box 11120, San Francisco, California 94101.

Grape and Wine

Varieties

ALEATICO Red muscat-flavored vinifera grape sparsely grown in California (169 acres). Rarely seen as a varietal.

ALICANTE BOUSCHET Thick-skinned red vinifera variety popular with home winemakers. Offered by 4 wineries; 4,956 acres in California.

ALIGOTÉ White vinifera grape of little distinction. All but phased out of production in France and California. Two Eastern wineries have offered it as a varietal.

ANGELICA A sweet, fortified wine traditionally produced from Mission grapes. Its name is reportedly derived from Ciudad de (City of) Los Angeles. Produced today primarily as a sacramental wine.

AURORA (or Aurore) Soft, fragrant, simple wines are generally produced from this white French hybrid, which is often used as a base for champagnes. 39 U.S. wineries produce a varietal.

BACO NOIR Very popular red French hybrid generally producing rather thin, fruity wines in most Northern states, but achieving a fuller, more mellow character in the Mid-Atlantic vineyards. At its best the variety offers vinous, slightly herbaceous qualities. 41 wineries offer it as a varietal.

BARBERA Red vinifera grape offered primarily as light-bodied, fruity, average-quality wine. Although most of the volume is in jug wine, a few producers offer limited quantities of Barbera in a traditional, robust style, high in acid and tannin and deeply colored in its youth. With bottle age it becomes softer and better balanced. 19,305 acres in California, of which 98% are in the Central Valley. Constitutes over 13% of the total production of California red wine. Produced as a varietal by 32 wineries.

BLANC DE BLANCS Literally, "white from whites." This term applies both to sparkling wines and to table wines made from white grapes. A few (but certainly not all) champagnes called Blanc de Blancs have substantial amounts of Chardonnay in their makeup.

BLANC DE NOIRS Literally interpreted, the term denotes white wine made from black-skinned grapes and applies to either champagne or still wines. It is seen increasingly on California table wines, partly due to the surplus of red wine grapes. In actuality, the color ranges from onion-skin to pink and sometimes even to light red. Since it lacks official definition, the phrase is often used as a prettier way to label lighter-hued rosés.

BURGER Pleasant, light, neutral wine used only for blending. Once the most widely planted white vinifera in California; now only 1,797 acres remain in production.

BURGUNDY Widely used generic name, invariably referring to inexpensive red wine blends unless specified as something else—such as White Burgundy or Sparkling Burgundy. Recently a few wineries have dropped the name in favor of Red Table Wine. Most California Burgundies are soft, slightly to medium sweet, and aimed at a broad market.

CABERNET FRANC An important red vinifera grape in France. Ignored until recently in the United States. Interest is now increasing in using the grape for blending with Cabernet Sauvignon and Merlot, its traditional use in Bordeaux. Still less than 200 acres in California. Few separately identified varietal bottlings have been offered to date.

CABERNET SAUVIGNON The most successful red vinifera grape in California, often yielding wines of world-class beauty and depth. In the best locations in Napa and Sonoma counties and the Santa Cruz Mountains, it develops ripe, almost black-currant concentration that is mixed occasionally with minty, weedy, herbaceous, and even vegetative overtones. Although frequently astringent when young, such wines soften gradually in the bottle (10–15 years for the biggest) until their full flavor shows through. These are the most expensive, and highly sought-after red wines of California.

The tradition of making high-quality Cabernets without blending has given way in recent years to blending experiments designed to emulate French practices with the grape. Today, many are blended with the Bordeaux varieties (Merlot, Cabernet Franc, Malbec, and Petit Verdot). In the medium price range, usually meant for earlier consumption, Cabernet wines are typically medium-bodied, only moderately tannic, and distinctively but less intensively flavored than the expensive top grade. In good vintages these wines can offer outstanding value. A few wineries offer rosé and Blanc de Noirs from Cabernet, and some are delightful. However, the occasional jug wine bearing the varietal name is Cabernet in name only.

The generally high quality of Cabernet wines is reflected in the rapid expansion of plantings: 24,000 acres (22,811 in CA), 615 in 1960. 302 wineries produce Cabernet, including 20 in the Pacific Northwest and 35 east of the Rockies.

CARIGNANE Red vinifera grape yielding well-balanced but ordinary, dull wines. Used primarily in California jug wines. As recently as 1969, Carignane composed over 30% of the total red wine crush (versus 15% in 1980). 11 California wineries produce Carignane as a varietal wine from 25,293 acres.

CARLOS Bronze muscadine cross released in 1970 by North Carolina Agriculture Experiment Station. Made as a varietal by wineries in North Carolina and Mississippi.

CARNELIAN Recently released (1972) red vinifera grape developed at the University of California, Davis. Its complex heritage includes Grenache, Carignane, and Cabernet Sauvignon. Most of the 2,749 acres in California are in the Central Valley, where the grape is expected to produce balanced wines with good color and body. However, no winery has yet made Carnelian a substantial part of its regular line.

CASCADE NOIR An early-ripening red French hybrid used for rosé and red table wine by a dozen Eastern wineries.

CATAWBA Red, white, and pink sweet wines with labrusca grapey flavors and aromas are produced from this popular, purplish-red native American hybrid. Made by some 45 wineries.

CAYUGA WHITE 16 wineries make wine from this white hybrid, developed by the New York Geneva Experiment Station.

CHABLIS Broadly used generic name for white table wine. A few wineries continue to use it on dry, crisp offerings that follow the style of wines from the Chablis region of France in some small way. Most, however, use it for inexpensive, slightly to quite sweet offerings blended primarily to sell in the jug wine market. One winery offers 5 Chablis (known in the trade as the Chablis quintet) that are identified by various colors and precious stones.

CHAMBOURCIN A relatively recent red French hybrid popular in France. Made as a varietal by 11 U.S. wineries. It yields light, simple red wines that have noticeable herbaceous qualities at their best.

CHAMPAGNE Synonymous with sparkling wine in the United States. The term applies to any wine whose carbon dioxide bubbles are derived naturally during a second fermentation in a closed container. Thus, if artificially carbonated, it cannot be called champagne. There are 3 ways to produce champagne: the *méthode champenoise*, the transfer method, and the bulk process.

CHANCELLOR NOIR Very agreeable dark red wine is produced from this French hybrid (which in France is the most popular of all the hybrids). 29 producers in the Eastern United States.

CHARBONO An all but unheard-of red vinifera grape yielding dark-colored, usually full-bodied, tart, and tannic wines in the hands of the half dozen producers who choose to offer it. For the most part, the wine's heaviness has not been accompanied by exceptional flavor. Less than 100 acres in California.

CHARDONNAY (also known as Pinot Chardonnay) White vinifera grape producing superb dry wines throughout the United States. Also widely grown in France in the Burgundy, Chablis, and Champagne regions. The character is fruity, sometimes appley, with good depth and intensity. Before being bottled, the wine is often aged in small oak barrels; this process increases its complexity. In the vineyard, yields are fairly low and the grapes command high prices.

The leading California Chardonnays have historically come from choice vineyards in Napa and Sonoma counties, and from a few isolated pockets in Santa Clara and Monterey counties. The 1970s planting boom expanded the geographical coverage of Chardonnay, and newer vineyards throughout the Central Coast are now matching and sometimes bettering efforts from more established areas. Regardless of heritage, such wines are ranked among the best in the world. They share a fat, rich style, full of fruit and possessing complex oak and ripe apple qualities, often with leafy or spicy dimensions. Lately another style of Chardonnay features less richness and higher acidity. These leaner, more angular wines, while often less complex than their full-bodied brethren, are usually easier to drink with the seafood and poultry featured in the new lighter-style cuisines. Wines of this latter type are often grown in the cooler vineyards of the Central Coast, in the Carneros district vineyards of Napa and Sonoma that front on San Francisco Bay, and in other North Coast vineyards relatively near the Pacific Ocean. The same style is prevalent in most of Oregon and throughout the northeastern United States. In whichever style produced, Chardonnay is typically the best dry white wine most regions have to offer.

Although most of the nation's Chardonnay acreage is in California (19,766 acres out of some 23,000 coast to coast), those other 3,000 acres represent the single largest commitment to a vinifera variety outside of California; 346 wineries offer Chardonnay, of which three-fourths are in California.

CHELOIS French hybrid that makes a fruity, dry red wine. Best when produced in a hearty style and aged 3 or 4 years. Produced by 26 U.S. wineries in the Northeast and Midwest.

CHENIN BLANC Popular white vinifera grape yielding fresh, fruity wine when grown in North and Central Coast vineyards. Delightful Chenin Blancs have flavors often compared to melons, pears, and peaches. Most are finished slightly sweet to medium sweet and are intended for early consumption. Dry-styled Chenin Blancs come mostly from smaller Napa and Sonoma producers, who often age their wines in small oak barrels. About 70% of California's 32,279 acres are in the Central Valley. Most of it shows up in wines from high-volume producers under a California appellation and is generally less expensive and less appealing than coastal-grown wines. 135 wineries offer Chenin Blanc, 119 of them in California.

CHIANTI A generic name borrowed from the popular Italian red wine and used by a few California producers for their heaviest, coarsest red jug wines. Usually overly sweet when offered by the largest producers.

CLARET A once popular generic name now used sparingly for red wines of no specific personality. By contrast, in international usage claret refers to the red wines of Bordeaux.

CONCORD Labrusca, grapey-tasting, usually sweet-finished wine comes from this native American hybrid, which is also the base for most grape juices, jellies, and candies. About 44 Eastern and Midwestern wineries produce it as a varietal wine. Concord is also the main grape in most kosher wines.

CYNTHIANA (also known as Norton) Grown commercially in Arkansas and Missouri, this red native hybrid is made into wine by 5 U.S. producers.

DE CHAUNAC An early-ripening, vigorous French hybrid yielding fruity, balanced red wines. 48 U.S. producers.

DELAWARE This native American hybrid grape is usually grown to produce sparkling wines and relatively dry, pleasantly fruity, white wines with a mild labrusca grapiness. 48 U.S. wineries produce it as a varietal.

DIAMOND Fairly aromatic, relatively dry, spicy-fruity wines with labrusca grapiness are produced from this white native American hybrid. 4 U.S. wineries offer it as a varietal.

DUTCHESS White native American hybrid producing fairly neutral, fruity, and relatively sweet wine with muted labrusca grapiness. 16 U.S. wineries.

EARLY BURGUNDY A dark-colored, medium-bodied wine without distinctive varietal character is made from this red vinifera grape. Usually used for blending. 572 acres in California. Occasionally seen as a varietal.

EMERALD RIESLING White vinifera grape developed by the University of California, Davis, by crossing Johannisberg Riesling with Muscadelle. Although available for the last two decades, only 2,832 acres have been planted, mainly in the Central Valley. About 16 wineries offer it as a varietal, usually in a light-bodied, slightly sweet style.

FINO A type of Spanish sherry, deriving its unique sharp, yeasty character from the development of a crusty, surface yeast called *flor*. In the United States almost all *fino* sherries derive their character from cultures of *flor* yeast introduced by the winemaker into the wine rather than from surface growths.

FLORA This white vinifera grape was developed by the University of California, Davis, by crossing Gewurztraminer with Semillon. It yields pleasant, flowery wines with a trace of spiciness and is used mainly for blending, often into Gewurztraminer. 372 bearing acres in California; 2 producers.

FOCH (or Maréchal Foch) Deep-colored, hearty red wine has been made from this early-ripening red French hybrid. Some winemakers are now moving toward producing lighter reds, reflecting the variety's Gamay origins. 40 U.S. wineries, primarily in the Northeast, offer Foch as a varietal.

FOLLE BLANCHE Light, vinous, tart wine without distinctive varietal character is produced from this white vinifera grape. The traditional variety for cognac. 354 bearing acres in California. 2 wineries.

FRANKEN RIESLING An infrequently used alternative name for the Sylvaner variety.

FRENCH COLOMBARD (also known as Colombard) Prolific, high-acid grape used primarily in generic jug wine and as the base for some inexpensive champagnes. It is first in total wine grape acreage in California and constitutes 41% of California's white wine grape crush. It generally has a fruity, vaguely weedy character that is easily submerged in blending. However, a few North Coast producers have managed to make interesting varietals with simple but pleasant fruitiness in both dry and sweet styles. The 44,252 acres in California are mainly in the Central Valley. 53 wineries offer it as a varietal.

FUMÉ BLANC Popular marketing name used for Sauvignon Blancs—usually dry-finished. The trend was started by the Robert Mondavi Winery in the late 1960s to signify a change to the fruity, crisp style of Sauvignon Blanc that now dominates the market.

GAMAY Another name used for the grape variety known popularly in California as Napa Gamay.

GAMAY BEAUJOLAIS Until the 1970s the red vinifera grape variety traditionally identified as Gamay Beaujolais was thought by California viticulturalists to be the true grape of France's Beaujolais region. Then it was reidentified as one of many versions (or clones) of Pinot Noir. It is a productive vine that requires cool growing conditions and can produce either a light- or medium-bodied red wine, depending on vineyard management and winemaking choices. Because of historical usage, the vines planted as Gamay Beaujolais have been allowed to retain the name if the proprietor prefers. Another grape, the Napa Gamay, is now thought to be from Beaujolais and may also be labeled as Gamay Beaujolais.

There are 59 U.S. wineries, mostly in California, producing wine under this name. There are 3,994 acres of the traditional Gamay Beaujolais (Pinot Noir) in California; 4,751 acres of Napa Gamay.

GEWURZTRAMINER Delicate to intensely spicy wines can be produced from this white vinifera grape. The wine is usually finished in a slightly sweet to medium sweet style to counter the grape's tendency toward bitterness, but dry versions have also shown quite well. Occasionally, the varietal grape will also be offered in a very sweet, late harvest style when the grapes are concentrated by *Botrytis.*

The key to capturing Gewurztraminer varietal character lies in choosing the right moment for picking. Harvested before maturity, the grapes produce wines with a delicate, floral character somewhat akin to Johannisberg Riesling. But for the winemaker with the patience to wait for the peak of ripeness, Gewurztraminer becomes intensely and distinctively spicy while still retaining much of its floral charm.

The grape's popularity has grown steadily during the last decade, and it is now offered by 124 wineries (including 19 in the Pacific Northwest and 22 east of the Rockies). There are 3,645 acres in California.

GOLDEN CHASSELAS Medium-bodied, dry to slightly sweet table wine of limited varietal character made from Palomino grapes. (Not related to Chasselas grape of Switzerland and Germany.)

GREEN HUNGARIAN A wine of simple vinous character is produced from this white vinifera. The 11 California producers have each created and popularized their own versions through generous blending with more distinctive varietals. These versions vary from dry to sweet. None are distinctive, interesting wines, and we suspect that the wine's appeal is related as much to habit and an interesting name as to quality considerations. 412 acres in California.

GRENACHE Almost entirely blended into generic rosé and red
jug wines, in which it often is identified by its distinctive
orange cast and the sweet, somewhat strawberrylike aroma
that it contributes. 25 West Coast wineries offer varietal
rosé and a few offer Grenache red table wines. Almost
17,560 acres are in California, and 300 acres are planted in
Washington.

GREY RIESLING Popular, modestly priced, simple-tasting white
vinifera wine produced from the grape known as Chauché
Gris in France, not a member of the Riesling family. The
widest-selling Grey Rieslings are offered in a dry, medium-
acid style with light fruity flavor and no oak-barrel aging.
They seem well suited for meals, especially seafood, and
have become mainstays on wine lists. Since the grape
has very muted flavors on its own, the better Grey Rieslings on the market are usually blended with a little
Sylvaner or Chenin Blanc to uplift their character. A few
slightly sweet and medium sweet versions are offered.
18 California wineries offer Grey Riesling. 2,424 acres
in California.

GRIGNOLINO In its few versions, this red varietal wine has a
light, spicy-fruity flavor and an orange hue. 3 California
producers and 55 acres.

ICE WINE Called Eiswein in Germany, it is produced from
grapes in which the juice (water) has frozen on the vine.
Thus, if pressed when still frozen, the must has a high
concentration of sugar. The wines are usually very sweet,
but the balance and quality vary. Ice wine is rarely made.

JOHANNISBERG RIESLING (also known as White Riesling in the
United States and simply as Riesling in Germany) A white
wine of distinctive varietal character, which is made in
every style from bone dry to very sweet dessert wine. The
typical character is fruity and delicate with a variety of
floral to fresh apple and apricot scents, depending on
where it is grown. In the 1960s most California wineries
produced this white vinifera in a dry, relatively austere,
high-alcohol style, sometimes with a hint of oak, usually at
the expense of the grape's subtle charms. The trend beginning in the 1970s, spurred by consumer demand and improved technology, has been to stress the grape's more
delicate qualities and to finish the wine in a slightly sweet
to medium sweet style. Another recent trend has been to
allow the grapes to be attacked by *Botrytis cinerea*, the
result being a luscious sweet wine. 203 producers of Johan-

nisberg Riesling (26 in the Northwest and 48 east of the Rockies); 10,186 acres in California.

KLEINBERGER RIESLING A light, fruity white wine is produced occasionally under this name by 1 winery. The grape may be a minor German variety.

LANDOT A red French hybrid that produces a light, fruity style of wine with faint labrusca notes. 6 Eastern producers.

LEON MILLOT A very early ripening red French hybrid similar to Foch. Produced by 6 Eastern wineries.

MAGNOLIA A muscadine with a strong flowery character used to produce a sweet white wine by 3 Southern wineries.

MALBEC Red vinifera. Important as a blending grape in California prior to Prohibition. There is some interest today in its revival for use in blending with Cabernet, based on the grape's use in Bordeaux. 57 acres in California.

MALVASIA BIANCA A somewhat perfumed table wine, usually finished medium sweet to sweet, is made from this white vinifera grape. 8 California wineries produce the varietal from 831 bearing acres.

MERLOT Long a variety of major importance in Bordeaux and in other wine-producing districts, Merlot has come into fashion in California only within the last decade. Indeed, it was during the Cabernet planting boom of the early 1970s that Merlot was sought and planted as a blending grape to round out, soften, and add some complexity to Cabernet. However, as the vines matured, several wineries discovered that Merlot was capable of yielding a wine that could stand on its own. The most critically acclaimed wines were medium-deep red to occasionally dark in color, had generous herbaceous-tinged aromas somewhat akin to Cabernet, but carried softer tannins and offered a more supple texture. Moreover, the best Merlots were rich and complex. As the result, the leading examples now command prices reaching toward the same levels asked for upper echelon Cabernets. Current acreage is 2,667, with 75 wineries involved, of which 13 are in the Pacific Northwest and 7 east of the Rockies.

MISSION Sweet white dessert wines are the traditional product from this red vinifera, which the mission padres introduced to California during the 1770s. Low acidity and weak color are two of the marks against it for table wine.

However, it is still planted in 16 California counties with 3,686 acres bearing; 7 wineries produce a varietal Mission.

MOSCATO (Moscato Amabile, Moscato d'Oro, Moscato Spumante) Italian spelling for muscat and name given to wines from muscat grapes by some California wineries. Usually in sweet style, they range from table wines to fortified wines and sparkling wines.

MOSCATO DI CANELLI Italian name for Muscat Blanc used by a number of wineries for their varietal wines.

MOSELLE Generic name used by a few U.S. wineries for medium sweet white wines. The name is borrowed from a German wine district noted for its delicate, floral wines.

MÜLLER-THURGAU White vinifera grape developed in Germany by crossing two strains of Johannisberg Riesling. The result is a grape that ripens with even less summer heat than Johannisberg Riesling and still exhibits much of its floral character. Müller-Thurgau has become the most widely planted grape in Germany and is being planted in Northern vineyards from Oregon to the East Coast. A few experimental plots exist in California, but there is not enough commercial acreage to be recorded.

MUSCADINE Common name for an American species native to the Southern states, of which the best-known variety is Scuppernong. 10 wineries offer Scuppernong or muscadine varietals, mostly as sweet white wines.

MUSCAT BLANC (also known as Moscato di Canelli and Muscat Frontignan) Light wine with strong muscatty, spicy aromas and distinctive flavors are produced from this white vinifera. Some producers have offered Muscat Blanc in a dry, crisp style, but most often it is finished slightly sweet to medium sweet and is suited to after-dinner use with fresh fruits. A few fortified wines. 1,397 acres in California; 21 producers.

MUSCAT FRONTIGNAN French name for Muscat Blanc used by some California wineries, primarily for sweet, fortified dessert wines.

MUSCAT OF ALEXANDRIA Aromatic, somewhat spicy table wines generally less interesting than Muscat Blanc are produced from this white vinifera, which is grown primarily for raisins and table fruit. Produced by 5 U.S. wineries (4 in California); 10,658 acres bearing in California.

MUSCAT OTTONEL A French hybrid with characteristics somewhat similar to Muscat Blanc. Planted in small quantities in Oregon and New York because it tends to ripen well in cool climates. 2 producers.

NAPA GAMAY Red vinifera grape long regarded as a poor Gamay relative in California vineyards, but recently gaining stature when identified (tentatively and possibly incorrectly) as the major Gamay grape of France's Beaujolais region. Amid the current confusion this grape is allowed to be called Gamay Beaujolais on labels and now commands a higher price per ton at harvest than the grape previously called Gamay Beaujolais. (See entries for Gamay and Gamay Beaujolais for more information on these interrelated wine names.) Napa Gamay yields fruity but simple wines that can be supple when produced in a light style, but are coarse and tannic when made heavier. Napa Gamay also yields rosés with good fruit and bright pink/ever so slightly orange color. 4,751 acres; 31 wineries offer a varietal.

NEBBIOLO This grape, responsible for the fine red wines from Italy's Piedmont region (Barolo, Gattinara, Barbaresco), was unfortunately dismissed decades ago in California because test plots yielded lightly colored, thin wines. New plantings in the early 1970s increased the bearing acreage to approximately 500, mostly in the hot Central Valley flatlands where the result will probably be lightly colored, thin wines. This grape deserves a better chance, and may receive it if experiments underway in Amador County and San Luis Obispo County pan out.

NIAGARA A popular white native hybrid. The wines possess a strong grapey labrusca flavor. Used in both relatively dry and sweet wines by 40 wineries centered in the East and Midwest.

NOBLE A recent muscadine cross, used to produce red wine by 4 Southern wineries.

PALOMINO (also known as Golden Chasselas) White vinifera grape used almost exclusively for sherry thanks to its natural tendency to produce high sugar and low acid and to oxidize easily. As recently as 1968, Palomino was the most widely planted of all white wine varieties in California. However, total acreage has steadily declined as a result of a public shift in taste from domestic sherry to table wines. There are now 3,746 acres in California.

PEDRO XIMÉNES White vinifera grape yielding intensely sweet, molasses candy–flavored wines. Important as a blending grape for cream sherries. There are 208 acres standing in California.

PETIT VERDOT Lightly grown grape used primarily for blending with Cabernet Sauvignon. A few stands of the grape exist, but not enough to be recorded.

PETITE SIRAH Long used in California as the backbone for blended North Coast burgundies, this red vinifera variety slowly came into its own during the early 1970s. Although there is some confusion over the grape's heritage (some say it is the minor French variety Duriff), most viticulturalists now agree that the grape is not the Syrah variety grown extensively in the Rhone region of France, as they once thought. Adding to the confusion are the several variants of Petite Sirah grown throughout California. Most Petite Sirahs on the market today come from coastal vineyards or from the Delta and Lodi regions, where the grape typically yields inky-colored wines that are high in tannin and have simple, vinous flavors and few complex nuances. Its popularity is based mainly on the ability of its brawny structure to stand up to hearty foods. There are 11,254 acres in California; about half lie in the warmest regions of the Central Valley, where the grape retains its role in blended jug reds. 82 wineries now produce Petite Sirah.

PINOT BLANC White vinifera grape that developed as a natural variant of Pinot Noir. It produces fruity, relatively subtle wines that are often compared to simple versions of Chardonnay. Coupled with its modest flavors, the grape's typical low yield in the vineyard has kept it from gaining popularity. The few outstanding examples come from the dedicated efforts of small wineries and often carry Chardonnay-like price tags. A number of large wineries use Pinot Blanc in their better champagnes because of its natural acidity and clean flavor. There are 1,930 acres, half in Monterey County. 24 wineries offer Pinot Blanc as a varietal wine. Recent research reports speculate that much of what is called Pinot Blanc in California is actually the Melon de Muscadet grape grown extensively in France's Loire Valley and source of the well-known Muscadet wines that go so well with shellfish.

PINOT GRIS Red, early-ripening variant of Pinot Noir. Offered by 9 wineries in Oregon and 3 in the Northeast.

PINOT MEUNIER (or Meunier). A red member of the Pinot family produced by 1 Oregon winery.

PINOT NOIR Red vinifera variety of high reputation in France —it is the principal red grape of Burgundy—that has proven a puzzle to California winemakers. In spite of large plantings (almost 10,000 acres) in a variety of soils and climates, California Pinot Noirs have too often been thin-flavored and simple. They have seldom offered the burgundian richness, complexity, and velvety texture on which the grape's reputation is based. Recent experiments with location, restricted crop level, fermentation technique, and clonal selections (over 200 strains of Pinot Noir exist) have begun to improve the wineries' performance—particularly for the producers with the patience and money to make a special effort. The favored vineyard locations are in cool areas, especially hillsides with limestone-enriched soils.

For the moment, however, the grape has lost its standing as California's number-two red variety (behind Cabernet), having been surpassed by Zinfandel for overall quality and popularity. The current surplus of Pinot Noir grapes has allowed the variety to be used increasingly and fairly successfully for Blanc de Noirs, rosé, and champagne. 149 wineries offer Pinot Noir, including 14 in the Pacific Northwest and 8 further east (Colorado to New York).

PINOT ST. GEORGE Red vinifera grape (unrelated to Pinot Noir) that yields simple, vinous wines whether made in a thin, fruity style or pushed into becoming more full-bodied and tannic. 638 acres in California.

PORT Generic name for sweet fortified wine, usually red, made in the style of the port produced in the Douro region of Portugal. Most U.S. ports are simple, cheap, quickly made sweet wines that are offered by large, full-line producers and bear little resemblance to their Portuguese namesakes. A handful of small wineries (and one or two of the big producers) treat the wine with more care and have offered ports that combine depth, richness, fruit, and aging potential.

RAVAT (VIGNOLES) A white French hybrid that is experiencing a popularity boom. The fruity aroma has an agreeable spicy note and there is a bit of complexity to the flavors. 13 producers, mainly in the Finger Lakes area of New York, but also being planted in Pennsylvania and Virginia.

RAVAT NOIR Several Pennsylvania wineries are leading a revival of interest in this French hybrid relative of Pinot Noir. The grape produces a fairly tasty red wine with a slight candy-like note in the aroma.

RED TABLE WINE Generic name increasingly used by North American wineries for their blended, inexpensive red wine—instead of the borrowed names, burgundy or claret.

RHINE In the United States, a generic term for ordinary white table wine. Usually sweet.

RIESLING A legally acceptable name for wine produced from any grape variety carrying Riesling in its name (Johannisberg, Sylvaner, Grey, and Kleinberger). In actual use, it is most often produced from one of the lesser varieties, since Johannisberg on the label would seem to carry more prestige than the term Riesling itself. The wine is usually slightly to medium sweet.

RKATSITELI A Russian white vinifera with small acreages in California and New York. The grape yields a neutral, well-balanced wine with good acidity.

ROSÉ Pink wine made for early consumption and usually oversweetened. The best achieve a fresh, fruity taste and carry enough acid to balance the sweetness that most rosés have. Many rosés carry varietal names (Zinfandel Rosé, for example), but rosés made from blends of grapes are not necessarily less attractive. The wine's color is achieved either by blending red wine into white or by keeping the juice of red wine grapes (which starts out white and acquires color during fermentation) from extensive contact with the grape skins. Either way, the trick is to acquire a pleasing pinkish hue that suggests a lighter body and taste than red wine. Use with food depends on the degree of sweetness.

ROSETTE (also known as Seibel 1000) Red French hybrid lacking intense color, frequently used to make rosé. A half-dozen producers in the East and Midwest.

RUBY CABERNET A red vinifera grape developed by the University of California, Davis, in a search for a more productive, Cabernet-style wine. The grape, a cross between Cabernet Sauvignon and Carignane, was expected to yield Cabernet character at Carignane's bountiful harvest levels. Unfortunately, it comes closer to the latter than the former

and usually produces vinous, soft wines of jug quality—perhaps because 96% of the 16,935 acres are in the Central Valley. 29 wineries offer Ruby Cabernet.

SAUTERNE Generic name used by a few U.S. producers for white wine, usually sweet, always of jug wine quality. Fewer California wineries seem to be using the name these days, but it remains a popular product for Eastern wineries.

SAUVIGNON BLANC Very popular white vinifera grape, second only to Chardonnay for the production of dry white wines in California (many of which are identified as Fumé Blanc on the label). The grape typically has distinctly weedy, sometimes grassy aromas and flavors and can be intensely fruity. When produced as a dry wine, it is often aged in small oak barrels to round out its somewhat monochromatic character. In the dry style, Sauvignon Blanc often makes a suitable companion to fish and shellfish. A few wineries offer sweeter versions, but the number is decreasing due to the rapidly growing demand for the dry, crisp style. An occasional late harvest wine also appears. The 7,269 acres of Sauvignon Blanc are concentrated in the coastal counties of California, although highly respectable wines have also come from the Sierra foothills and from the Pasco area of Washington State. There are 163 producers of Sauvignon Blanc, mostly in California.

SAUVIGNON VERT All-but-forgotten white vinifera of modest aroma and flavor that is no longer grown commercially in France and is diminishing in California. 3 producers and 528 acres in California.

SCHEUREBE A cross between Sylvaner and Johannisberg Riesling developed in 1916 by German botanist Scheu. It is widely planted in Germany and is now attracting some interest in California where 2 wineries are making a varietal. This white grape ripens under cool conditions and is capable of developing late harvest characteristics.

SCUPPERNONG Native American variety of the muscadine species grown mostly in Southeast and Gulf Coast states. It has a unique musky flavor and is usually sweet-finished. 5 wineries offer Scuppernong, commercially cultivated as early as 1809.

SEMILLON Vinifera grape popular from the 1930s through the 1960s as a dry, white, medium-bodied table wine with a figlike perfume. Acreage has expanded very slowly during the past decade, and the grape has been surpassed as a dry wine by Chardonnay and Sauvignon Blanc. A few very sweet dessert wines are made from Semillon. There are 15 producers in California, 5 in the Northwest, and 3 in Virginia. 2,848 acres in California.

SEYVAL BLANC This white French hybrid has become one of the mainstays of Eastern winemaking. It takes well to cold climates where it can be counted on to yield fruity, crisp wines. There are 69 wineries producing Seyval Blanc, mainly east of the Rockies; limited amounts are grown in the Northwest.

SEYVE-VILLARD Wine made from several varieties developed by French hybridist Seyve-Villard are labeled with his name by 3 wineries.

SHERRY Generic name in the United States for any fortified wine styled more or less after Spanish sherry. Though some follow the traditional *solera* system of aging, most U.S. sherries are "baked," or heated and briefly aged. The cream-style sweet sherries have been the best of the domestic products. The drier-style sherries are not competitive with the Spanish imports.

SOUZAO Portuguese grape used sparingly for port in California (197 acres). 2 wineries offer it as a varietal port.

SPARKLING BURGUNDY A generic name used for red sparkling wines in the United States. Some are attractive; none outstanding.

STEUBEN Native red hybrid made as varietal wine by 4 Midwestern and Eastern wineries. It has a light, grapey quality.

SYLVANER (also called Sylvaner Riesling and Franken Riesling) Not a Riesling at all, this white vinifera once enjoyed great popularity in California for its lightly spicy and floral qualities. However, increasing sophistication among wine drinkers and the change in style for Johannisberg Riesling seem to have reduced its popularity. Acreage has remained low: only 1,411 acres are planted. 10 wineries now offer it as a varietal.

SYRAH (also known as French Syrah and Shiraz) Low-producing grape of the Côtes du Rhône in France, yielding Hermitage wines among others, this red vinifera is attracting new attention among California winemakers who for years thought their Petite Sirah vines were this variety. 4 wineries make small lots of varietal wines. Less than 100 acres in California.

THOMPSON SEEDLESS Very versatile warm-climate white vinifera that produces wine with a bland character. It is widely used in common white blends as a base for inexpensive sparkling wine and brandy. However, more than half the world's raisins are made from this variety, and it is also the foundation of California's fresh table grape business. 259,513 acres, over half in Fresno County.

TINTA MADEIRA Red vinifera grape used in some California ports for its rich flavor and deep color. 658 acres, mostly in the Central Valley.

TRAMINER A name used in California for various white varietal wines. Two decades ago, the name was mistakenly applied to the now abandoned Red Veltliner variety. Later the name Traminer was correctly used for the grape variety originating in Europe and grown sparsely in California. It is the parent of the now popular clone Gewurztraminer, which is far more intense and spicy than its progenitor. The term Traminer has disappeared except for references in wine books.

VIDAL BLANC This white French hybrid is rapidly gaining popularity because of its pleasant, fruity flavors and good balance. Successful versions, offered both in soft, slightly sweet and dry, crisp styles, are among America's most enjoyable wines coming from nonvinifera grapes. 38 wineries east of the Rockies produce Vidal Blanc.

VIGNOLES (also known as Ravat 51) 13 wineries vinify this white French hybrid, usually in a relatively dry, crisp style.

VILLARD BLANC Simple, fruity wine is made from this white French hybrid. 14 producers east of the Rockies. Interestingly, it is the most widely planted white hybrid in France.

WHITE RIESLING (known popularly as Johannisberg Riesling) The legally required name in the state of Oregon; used also by many vineyardists and wineries in other states when an alternative to the borrowed Johannisberg name is desired.

ZINFANDEL Often called "the mystery grape" because its origins are unknown, Zinfandel is the most widely planted red vinifera (29,148 acres) and also the most versatile wine grape grown in California. In medium-warmth coastal locations, especially sheltered hillsides, Zinfandel can yield full-bodied, intensely flavored wines with substantial tannin. The best wines of this type show Zinfandel's vigorous, berrylike, sometimes spicy varietal character. Late harvest Zinfandels (usually high in alcohol, occasionally sweet) can come from coastal locations also.

Parts of Sonoma County—notably the Dry Creek Valley and the Geyserville area—as well as Amador County in the Sierra foothills have yielded most of the exceptional Zinfandels of the last decade. The grape is also widely grown in the Central Valley, including the Lodi area, which contains almost 40% of the state's total plantings. Lodi Zinfandels often display the variety's berrylike character, but tend toward flatter, earthier qualities at the expense of the lively, vigorous character found in other regions. Jug wine Zinfandels exhibit the same lack of virtue found in most wines of the area.

A versatile grape, Zinfandel has proven successful in a variety of other styles, including light fruity red wine, rosé, Blanc de Noirs, and Nouveau, and even as the base for champagne. There are 196 producers of Zinfandel, including several (Ridge, Fetzer, and Monterey Peninsula) who offer up to a half-dozen separate vineyard-designated Zinfandels.

California Vintages

Cabernet Sauvignon

1968 Copious vintage yielding wines that have big flavors, are
tannic and long-lived. A number of successful bottlings
offered a ripe, classic style. Many have reached their peak,
but a few are still developing. Excellent vintage.

1969 An underrated vintage at first with most wines seeming
light, short-lived, and lacking in full ripeness. With time
the wines developed into nicely flavored, soft, and very
likable Cabernets. Generally a good vintage, and a few
wineries using hillside grapes offered very good quality.
Most have peaked.

1970 A mild wet winter followed by severe spring frosts that
reduced the crop by half. Fine warm late summer weather
brought the grapes to full ripeness. Many wines are intense
and ripe in character, but are revealing a lack of balance
with aging. Most are ready now, whereas others remain
magnificent and long-lived. An excellent vintage generally
less classically styled than 1968.

1971 A cool spring followed by a long, unusually cool growing
season. Good-sized crop. Most wines were average in quality, with the best coming from hillside and mountain vineyards. Generally on the thin, simple side and ready now.

1972 July heat spells reduced the crop. Late-season rains hurt
the quality by creating mold. Most wines lacked varietal
character and depth; they tended to be simple and short-
lived. Quality generally ranged from dull to disastrous. A
few exceptions were quite pleasant. Drink up.

1973 Wet, cool winter followed by a warm spring and lovely
long, moderate weather during the late season. The crop

was large, and after some aging the quality now approaches excellent. Many wines possess fine character, balance, and harmony and have both tannin and a firm structure to hold for several more years. Above-average to excellent year.

1974 Cool spring and summer weather culminated in a warm harvest. The crop was large, and the grapes became very ripe. The best are dark, concentrated, tannic, and potentially long-lived. But some of the biggest, most tannic wines are fat and ponderous. Many medium-priced, less tannic versions are drinkable now, but will hold to 1983–85. A few of the special bottling types will mature close to 1990 and may last until the next century.

1975 Early frosts and rains were followed by a cool, unusually long season. Most wines are proving to be lightweights—pleasant, sometimes elegant—but few are superb versions. Straightforward in character, without great depth, the wines are likable and similar to the 1969s. Some are ready now, but the best have 4–8 years to go.

1976 First drought year, combined with heat spells and late rains. The grapes were tiny with high sugar levels and low acidity. The wines are dark, tannic, and high in alcohol, but generally lack intense fruit and firm structure. The best should peak in 1985–86; the majority before then. Atypical vintage.

1977 The second drought year was both drier and cooler. Wineries were better prepared, but the harvest experienced sporadic rains. The wines are better balanced than the 1976s, also less tannic and alcoholic. Generally average in varietal character, but lacking in depth and longevity. Average quality.

1978 Late September heat waves sent sugar levels soaring, sometimes too high. The crop was large. Many wines are ripe and tannic with high alcohol levels and over-ripe flavors. Those lower in alcohol often lack classic Cabernet depth. Less age-worthy than '74. Above-average to good quality overall.

1979 Heat waves followed by prolonged and persistent rains throughout September created problems. Many vineyards developed rot; some went unpicked, especially in the North Coast. A number of wines turned out better than expected, though quality appears to be uneven. Average to slightly below-average quality.

1980 Unusual combination of high sugar and acid levels created early enthusiasm. Could become an exciting vintage for big-style, ripe, tannic wines. Rapid maturation of the grapes suggests less aging potential than either 1973 or 1974. Style similar to that of 1978. Above-average quality likely.

1981 Intense June heat spell reduced the crop by 20% or more. Early harvesting raises questions of varietal character. Most wines possess adequate color and acidity, pointing toward early maturity. Likely to become an average quality, light style vintage.

Chardonnay

1972 Small crop due to hot July weather, but rather impressive quality. Almost all Chardonnay was picked before the mid-harvest rains. Many Napa versions were ripe, richly flavored, and oily in texture. They have also aged well. A fine vintage and probably the first with more than a handful of excellent renditions. Most are mature by now.

1973 Some frosts and a warm July. The grapes matured early, and it was a good-sized crop. Most wines possessed good varietal fruit and intensity, decent balance. The best are as developed as possible; some are faded by now. Above average.

1974 Odd—cold, wet, then a cool July. Adequate ripeness, decent acidity, generally average quality. Somewhat simple, light, fruity varietals. Virtually all reached an early peak. Few exceptions.

1975 Good rainfall, a few frost scares, only light damage. Ideal May and June weather allowed a long, cool growing period perfect for Chardonnay. Ripe wines with tremendous flavors, complex, yet well balanced. Began as nicely structured, closed-in wines; now blossoming as harmonious, flavorful wines. Several long-agers from this exceptional vintage.

1976 Drought and dehydration; tiny berries and uneven ripeness. Picked during or after intense heat spell. Some Botrytis in Napa. Wines are ripe, fragrant, powerful, often low in fruit with insufficient acid to balance the high alcohol level. A real contrast to the classic 1975s. Best to drink soon.

1977 Second drought year with unexpected late August rains forcing some early harvesting of marginally ripe fruit. Those who delayed in this on-again, off-again vintage achieved more flavorful, better-balanced wines. A surprising number of successes with above-average intensity, depth, and balance in a pleasantly restrained style. The best will not develop until 1982–83. Many above-average wines; very few classics.

1978 Enormous rainfall (55 inches) and a cool spring without frost damage. September was warm, sending sugars very high, very quickly. Many wines are ripe and fragrant, full-bodied, but often excessively alcoholic. Some lack acid balance. The quality is above average, but the lack of balance makes longevity questionable.

1979 Despite perils of mid-harvest rains, the quality turned out better than expected. The style is moderately ripe, fruity, with good acid balance. Napa and Sonoma wines are surprisingly rich and balanced. Several fine examples came from Monterey, Edna Valley, and Santa Barbara grapes. The best will age until 1983–85.

1980 Early enthusiasm over high sugars and acids was dampened by difficult, sluggish fermentations in the North Coast. Those fermented dry could prove to be big, rich, concentrated wines. The crop from the Central Coast was reduced, but the wines range in quality from average to above average with very few exceptions.

1981 Record-setting heat waves caused sunburn and diminished the crop. Mild August and early September weather may have saved the wine. The sugar levels were high in the North Coast areas, but acidity varied, usually being low. The Central Coast experienced a small crop, but the sugar and acid levels were better balanced. Should compare in quality to '78, though with less intensity. Questionable for longevity.

Pinot Noir

1971 Cool weather prevailed during the early season, enabling several wineries to produce above-average-quality versions. Even the best (Chalone, Hanzell, Sonoma Vineyards, Inglenook Cask, and Sterling) are ready now.

1972 An average, uneventful year overall with mostly dull wines. Hanzell, Mount Eden, Swan, and ZD excelled. Drink now with few exceptions.

1973 Another average-quality year offering many ordinary wines. Several rose above ordinary—Hoffman Mountain Ranch, Mondavi, Kenwood, and Chalone. Mount Eden was superb. All others are now ready.

1974 A very consistent year yielding wines uniformly lackluster in character. Only Mount Eden, Swan, Fetzer, and Chalone offered wines of ❀❀ or better quality.

1975 The coolish, elongated growing season offered hope for major breakthroughs, but the quality was just above average overall. Santa Cruz Mountain Vineyard's wine was superb. All others should be ready now.

1976 Drought, dryness, and the first fruits of long-term experiments combined to make this an unusual vintage. Fine wines were made by Carneros Creek, Caymus, Burgess, and Hoffman Mountain Ranch. Others showed improvement, though suffering somewhat from a lack of balance.

1977 The crop was small, picked before the rains. The vintage produced more successes than 1976, and several wines have better depth and balance. This could prove to be a watershed vintage for Pinot Noir. Initial enthusiasm was confirmed by the releases from Carneros Creek, Chalone, Firestone, Kenwood, ZD, and many others.

1978 Many vineyards were maturing when the heat spell arrived, and the grapes ripened quickly, reaching high sugar levels. The wines possess good color and strong alcohol, but balance is a problem for longevity. Chalone, Firestone, and Carneros Creek are exceptions to the general above-average ranking.

1979 Variable quality due to mid-season rains. A few vineyards were harvested too early before the storms; several too late afterward. Sugars were not as high as in 1978, with acidity about average. A few exceptional wines are flavorful, balanced, and excellent in quality. In general, quality ranges from average to slightly above. Newcomers Acacia, Calera, and De Loach advance the cause.

1980 Early cool weather prolonged the maturation and delayed the harvest. High sugars and fine balancing acidity raise hopes for a banner vintage. The wines have deep color and moderately intense flavors. Early signs are encouraging for wines of fine character and good aging ability.

1981 Excessive heat and a short growing season dashed most hopes. Many wines lack color and varietal flavor, and will struggle to reach average quality. The only exceptions are likely to come from the Carneros region and parts of the Central Coast.

Zinfandel

1970 Hot summer weather brought Zinfandel to full ripeness, but few wineries were taking the varietal seriously. Those who did made rich, well-flavored wines. Most have reached their peak.

1971 A cool vintage yielding wines of moderate ripeness. Joseph Swan and Kenwood's Lot #1 excelled, joining Ridge and Sutter Home as quality leaders. Others were generally of average quality. Wines now at peak or beginning to fade.

1972 Late-season rains hindered quality overall. Many wines were thin and early-maturing. Clos du Val, Ridge, and Fetzer Vineyards proved to be exceptions. Drink now.

1973 An ideal warm harvest without any rains led to many successful barrel-aged, ripe fruit Zinfandels. Uniformly good conditions in Napa, Sonoma, Mendocino, and Amador counties. Many new wineries entered the field, and both Amador and Sonoma counties won recognition in 1973. Many ❀ versions and several were of ❀❀❀ quality. Excellent year. Most ready to drink now.

1974 Another fine, warm year resulting in numerous ripe, full-flavored Zinfandels. All regions fared well, but quality overall was just a shade below 1973. Many are near full maturity.

1975 Generally cool with late-season showers. Napa versions were less intense; those from Sonoma and Amador generally above average in quality, but early-maturing. Ready now except for the most tannic.

1976 Drought and heat waves brought Zinfandel to extreme ripeness, making it the greatest success of the vintage. Many late harvest versions were offered. Others were heavy, intense, and tannic. An excellent vintage, the best of which need further cellaring.

1977 Another drought-year extravaganza for Zinfandel. Many outstanding ripe and balanced wines from Sonoma County. Again, an abundance of late harvest wines. Cellaring required for most.

1978 Most wines are ripe, fruity, substantial in tannins and alcohol, but reasonably well-balanced for their size. Many late harvest versions are dry, with several made slightly sweet, but even they are somewhat balanced. Well above average quality from Sonoma, Amador, Napa, and Mendocino.

1979 Very mixed quality. Some wines made from grapes picked before the heavy September rains are of average quality. Those made from grapes picked later are high in alcohol and tannin, but many are low in acidity. Amador fared better than most for concentrated character; Napa and Sonoma are more variable.

1980 Many vineyards reported high to runaway sugar levels. Ripe, warm, tannic, and likely to range from concentrated to late harvest, slightly raisined. Amador seems under control, with Napa bordering on very ripe and Sonoma wines better than average in quality.

1981 Early signs were gloomy with "spotty quality" a generous judgment. Many North Coast vineyards refused to ripen fully; others got caught in late September rains. Napa was hard hit, and Sonoma less so. Mendocino and Amador counties are the best early bets for balance and flavor.

Amador County Zinfandel

1970 Only Sutter Home was involved to any extent. Above-average quality.

1971 Generally less ripe and average in quality. Matured early.

1972 An uneventful vintage of average-quality wines. Mayacamas late harvest Zinfandel was the only exception. Most are past prime.

1973 An above-average vintage. Monteviña joins Sutter Home and Harbor to focus greater attention on Amador. These wines are now fully developed.

1974 A warm year, but ideal. Many coastal wineries purchased Amador grapes and brought forth ripe, briary, sometimes brawny Zinfandels, often the vintage's finest. Carneros Creek, Mount Veeder, and Ridge contribute to the region's success. Many ❀ and several ❀❀ Zinfandels. Excellent vintage. Most are close to ready.

1975 Average quality, generally less intense than 1974. The best, however, were powerful, high-alcohol wines. San Martin and Monterey Peninsula entered the Amador sweepstakes. Most are drinking well now.

1976 Powerful, very ripe wines resulted from the drought conditions. Several late harvest Zinfandels were made. The style was heavy, tannic, and high in alcohol. Some versions are too dried out and lack fruit. The best will develop to 1983–84.

1977 Fairly ripe grapes again, but the wines are better balanced than in 1976. The crop was reduced by drought conditions. The wines have good color, moderate tannins, and average fruitiness. Quality ranges from average to good, with short aging potential.

1978 Good winter rainfall and a warm spring and summer. Rains in early September delayed the harvest and deprived the grapes of their usual dehydration. Many are balanced with ample flavors, but lighter in body and tannin than in previous vintages. Vintners who waited were able to make late harvest wines. Above-average quality.

1979 A rather normal vintage, meaning wet in the winter and warm and dry in the summer months. Amador escaped the rains but not the September heat wave. The crop size was average. The wines are generally fruity and moderate in tannins with fairly high alcohol. They lack the intensity of 1974. Several new local wineries join in and earn ❀ rating. Above average, but early maturing.

1980 A cool early season followed by blasts of heat near the harvest produced a large crop. The sugar levels were in the modest 22°–23½° range, but the acids were high. The wines are intensely fruity, moderately tannic, and nicely balanced. Above-average quality, ranking just behind 1978. Should develop to 1984–85.

1981 Harvesting began about one month early, and the early hot spells reduced the quantity by 20% on average. Because the sugar level was less than usual, most wines will be under 14% alcohol and balanced, with medium intensity of flavor. Few late harvest versions. Slightly above average for now.

Wine Geography

*Place names listed here are in California, unless
otherwise noted. Counties are indicated in parentheses
following the place name.*

ALAMEDA COUNTY Across the bay from San Francisco, this
county has 2,000 acres of grapes grown primarily in the
Livermore Valley and owned in large part by local winery
interests, including Wente and Concannon. The leading
varieties are Grey Riesling and Semillon (about 300 acres
each). Other important varieties are Chardonnay, Chenin
Blanc, Petite Sirah, Sauvignon Blanc, and Zinfandel (100–
150 acres each). In the last several years, about a dozen
small- to medium-sized wineries have sprung up in the
Oakland-Berkeley area, the result of home winemakers'
turning commercial. A few have full-time staff, but most are
still at the hobby stage.

ALEXANDER VALLEY (Sonoma) Lying along the course of the
Russian River from the point where it passes Cloverdale in
the north until it sidles around Healdsburg before turning
toward the sea, the Alexander Valley is a landlocked piece
of topography every bit as temperate and hospitable as the
Napa Valley. Near Geyserville, heat-loving varieties like
Zinfandel bask in long sunny days and reach levels of ripeness similar to the adjacent Dry Creek Valley. In other
pockets, especially those near the river and those at the
southwestern corner of the valley near Healdsburg, growers do very well with Gewurztraminer and Johannisberg
Riesling. There are more than a dozen wineries in this area,
including such important names as Simi, Alexander Valley
Vineyards, Jordan, and Souverain. About half of Sonoma
County's vineyard acreage is in the Alexander Valley.

AMADOR COUNTY Tucked into the Sierra foothills in an area
southeast of Sacramento, logging- and vacation-oriented
Amador County would be indistinguishable from all the
other gold-country foothill locations save for the Zinfandel

grown there. The major grape-growing areas are in the Shenandoah Valley and in Fiddletown (both near the town of Plymouth). It was the rediscovery of Shenandoah Valley Zinfandel in the late 1960s that put Amador County on the wine map and encouraged more than a dozen coastal wineries to go there for grapes. Now, many of the grapes are used by the several new, small wineries that have recently come into existence. Amador County has about 1,100 acres in vineyard, of which 450 were in existence prior to the vinous rebirth of the area. Zinfandel is 82% of the acreage.

AMERICAN The least specific appellation of origin. It usually suggests that the wine was blended from grapes grown in 2 or more states.

ANDERSON VALLEY (Mendocino) Tucked into a narrow valley halfway between Ukiah and the Pacific Ocean is the very cool (Region I and Region II) Anderson Valley. Its 500 acres are mostly devoted to Gewurztraminer, Chardonnay, and Pinot Noir, with limited amounts of Zinfandel and Cabernet Sauvignon. Edmeades, Husch, and Navarro wineries are located in the Anderson Valley.

ARROYO SECO (Monterey) Lying west of Greenfield in a protected area nestling against the foothills of the coastal mountains, the Arroyo Seco area has, in its first decade as a wine-growing area, yielded the superb late harvest Rieslings from Wente and a brace of exciting Chardonnays grown in the Ventana Vineyard and produced by MEV, La Crema Vinera, Sarah's Vineyard, Leeward, and by Ventana itself. Wente, Masson, and Mirassou are also major growers in Arroyo Seco.

AUGUSTA *Missouri* Historic winegrowing area west of St. Louis undergoing a modest revival movement. The name has received official governmental recognition for use on wine labels as much for nostalgia as for present achievement.

CALIFORNIA The number-one state in population, cars per capita, wine and beer consumption, and natural beauty, California is also number one in vineyard acreage. Some 85% of all wine produced in the United States is grown there and, by some estimates, 95% of the premium wine is Californian by origin. Wine grapes are grown in 41 of California's 58 counties and are the third most important agriculture crop of the state. Today, California boasts more than 330,000 acres planted to wine grapes and produces 400 million gallons of wine annually. In the last decade,

California's reputation for premium wine has gained nationwide and even worldwide acceptance. However, California specializes in the production of everyday table wine —as much as 80% of the annual output.

On wine labels the name California means that the grapes come from anywhere within the state and usually signifies a blend of grapes from areas that very often include the hot Central Valley. (See table on pages 228–29 for grape acreage by county and variety.)

CALISTOGA (Napa) As the Napa Valley floor fans out north of St. Helena, the climate becomes increasingly warm. With few exceptions, the area around the city of Calistoga is rated medium to high Region III in heat accumulation and is most noted for Zinfandel and fat-styled Cabernet Sauvignon. Wineries located in the Calistoga area include Sterling, Cuvaison, Stonegate, Chateau Montelena, and Robert Pecota.

CARMEL VALLEY (Monterey) Twisting inward from the Pacific Ocean near the town of Carmel is the Carmel Valley. The few vineyards occupy the uplands and receive enough sunlight and warmth to be somewhat more hospitable for red wine grapes than the Salinas Valley, several miles directly inland.

CARNEROS (Napa and Sonoma) Stretching across the southernmost parts of Napa and Sonoma counties, immediately adjoining San Francisco Bay, Carneros is a cold growing area (Region I and low Region II) by California standards and is suited mostly to early-ripening varieties: Chardonnay, Johannisberg Riesling, Gewurztraminer, and Pinot Noir. The climate is tempered by lingering fogs and early afternoon breezes off the bay. Much of the early wine activity of the Napa and Sonoma valleys was centered in Carneros. Today, such important wineries as Charles Krug, Beaulieu, Louis Martini, Chandon, Buena Vista, Acacia, and Carneros Creek have substantial vineyard holdings in Carneros. In addition, Carneros has been identified on labels as the place of origin for a number of wines produced by Kistler, Martin Ray, Veedercrest, and Berkeley Wine Cellars.

CENTRAL COAST The territory lying south of San Francisco and north of the city of Santa Barbara—San Mateo, Santa Cruz, Santa Clara, San Benito, Monterey, San Luis Obispo, and Santa Barbara counties—is known as the Central Coast. After a brief flirtation with the term North Coast, most wineries in this area are now proudly identifying their wines with specific Central Coast appellations. In addition, many Napa and Sonoma producers have added Central Coast wines to their lists.

CENTRAL VALLEY California's Central Valley, the most productive agricultural area in the state, consists of 2 major sections. The Sacramento Valley runs north of Sacramento almost to the Oregon border; the San Joaquin Valley stretches south from the Sacramento-Stockton area to Bakersfield. There are isolated pockets of grapes in the north amounting perhaps to 8,000 acres. In the southern portion of the Central Valley, spread across 8 counties, are approximately 195,000 acres of grapes—about 60% of California's total. Until recently, Central Valley wines were very often bad: low in acid, oversweetened to hide a multitude of faults, and possessing a cooked quality in aroma and flavors. The bad days are not totally past, but things have certainly changed. Varieties with higher natural acidity (French Colombard, Barbera, and Chenin Blanc) have been planted where once Carignane, Mission, and Grenache ruled. Grapes are picked with more care so that balance and ripeness are achieved. And the modern technology of temperature-controlled, stainless-steel fermentation keeps the fruit cleaner and retains whatever freshness is brought into the winery from the vineyard.
Central Valley products at their best are the cleanest, most flavorful everyday drinking wines in the world. Of course, at their worst they remain as unpalatable as ever.

CLARKSBURG (Yolo) Lying at the eastern edge of the Delta region, Clarksburg-area vineyards are heavily oriented toward Petite Sirah and Chenin Blanc. The area is fairly warm (Region III to low Region IV).

CLEMENTS DISTRICT (San Joaquin) Every now and then a winery will get hold of some Zinfandel from the Clements district, in the foothills east of Lodi, and bottle it up with its own appellation. We have never been fond of the results and apparently neither are they—judging by the one-time nature of most experiments.

CUCAMONGA (San Bernardino) This once burgeoning vine-growing region clings tenaciously to life in spite of air pollution and urban encroachment. The vineyards are old and fast disappearing, having dropped from 25,000 acres before World War II to under 8,000 acres now. Most wine from the area is of bulk quality, and even that which bears varietal nomenclature lacks interest. A sad fate for a proud winegrowing region.

DAVIS (Yolo) 90 miles northwest of San Francisco, on the doorstep of Sacramento, sits the pretty university town of Davis, home of the University of California, Davis. Its Viticulture and Oenology Department, the best in the country, has trained winemakers for more than half the premium wineries in the state and has contributed substantially to the high-technology orientation of most California wineries. The university is a world leader in studies of grapevine diseases, vineyard problems, and grape clones.

DELTA The watery lowlands lying in the triangle formed by the confluence of the San Joaquin and Sacramento rivers is known as the Delta. On some of the many islands and on the surrounding hills, there is a small but moderately successful winegrowing industry. The Delta is warm (Region III to low Region IV) but more moderate than its Central Valley neighbors because of the San Francisco Bay fog and wind that cool it. Its prominent grape-growing locations are Clarksburg in southern Yolo County and Mandeville Island in northern San Joaquin County.

DRY CREEK VALLEY (Sonoma) 6 miles long and (on the average) 1 mile wide, this valley runs northwest-southeast in Sonoma County near Santa Rosa and Geyserville. It has a medium temperature range and long growing season and is home of Dry Creek, Preston, Lambert Bridge, and A. Rafanelli wineries. Most noted for the very fine Zinfandel (among California's best) grown on benchlands with southern and southwestern exposure. Dry Creek Zinfandels often exhibit archetypical, ripe Zinfandel flavors and are full-bodied and well-balanced with good aging potential. Its use as an appellation is spotty, but growing. Sauvignon Blanc and Chenin Blanc are often successful in cooler, lower grounds and in areas near the valley mouth bordering the Russian River Valley. The Lytton Springs area is immediately adjacent.

EDNA VALLEY (San Luis Obispo) In this coastal plain bordering the western edge of the Coast Range, about 600 acres have recently been planted. Most of the acreage is owned by Paragon Vineyards, which commits the bulk of its Chardonnay and Pinot Noir to the Edna Valley Vineyard winery. However, Paragon's other grapes are sold to many Central and North Coast wineries.

EISELE VINEYARD (Napa) This well-known Cabernet Sauvignon vineyard in the warm Calistoga area produces fat, generously flavored wines in years like 1971 and 1975, when wines from cooler climates tend to turn out on the thin side. In recent years, grapes from this vineyard have gone to the Joseph Phelps winery. They had gone to Ridge, Souverain (of Rutherford), and Conn Creek earlier.

EL DORADO COUNTY During the 19th-century Gold Rush days, El Dorado is said to have contained 5,000 acres of vineyards. While the current 200 acres is not much by comparison, most of it has been planted in the last decade, and half a dozen wineries have also come into existence. Zinfandel is one-third of the plantings and the most successful varietal to date.

FIDDLETOWN (Amador) Lying just across the ridge from the Shenandoah Valley, this area yields typical, ripe, concentrated Zinfandels in the Amador County style, but possibly a little less forceful in flavor and alcohol than those of the Shenandoah Valley.

FINGER LAKES REGION *New York* The largest wine region in New York, producing over 80% of its wines. Most of the 10,000 acres of vineyards are clustered around Keuka, Canandaigua, and Seneca lakes. Though moderated by the lakes themselves and Lake Ontario to the north, the weather is freezing in winter. The growing season is very short for wine grapes. Most of the state's vinifera are in this region. Labruscas, mainly Concord, predominate, but French hybrids now represent about 15% of the total acreage and are increasing. The region's wine production is primarily in the hands of Taylor, Gold Seal, Great Western, and Widmer's. Bully Hill, Glenora, Heron Hill, and Konstantin Frank are small, prestigious producers.

FRESNO COUNTY 38,700 acres of grapes grow in hot Fresno County; most are converted into jug and dessert wines. The list of plantings is typical of the Central Valley: French Colombard (8,700 acres), Barbera (6,000 acres), Ruby Cabernet (4,100 acres), Chenin Blanc (2,800 acres), Grenache (2,800 acres). At the other end of the scale is Chardonnay (127 acres).

GEYSERVILLE (Sonoma) Sitting on the northwestern edge of the Alexander Valley, Geyserville is the source of excellent Zinfandels, notably from Ridge Vineyards, and of fat-styled Cabernet Sauvignons. In low-lying areas, especially near the river, growers seem to succeed with Chardonnay and Gewurztraminer. The Geyserville area is the home of the Souverain, Geyser Peak, and Pedroncelli wineries.

GILROY (Santa Clara) The agricultural center of the southern Santa Clara Valley, Gilroy has long been home for a number of jug wine producers and small, family-owned wineries operating on a shoestring. The valley floor near Gilroy has substantial vineyard acreage, but the majority of the nearby wineries are located in the hills to the west in the Hecker Pass area.

GLEN ELLEN (Sonoma) North of the city of Sonoma, about halfway to Kenwood, the Sonoma Valley floor becomes a series of rolling hills and gullies. Recent experience in the area suggests that the tops of these "moguls" are warm enough to ripen Zinfandel and Cabernet Sauvignon, but the gullies are more appropriately planted to early-ripening varieties. Grand Cru Vineyards, J. J. Haraszthy, and Valley of the Moon are the major wineries in Glen Ellen.

GONZALES (Monterey) In the northern end of the Salinas Valley, this small community boasts 1 winery, 1 giant freestanding bottling facility, and a host of plantings in what is surely one of the windiest and coolest vineyard locations in California. The winery is the Monterey Vineyard (owned by Coca-Cola of Atlanta), and the bottling facility, which is nearby, is dedicated to the Taylor California Cellars label (also owned by Coke). At the beginning of the 1970s, when the area was planted, the emphasis was on red grapes, particularly Cabernet Sauvignon. These proved unsatisfactory and have now been grafted over to whites or removed. Although many other locations in the Salinas Valley have now begun to produce wines of great merit, it is still rare to see Gonzales referenced as the vineyard source for any winery's offerings.

GRAND TRAVERSE REGION *Michigan* Located in the northwest corner of the state, the region includes the Leelanau Peninsula and the Old Mission Peninsula, both running into Lake Michigan. The "lake effect" provides cooler summers and warmer winters than elsewhere in the state. The first vineyards were established here in the mid-1960s, and total acreage now exceeds 100. The predominant grapes are French hybrids; Chardonnay and Johannisberg Riesling are the only vinifera varieties of consequence. 5 wineries.

GREENFIELD (Monterey) A town in the northern Salinas Valley,

Greenfield received heavy plantings of red and white varieties during the early 1970s. The first results in this cool growing area suggest that the whites will prosper, but reds may not. J. Lohr is the most visible producer and has indeed converted much of its red grape acreage to whites. A new winery, Jekel Vineyards, has also enjoyed early success with white wines. Greenfield is capable of producing fruity, high-acid Pinot Blancs and Chardonnays, and floral, delicate Rieslings. In good years, it is likely that a few stands of Cabernet may also succeed. However, it appears that most producers will look farther south in the valley for their Cabernet. Arroyo Seco is immediately adjacent to Greenfield.

GUENOC VALLEY (Lake) In the southern portion of Lake County near Middletown, the Guenoc Valley is home to one grower/winery appropriately named Guenoc Ranch. The valley, about fifteen miles north of Calistoga, was an active winemaking region at the turn of the century.

HEALDSBURG (Sonoma) About 20 miles north of Santa Rosa, the Healdsburg area is home to some 2 dozen wineries. 3 unique and important vineyard districts are nearby: the Alexander Valley to the east and north; the Dry Creek Valley to the northwest; and the Russian River Valley to the south and southwest.

HECKER PASS (Santa Clara) The Coast Range Mountains to the west of Gilroy open up ever so slightly to the coastal plain. This area, called Hecker Pass, is the location of a dozen wineries, most of which produce fair to indifferent jug wines and an occasional heavy red wine of interest. In recent years, a few small producers with higher aspirations have emerged.

HUDSON RIVER VALLEY *New York* This valley claims to be "America's oldest wine region." Attempts to grow vinifera in 1677 failed here; and until the 1950s, labrusca varieties were the rule. Today it has over 1,500 acres planted to French hybrids, mainly along the west bank of the Hudson River about 75 miles north of New York City. Concord still predominates, but is decreasing in acreage. Seyval Blanc and Baco Noir are the most successful varieties. Presently home to 13 wineries.

ISLE ST. GEORGE *Ohio* On this island, nine miles out in Lake Erie northwest of Sandusky, grapes have been grown for more than a century. All the grapes go to Meier's Wine Cellars.

KENWOOD (Sonoma) Midway between the cities of Sonoma and Santa Rosa in the Sonoma Valley is the whistle-stop town of Kenwood. It is the home of Kenwood Vineyards, Chateau St. Jean, and the new St. Francis Winery. Most St. Francis wine comes from grapes grown near the winery in cooler vineyards lying at the lowest, least sunny section of the valley floor. The other two wineries derive only a small portion of their crushes from local grapes.

KERN COUNTY 38,000 acres of grapes located here in the hottest, driest part of the Central Valley are oriented toward jug and dessert wines. Some vineyards are planted in the foothills above the valley floor, where the climate is thought to be more moderate. But one can scarcely detect the difference in Kern County wines that claim hillside provenance. The vineyards have the typical Central Valley mix: Ruby Cabernet (4,500 acres), French Colombard (6,300 acres), Chenin Blanc (5,200 acres), and Barbera (3,500 acres). Surprisingly, there are also 850 acres of Cabernet Sauvignon.

KING CITY (Monterey) Toward the southern end of the Salinas Valley, the temperatures become more hospitable for the medium-heat varieties that fail to ripen adequately farther north. The most enjoyable Petite Sirahs and Cabernet Sauvignons from Monterey County have been grown in the King City area.

KNIGHT'S VALLEY (Sonoma) Occupying its own bowl midway between the southern end of the Alexander Valley and the northern end of the Napa Valley is the small but increasingly vineyarded Knight's Valley. The area is cooled by tenacious morning fogs and afternoon breezes. Knight's Valley appears as the appellation of some Beringer wines.

LAKE COUNTY A northern coastal county lying inland from Mendocino County and north of Napa County, Lake County had about 100 acres of wine grapes 10 years ago; now, the total is close to 2,500. The expansion occurred in 1973 and 1974 with moderate growth after that. About 40% of the acreage is planted to Cabernet Sauvignon with another 40% split between Zinfandel, Napa Gamay, and Sauvignon Blanc. Everything else is planted in minuscule amounts. The few red wines from Lake County have, to date, been on the thin side, although there is reason to believe that some well-exposed vineyards will be able to ripen the medium-heat reds that dominate the current plantings. A few wineries have begun operations, the largest of which is Guenoc in the Middletown area.

LIVERMORE VALLEY (Alameda) Southeast of San Francisco, lying in its own enclosed pocket, is the Livermore Valley. Urban expansion has whittled away at vineyard holdings here, but both Wente and Concannon remain in the area and continue to emphasize estate-bottled wines. Agricultural zoning has slowed the onslaught and encouraged new plantings. The valley is marked by medium-warm growing conditions (low Region III) and rocky soil. Almost 1,900 acres of vineyard survive.

LODI (San Joaquin) Located at the northern end of the grape-searing, hot San Joaquin Valley and cooled by the same coastal breezes as the Delta area, Lodi has produced heavyweight, sometimes overripe Zinfandels and Petite Sirahs. Flame Tokay grapes from Lodi, highly praised for table use, also find their way into bulk method champagnes, sherry, and brandy.

LYTTON SPRINGS (Sonoma) Small winegrowing area lying in the low hills that separate the Dry Creek Valley from the Geyserville area of the Alexander Valley. Zinfandel is the leading wine.

MADERA COUNTY 32,000 acres of wine grapes are planted in Madera County, and 2 wineries there, Ficklin and Angelo Papagni, are among the quality leaders of the Central Valley. Papagni is the only winery in the area that proudly displays its local appellation instead of the more general California appellation. The major plantings in the county consist of: French Colombard (7,300 acres), Carignane (5,300 acres), Chenin Blanc (4,000 acres), Barbera (3,600 acres), and Ruby Cabernet (2,000 acres).

MANDEVILLE ISLAND (San Joaquin) This peat bog of an island in the Delta region produces grapes that go to a variety of wineries. The combination of medium-warm temperature and rich soil yields good but rarely great wines; Chenin Blanc, Petite Sirah, and Cabernet Sauvignon are the main varieties.

MARTHA'S VINEYARD (Napa) This most famous Cabernet Sauvignon vineyard in California yields moderate amounts of exceptional wine from Heitz Cellars. The vineyard is located on the Rutherford benchlands along the western edge of the Napa Valley just north of Oakville and yields balanced, fairly hard wines marked by a distinctive blend of black currants and mint in aroma and flavors.

MAYACAMAS MOUNTAINS The mountain range, running north from San Francisco Bay, that forms the geographical boundary between the Napa and Sonoma valleys. Important vineyards and wineries are located on the mountainsides in both counties, including the Spring Mountain and Mount Veeder areas.

MCDOWELL VALLEY (Mendocino) This one-winery viticultural area lies in southeastern Mendocino County. All the grapes belong to the winery, McDowell Valley Vineyards.

MENDOCINO COUNTY The northernmost of the coastal wine producers, Mendocino County has established a vinous identity of its own only in the past decade. Rough timber country, it has limited tillable acreage tucked away in a series of isolated valleys and canyons cut into the hills by the Russian River, including Anderson Valley, Redwood Valley, Potter Valley, and the Talmage and Ukiah areas. The growing season in Mendocino is generally shorter than elsewhere in California, but varies from very cool (Region I) near the coast to fairly warm (Region III) inland. Grape acreage has increased by 70% in the last decade to 10,300. The pre-1970 plantings of Carignane (1,900 acres) and French Colombard (1,100 acres) still show the way in Mendocino, but Zinfandel (1,300 acres), Cabernet Sauvignon (900 acres), and Chardonnay (900 acres) are making headway. The leading wineries are Parducci, Fetzer, McDowell Valley, and Edmeades.

MODESTO (Stanislaus) The incredible assortment of labels from Modesto, including Red Mountain, Carlo Rossi, André Champagne, Boone's Farm, and Madria-Madria Sangria, are all products of the Gallo Winery.

MONTE BELLO (Santa Clara) This is the famed home of Ridge Vineyards in the Santa Cruz Mountains west of San Jose. Both Cabernet and Zinfandel produce flavorful, full-bodied wines on Monte Bello Ridge.

MONTEREY COUNTY Grape growing in Monterey County (32,200 acres) is mainly in the Salinas Valley; a few hundred acres exist also in the Carmel Valley and the mountains near the Pinnacles National Monument. The county rates as cool (Region I to Region II) in its northern two-thirds to moderately warm (Region III) in its southern extremes.

All but 2,000 acres are new since 1970, and initially 60% were in red varieties. However, the white varieties have seemed to fare best in the cool, windy climate, and some 5,000 acres of whites have been added in the last two years, while substantial amounts of reds have been removed. As a result, whites are now 55% of Monterey's

plantings. Johannisberg Riesling and Gewurztraminer
have succeeded because of the intense fruitiness they develop. The fuller-bodied whites—Chardonnay, Sauvignon
Blanc, and Pinot Blanc—have generally been less well received, although wineries like Jekel and Ventana have
been able to coax big wines out of their vineyards. The
reds are a different story. Thousands of acres of Cabernet
Sauvignon, Zinfandel, and Petite Sirah were planted in
locations too cool to ripen the grapes adequately in most
years. The wines also displayed bothersome vegetal smells,
although this problem is being eliminated to some extent
as the vines mature. Even in the most hospitable areas, few
red wines from Monterey rise above ✪ rankings.
Monterey County plantings in order of acreage are Cabernet Sauvignon (3,600 acres), Chenin Blanc (4,500 acres),
Chardonnay (4,300 acres), Johannisberg Riesling (3,350
acres), Zinfandel (2,400 acres), Petite Sirah (2,200 acres),
and Pinot Noir (2,000 acres). Important Monterey County
growing areas include Arroyo Seco, Carmel Valley,
Gonzales, Greenfield, King City, Salinas Valley, and
Soledad.

MORGAN HILL (Santa Clara) The first town south of San Jose in
the southern portion of the Santa Clara Valley, Morgan Hill
has a few wineries with poor to fair track records.

NAPA (Napa) A few wineries and a few vines lie within the city
of Napa. Its major importance is as the urban center (if a
town of 25,000 can be so described) for the Napa Valley,
whose vineyards lie to the west and north.

NAPA COUNTY For years, wine labels reading Napa Valley have
been allowed to refer to grapes from any location in Napa
County. And although it is true that 95% of the 25,400
planted acres in the county actually lie in the valley
proper, new wine laws could have ruled out the remaining
5%, but, because of historic usage, even these non-Napa
Valley names may carry the name. With almost no exception among present plantings, these other areas have generally warmer climates and shorter growing seasons than
the Napa Valley. Some, such as Pope Valley, already appear on wine labels, while others, Gordon Valley and
Wooden Valley, have not achieved separate recognition.
As a way of calling attention to the nonvalley-floor origin
of their grapes, a few wineries have chosen to use Napa
County as an appellation in cases where their grapes come
from the surrounding hills or from the Carneros region.
The most widely planted varieties here are Cabernet Sauvignon (5,600 acres), Chardonnay (4,300 acres), Pinot Noir

(2,400 acres), Zinfandel (2,100 acres), Sauvignon Blanc (1,700 acres), and Johannisberg Riesling (1,500 acres).

NAPA VALLEY (Napa) The most famous winegrowing area in the United States, this land lives up to its Indian moniker of "the Valley of Plenty." It begins at the base of Mount St. Helena in the north, dissolving some 30 miles to the south into a flood plain as the Napa River enters San Francisco Bay. From Mount St. Helena to the city of Napa, the valley is defined by 2 north-south ridge lines of the Coast Range Mountains. The valley floor varies from 3 to 4 miles in width in the south to 1 mile or less in the north.

From its earliest days, the Napa Valley has been the home of some of California's most famous wine estates, including such well-known producers as Charles Krug, Beringer Brothers, Schramsberg, and Inglenook. Today, the valley boasts upward of 23,000 acres planted to wine grapes, making it California's most intensively farmed viticultural area. More than 100 wineries are in the Napa Valley, and most offer high-caliber, often expensive wines.

With few exceptions, the best California Chardonnays and Cabernet Sauvignons come from the Napa Valley, and much of the reputation of the valley is based on the success of these two varietals. But the valley is large and filled with varied growing conditions. The cold Carneros region by San Francisco Bay yields good Chardonnay and Riesling, shows great promise for Pinot Noir, but rarely produces well-ripened Cabernet Sauvignon. By the same token, the warm Calistoga region can produce nicely ripe Zinfandel, Gamay, and Petite Sirah, but overcooks Pinot Noir and the other heat-sensitive varieties. On wine labels the term Napa Valley has historically included all areas within Napa County. A recent change in federal wine-labeling rules excludes only the most outlying areas of the county from using the Napa Valley name.

Over 20 major subareas have been identified within the Napa Valley; 12 are already important for viticulture and are described in the adjoining pages (see Carneros, Calistoga, Napa, Stag's Leap, Rutherford, St. Helena, Yountville, Spring Mountain, Mount Veeder, Silverado Trail, Oakville, and Pope Valley).

NEW YORK STATE The second most important wine-producing state in the United States now has close to 50 wineries, including several of the country's largest. Its vineyards are planted to labruscas, French hybrids, and vinifera, but are predominantly Concord. Only half of the total acreage (50,000) is harvested for wine production. The other half goes into assorted fruit juices, jams, and jellies. The most important regions for winemaking are the Finger Lakes (about 80% of the state's total) and the Hudson River Valley. New York State as an appellation means that at least 75% of the wine's volume was derived from New York–grown grapes. New York is the second biggest wine-consuming state on a per capita basis.

NORTH COAST Once used to indicate the coastal counties north of San Francisco, this ill-defined suggestion of geographical heritage and wine quality came to mean any portion of California north of Bakersfield and Santa Barbara and as far inland as the distinctly noncoastal Central Valley. It might be appropriate for the term to pass totally out of use, and there is some indication that government rule makers will force that to happen. However, if the name continues to be employed, there is every chance that it will once again come to mean that the wine is from Mendocino, Sonoma, or Napa County.

NORTHERN CALIFORNIA One occasionally sees this appellation on wine labels. By most definitions it covers everything north of Los Angeles, or 97% of the grapes grown in the state. For all practical purposes, this term on a label is no more meaningful than the word California.

OAKVILLE (Napa) Situated in the southern end of the Napa Valley, halfway between Yountville and Rutherford, this way station is the home of several wineries (foremost among them the Robert Mondavi Winery) and adjoins some of the Napa Valley's best Cabernet growing turf. The superb Martha's Vineyard produced by Heitz Cellars and a substantial portion of the Robert Mondavi Cabernet vineyards are in Oakville, along the western edge of the valley floor. Other wineries in the area are Villa Mt. Eden and an Inglenook production and bottling plant.

OREGON 30 small wineries and over 200 growers have become active since the early 1960s. Most vineyards are less than 5 acres, and many wineries depend on eastern Washington for grapes. The total acreage was approximately 1,300 acres; two-thirds of which lay on the western side of the Willamette Valley, west and south of Portland. The other major wine area is the Umpqua Valley in Douglas County. Almost all Oregon vineyards are dry farmed on shallow, light soils, on hilly sites. Predominant grape varieties are Chardonnay, Pinot Noir, and White Riesling.

PACIFIC NORTHWEST Burgeoning winegrowing area covering Oregon, Washington, and Idaho. Upward of 5,000 acres of

grapes (approximately 75% in Washington; 23% in Oregon; 2% in Idaho) and 45 wineries. California has been a
major influence, but winemakers and growers are increasingly successful at adopting their own special techniques
to the problems and opportunities of cool climates, shorter
growing seasons, and longer daylight hours in summer.
Whites (especially Chardonnay, Sauvignon Blanc, and
White Riesling) have been more successful than reds and
dominate the plantings.

PASO ROBLES (San Luis Obispo) Lying in the lee of the Coast
Range area is a series of vineyards near Paso Robles. The
Hoffman Mountain Ranch, located in the hills to the west,
is the major winery in the immediate Paso Robles area,
which is also home to a number of new, small producers.
Others are nearby in Templeton, and the Estrella River
Winery lies on the rolling hills to the east. Grapes from the
entire area are often labeled as being from Paso Robles.

POPE VALLEY (Napa) Nestled in the mountains east and north
of the Napa Valley is the small, hot depression of land
called Pope Valley. A few hundred acres of vines and 1
winery occupy this rustic area, removed from the sophistication of the Napa Valley floor. Zinfandel grows well, and
there has been talk of planting Barbera. The area's lone
winery, Pope Valley Winery, is suitably quaint.

POTTER VALLEY (Mendocino) The most northerly and highest
in elevation of the county's grape-growing areas, Potter
Valley contains approximately 700 acres of mostly new
vineyard. Chateau St. Jean has produced late harvest Rieslings from the area, and Fetzer and Felton-Empire have
made soft Rieslings.

RANCHO CALIFORNIA (Riverside) Another name for the new
grape-growing area northeast of San Diego, which is more
frequently called Temecula.

REDWOOD VALLEY (Mendocino) Among the most northerly and
coolest of the many grape-growing valleys framing the
Russian River, this moderately cool wine-growing area
seems able to ripen most varieties adequately. The hills
yield good Zinfandel and Petite Sirah, whereas the cooler
valley floor is more suited to whites. The name Redwood
Valley appears on many Fetzer wines.

RUSSIAN RIVER VALLEY (Sonoma) The Russian River is an important influence in several viticultural parts of Sonoma
County—and each of these is a valley bearing its own

name. As an appellation of origin, however, the name Russian River Valley has commonly been used to describe the low-lying, flat plain near Healdsburg that extends south and west and follows the river as it turns toward the Pacific Ocean. At Guerneville the coastal hills close off the area and mark its western boundary. Plantings are oriented to early-ripening varieties, especially Chardonnay and Johannisberg Riesling. Some Merlot and Pinot Noir also thrive in the coolest areas near the river. In the sheltered areas and hillsides, decent-quality red varieties can be grown. There are over a dozen wineries in the area, including the well-known Korbel and Sonoma Vineyards. Most, however, are new and small.

RUTHERFORD (Napa) Small community located in south-central Napa Valley between Oakville and St. Helena in a temperate Region II climate. Heat-retaining soils keep the hillsides warm; high clay content along the valley floor near Napa River and Conn Creek provides cooler growing conditions. The area is home for many important wineries—Beaulieu, Inglenook, Caymus, Rutherford Hill—and yields exceptional (up to ✪✪✪) Cabernet Sauvignon along benchlands at the western edge and also from scattered sites across the valley floor. Freemark Abbey and Spring Mountain have major vineyard holdings in slightly cool locations that yield good to excellent Chardonnay. The east-side hills have medium heat (up to Region III) suited to Zinfandel and Petite Sirah. West Rutherford (Benchlands) should become an appellation of origin recognized for its superb Cabernet Sauvignon in the next decade.

SAGEMOOR FARMS (Washington) South Columbia Basin vineyard name appearing on some of the best wines produced in the Pacific Northwest. Sagemoor Farms has 465 acres and regularly sells to more than 20 wineries in the northern states and Canada, including Chateau Ste. Michelle, Preston, Ste. Chapelle, Sokol Blosser, and Eyrie. A third of the total acreage is in Cabernet Sauvignon and Merlot. Most of the remaining acreage is in white varieties, led by Johannisberg Riesling (96 acres) and Chardonnay (65 acres).

ST. HELENA (Napa) This picturesque town and its environs are home to no fewer than 40 wineries, including such historically important producers as Beringer, Charles Krug, Christian Brothers, and Louis Martini. Among newer properties, St. Helena can boast Freemark Abbey, Heitz Cellars, and Joseph Phelps. The vineyards surrounding St. Helena are not the valley's most noteworthy. On the valley floor east of the city, heavy soils and increased temperatures limit the area's suitability for the noble grape varieties.

But there are exceptions. The low-lying, wet clay soils that abut the Napa River have yielded above average to superb Chardonnays (up to ❈❈❈) and very likable Johannisberg Rieslings. The low hillside slopes west of the valley floor contain areas similar in exposure and soil to the best Cabernet Sauvignon vineyards of Rutherford and are expected to yield fine wines when the vineyards mature. The eastern side hills get the hot late-afternoon sun and are amenable hosts to Zinfandel and Petite Sirah.

SALINAS VALLEY (Monterey) Lying on a north-south axis behind the Coast Range hills, which protect it from direct ocean influence, the Salinas Valley contains almost all of Monterey County's 30,000-plus acres of grapes.

SAN BENITO COUNTY This is Almadén country. When its grape needs could no longer be met by Santa Clara vineyards, Almadén made a major commitment to San Benito County that now approaches 4,600 acres. There are a few other growers and producers in San Benito, but their output is small. This warm, dry area is planted substantially to early-ripening varieties that have fared only moderately well—like Chardonnay (1,000 acres), Pinot Noir (800 acres), Gamay Beaujolais (500 acres), Johannisberg Riesling (300 acres), Gewurztraminer (300 acres), and Pinot Blanc (200 acres). The later-ripening varieties planted there, Cabernet Sauvignon (500 acres) and Zinfandel (200 acres), have similarly failed to yield particularly interesting results. A few small wineries have developed in the hills that separate San Benito from Monterey. The most prominent is Calera.

SAN BERNARDINO COUNTY The remaining 7,100 acres of vineyard of the once vibrant Cucamonga district east of Los Angeles make up the plantings in San Bernardino County. The vines are old, the varieties are old-fashioned, and the grapes are made into wines of indifferent quality by local wineries. The leading varieties are Zinfandel (2,300 acres), Mission (1,500 acres), Grenache (800 acres), Palomino (800 acres), Burger (400 acres), and Alicante Bouschet (300 acres). There have been very few plantings in San Bernardino County in the last decade.

SAN JOAQUIN COUNTY The northernmost of the major Central Valley counties, San Joaquin (especially in the Lodi and Delta areas) is occasionally cooled by fog and winds flowing in from San Francisco Bay. This may account for the somewhat higher quality of its wines in comparison to its even hotter neighbors to the south. The plantings in the 39,000-acre San Joaquin County vineyards are a mix of old-fashioned varieties, of coastal grapes hoping to benefit from the occasional fog, and of the typical high-acid choices for new Central Valley plantings. 11,100 acres of Zinfandel concentrated in the Lodi area yield over 40% of the entire California crop. Other grapes include Carignane (6,600 acres), French Colombard (5,400 acres), Chenin Blanc (3,000 acres), Grenache (2,500 acres), Petite Sirah (1,600 acres), Barbera (1,100 acres), and Cabernet Sauvignon (700 acres).

SAN JOAQUIN VALLEY The southern portion of the Central Valley. Running south from the Sacramento-Stockton area to Bakersfield and containing San Joaquin, Stanislaus, Merced, Madera, Fresno, Tulare, Kings, and Kern counties, the San Joaquin Valley is the source of most California jug wine. A medium-warm area at the northern end of the valley (see Lodi and Delta) is cooled by breezes that flow in from the coast; Zinfandel, Petite Sirah, and Chenin Blanc grow well here. The rest of the valley is extremely hot in the summer (up to Region V) and rarely produces exceptional wine; it is common to refer to grapes and wines from this area as Central Valley.

SAN JOSE (Santa Clara) This major urban area (population 700,000) is home to 3 important wineries—Almadén, Mirassou, and J. Lohr. It also houses facilities for Paul Masson and Llords & Elwood.

SAN LUIS OBISPO COUNTY A recently developed major California grape-growing region, San Luis Obispo County contains approximately 4,700 acres located in 4 distinct areas. The newest are the Shandon region in the northern end of the county and the Edna Valley, stretching south from the city of San Luis Obispo toward Santa Barbara County. The wines of these areas have been of average to above average quality to date, with the exception of Edna Valley–grown Chardonnay, which has shown the potential for excellence. The older areas, Paso Robles and Templeton in the western foothills of the county, have a longer but no more distinguished history. The county's main grapes are Zinfandel (1,000 acres), Cabernet Sauvignon (900 acres), Chardonnay (500 acres), Sauvignon Blanc (500 acres), Chenin Blanc (500 acres), and Johannisberg Riesling (200 acres).

SAN PASQUAL VALLEY (San Diego) Within the city limits but lying about 20 miles northeast of the downtown section, the San Pasqual Valley sports avocados in the foothills, cows and truck farming in the flatlands, and one major vineyard. The area, warm Region III in temperature, has been hospitable to Chenin Blanc and Sauvignon Blanc.

SANTA BARBARA COUNTY This coastal county north of Los Angeles is among the last decade's newcomers to grape growing. Its 117 acres in 1969 increased to 4,700 in 1973 and to over 7,000 today. The plantings are located in the Santa Ynez Valley, some 20 miles removed from the coast; in the Santa Maria area farther north and inland; and to a limited extent in cooler, more coastally oriented climes. Approximately 70% of the acreage is in 4 varieties: Johannisberg Riesling (1,700 acres), Chardonnay (1,500 acres), Cabernet Sauvignon (1,100 acres), and Pinot Noir (700 acres).

SANTA CLARA COUNTY This fast-urbanizing area was once among the highest production winegrowing regions in California. Now its 1,600 acres of grapes represent about 0.5% of all vineyards. The once abundant vineyards to the north and east of San Jose are all but gone. The one remaining concentration of grapes, in the southern end of the Santa Clara Valley near Gilroy, serves the cluster of small, local wineries. The bigger wineries of Santa Clara County have stayed in place. Paul Masson, Almadén, and Mirassou all maintain large production facilities in the San Jose area, and they are joined by a growing list of small and medium-sized operations up and down the length of the valley. The leading grape in number of acres is Cabernet Sauvignon (about 200 acres). Others with more than 100 acres are Carignane, Cabernet Sauvignon, French Colombard, Petite Sirah, and Zinfandel.

To supply their needs, many large and medium-sized wineries in Santa Clara County have invested heavily in vineyards in Monterey County and are major buyers of grapes from San Luis Obispo and Santa Barbara counties. The larger wineries also rely on grapes from the Central Valley.

SANTA CLARA VALLEY (Santa Clara) Nearly all the identifiable vineyard acreage of this county lies within the Santa Clara Valley. A few small but important mountain vineyards exist north and west of San Jose, but the bulk of the valley's northernmost winegrowing has faded under urban onslaught. A bit more than a thousand acres remain in production where the valley narrows south of San Jose in the Morgan Hill, Gilroy, and Hecker Pass areas.

SANTA CRUZ COUNTY A cool, coastal county south of San Francisco and north of Monterey. Fewer than 100 acres of grapes are made into wine here by a dozen small but dedicated wineries. The more successful varieties are Chardonnay, Johannisberg Riesling, and Pinot Noir. Grapes are brought in for crushing by most wineries to make up for the inadequate supply of local grapes.

SANTA CRUZ MOUNTAINS The coastal mountain range running south of San Francisco past San Jose has long been a hotbed of winemaking activity. Today, the two dozen wineries of the area, all fairly small, are scattered throughout southern San Mateo County and the low mountains west of San Jose on both the Santa Clara and the Santa Cruz sides of the ridge line. There is agreement among the wineries to call the entire area Santa Cruz Mountains, and the name has been appearing as an appellation of origin on a few wines from the area. Prominent wineries include Ridge, David Bruce, Felton-Empire, Mount Eden, and Roudon-Smith.

SANTA MARIA VALLEY (Santa Barbara and San Luis Obispo) Lying south and east of Santa Maria, this valley has cool Region II growing characteristics that have made it a suitable location for Johannisberg Riesling and Chardonnay. The substantial plantings known as Tepusquet Vineyards are located here.

SANTA YNEZ VALLEY (Santa Barbara) In this new cold-climate vineyard area in the low mountains of Solvang, initial experience shows frequent success with whites and Pinot Noir, but less satisfactory results with other reds. The leading wineries of the area—Firestone, Zaca Mesa, and Santa Ynez Valley—are well financed and quality-oriented.

SHENANDOAH VALLEY (Amador) This major grape-growing district of Amador County was rediscovered in the late 1960s by the Sutter Home Winery. Its mature Zinfandel vines have become highly prized for the ripe, intense wines they yield. Shenandoah Valley grapes, mostly Zinfandel, are used now by half a dozen wineries, including Monterey Peninsula and Ridge. In the early 1970s the new Monteviña Winery opened and began experiments with many varieties, including Nebbiolo. An older winery, D'Agostini, has been in business for over 100 years, making wines of indifferent quality. The Deaver, Esola, and Ferrero vineyards are important sources of grapes.

SIERRA FOOTHILLS East of the Central Valley rise the majestic 10,000-foot-high Sierra Nevada Mountains. During the

Gold Rush era, places like El Dorado, Placer, Calaveras, and Amador counties in the Sierra foothills developed a burgeoning wine industry that reached 10,000 acres at its peak. In 1970 less than 1,000 acres remained, and most was in Amador. Recent years have seen a return to those foothill counties by vineyardists and winemakers alike, raising the foothill acreage to 1,500. El Dorado County, which had 5,000 acres of vines during the Gold Rush, seems likely to come back into prominence.

SILVERADO TRAIL (Napa) Technically not a wine district, the Silverado Trail is a lightly traveled roadway that traverses the eastern edge of the Napa Valley starting in the city of Napa and extending northward to the city of Calistoga. The vineyards east of the trail generally support grape varieties needing warmer growing conditions than those found in corresponding locations on the valley floor.

SOLEDAD (Monterey) Located in the middle of the Salinas Valley wind tunnel, the area around Soledad is definitely a cold winegrowing area. Many large wineries have holdings in the area, but none so large as Paul Masson, which has produced a series of vintage-dated wines from its vineyards near Soledad.

SONOMA (Sonoma) The home of the Sebastiani, Hacienda, and Buena Vista wineries. This quaint town was the wine capital of the North Coast from the 1830s to the 1860s, when it sported the most successful and progressive vineyards of the area. Vineyards to the south and west of Sonoma are cooled by proximity to San Francisco Bay, making them suitable for white grapes. The hills north of Sonoma are more sheltered and have direct southern exposure. For almost 150 years they have produced good to very good Cabernets and Zinfandels.

SONOMA COUNTY Except for the mid-1800s, when North Coast winemaking was centered in the city of Sonoma, the nicely situated vineyards of Sonoma County have somehow always taken a back seat to the Napa Valley. In the late 1960s the vineyards of Sonoma County were still more heavily oriented toward jug wines than fine varietals. Almost 30% of the county's 14,000 vineyard acres were in Zinfandel, which had yet to be recognized as an important varietal wine. Another 30% was in Carignane, French Colombard, and Petite Sirah (another as yet unrecognized variety). Less than 25% of the vineyards were devoted to premium table wine varieties. At the time, only 6 of the then two dozen producers in Sonoma County offered varietal wines.

But what a difference a decade makes. Today, Sonoma County's acreage has increased to 27,800, and almost all of the new plantings are in the better varieties. In addition, the new popularity of Zinfandel and Petite Sirah has created a legacy of mature vineyards in outstanding locations. Superb wines from distinctly identified appellations —Carneros, Sonoma Valley, Russian River Valley, Alexander Valley, and Dry Creek Valley—are coming to market from 90 new and refurbished wineries. Among the great wines of Sonoma County are ripe, distinctive Zinfandels; lush late harvest Rieslings; forward, spicy Gewurztraminers; and fruity, forward Chardonnays.

SONOMA VALLEY (Sonoma) Almost one-quarter of Sonoma County's planted vineyards lie in the picturesque Sonoma Valley. The area contains a mix of climatic, topographical, and soil variations that may one day be divided into a dozen or so separate appellations of origin. Sonoma Valley's 6,000 acres of grapes stretch from San Francisco Bay northward through the narrow valley until they reach the suburban outskirts of the city of Santa Rosa. The coolest growing district, Carneros, abuts San Francisco Bay and is best suited to early-ripening varieties. Following the valley northward, one passes through the cities of Sonoma, Glen Ellen, and Kenwood. The hills that line the valley regularly produce good Cabernet Sauvignon and Zinfandel, whereas the valley floor is generally cooler and is more heavily devoted to whites.

There are almost 20 producing wineries in the Sonoma Valley, of which the oldest is Buena Vista and the biggest Sebastiani. Although the Sonoma Valley was the first wine-growing area to develop north of San Francisco, during the early to mid 1800s, it was soon surpassed by neighboring Napa Valley, losing its prominence by the early 1900s. Almost two-thirds of the current plantings in the Sonoma Valley, as well as 80% of its wineries, are relatively new.

SOUTH COLUMBIA BASIN *Washington* Rather large horseshoe-shaped land mass in eastern Washington defined by the course of the Columbia River as it heads toward the Oregon border and then reaches west for the Pacific Ocean. The region is arid, mountain desert relying on heavy irrigation of the sandy soils for agriculture. The several wineries and growers cultivating sites ranging up to hundreds of acres include Chateau Ste. Michelle, Preston Wine Cellars, and Sagemoor Farms (a grower only). Temperatures are moderately warm but not excessive, allowing most whites and many reds to ripen well with high levels of acidity.

SOUTHERN CALIFORNIA To a Californian, anything south of Santa Barbara is part of Southern California. As a grape-growing area, sometimes called South Coast, it consists of the Temecula area in the southwestern corner of Riverside County, the vineyards in the Cucamonga district, and the coastal vineyards of San Diego County.

SPRING MOUNTAIN (Napa) A distinctly identifiable watershed area known as Spring Mountain lies west of St. Helena in the Napa Valley and forms part of the Mayacamas Mountain Range, the boundary between the Napa and Sonoma valleys. This picturesque stretch of hillside has a long and fabled history of grape growing that dates back to the nineteenth century. It maintained itself fitfully after Prohibition, but many of Spring Mountain's great estates are only now being reopened and put back into winegrowing. (Chateau Chevalier and Spring Mountain Vineyard occupy two of the loveliest refurbished properties.) Soils and exposures on Spring Mountain vary considerably, allowing the successful cultivation of most varieties. York Creek Vineyard is near the top of Spring Mountain. Other wineries here include Yverdon, Keenan, and Smith-Madrone.

STAG'S LEAP (Napa County) About a mile east of Yountville is the picturesque Stag's Leap area. Known primarily for Cabernet Sauvignon, this superb viticultural pocket has distinctly red soil and is bounded on the east by a rocky knoll with red rock outcroppings. It is thought that the red soil and rock absorb heat and keep the vines at moderate growing temperatures long after the sun's warming rays are lost. Although only 400–600 acres of vines exist in the Stag's Leap area, the quality of wines produced by Clos du Val, Stag's Leap Wine Cellars, and Stags' Leap Vineyards makes it one of California's most important winegrowing microclimates.

STANISLAUS COUNTY 19,000 acres of grapes in the hot Central Valley geared primarily to bulk and dessert wine production: French Colombard (3,700 acres), Chenin Blanc (2,500 acres), Ruby Cabernet (2,200 acres), and Grenache (2,000 acres). Located in this county is Modesto, the home of Gallo.

STEINER VINEYARD (Sonoma) Halfway up the slope of Sonoma Mountain on the west side of the Sonoma Valley lies the Steiner Vineyard, whose Cabernet has been bottled recently by Stonegate, Roudon-Smith, and Kenwood (as part of its Artist Series bottling).

STELTZNER VINEYARD (Napa) This Stag's Leap area vineyard has yielded dry, full-bodied Chenin Blancs and round, inviting Cabernets typical of its viticultural area. Wineries using grapes from this vineyard have included Burgess, Markham, and Martin Ray.

TALMAGE (Mendocino) Near Ukiah, on a broad fan of land that extends to the east and south and occupies the foothills as well, are some 4,000 planted acres of grapes in the Talmage area. The majority of plantings (most of which are less than a dozen years old) are in the medium-warm reds—Zinfandel, Cabernet, and Petite Sirah. Sprinklings of whites, mainly Chardonnay, French Colombard, and Chenin Blanc, also appear.

TEMECULA (Riverside) This burgeoning winegrowing area inland from the ocean north of San Diego is home to the Callaway Winery and several newer and smaller enterprises. Grape-growing conditions seem to be suitable for cool to medium-warmth varieties of reds and whites, but the current track record is spotty indeed. Rancho California is another name used to denote the area.

TEMPLETON (San Luis Obispo) Just south of Paso Robles, located in the Santa Lucia Mountains, sit the 3 wineries of the Templeton area—York Mountain, Pesenti, and Las Tablas. These old-line establishments survive mainly on local clientele and the tourist trade that passes through. The area is noted for Zinfandel.

TEPUSQUET VINEYARDS (Santa Barbara and San Luis Obispo) 1,800-acre planting in the Santa Maria Valley area containing a wide range of varieties. The most successful to date have been Johannisberg Riesling and Chardonnay.

UKIAH (Mendocino) The urban center of the Mendocino County winegrowing areas and home of the Parducci, Weibel, and Cresta Blanca wineries. About 1,000 acres of grapes are grown directly north of Ukiah in the light bench soils and hillsides above the Russian River.

UMPQUA VALLEY *Oregon* Contemporary winemaking began in this valley, the watershed of the Umpqua River, when Hillcrest Vineyard established vineyards in 1961. 6 wineries and about 17 growers (200 acres) now exist. The area is a cool Region I, well suited to its major variety, White Riesling.

VALLEY OF THE MOON (Sonoma) The name given to the Sonoma Valley by author Jack London (whose winery existed there until the early 1900s) derived from the Indian expression "Valley of the Seven Moons." The moon would appear and disappear behind 7 hilltops as it rose.

VENTANA VINEYARDS (Monterey) This 300-acre vineyard in Soledad was planted to 8 varieties in 1973. The leading grapes are Chardonnay (46 acres), Pinot Noir (44 acres), Chenin Blanc (40 acres), and Johannisberg Riesling (33 acres). Grapes are sold to many small wineries, including Chardonnay to MEV, La Crema Vinera, Leeward, and Pendleton. 34 new acres of Chardonnay were added in 1980.

WASHINGTON Most of Washington's grape vines are Concords (19,000 of 24,000 acres). The Yakima Valley (Yakima and Benton counties) and the South Columbia Basin area farther east—where the Columbia, Snake, and Yakima rivers converge (Benton, Franklin, and Walla Walla counties)—are the centers for grape growing. These are dry areas with barren hills, warm summer temperatures, and cold winters. The acreage in vinifera wine grapes more than doubled, to 4,000 acres, between 1975 and 1980. Major varieties are Riesling and Cabernet, and other large plantings include Grenache, Chardonnay, Chenin Blanc, Gewurztraminer, Sauvignon Blanc, and Semillon. The largest blocks of vineyards belong to Chateau Ste. Michelle with approximately 2,000 acres, Sagemoor Farms with 500 acres, and Preston Wine Cellars with 200 acres. 15 wineries.

WILLAMETTE VALLEY *Oregon* Principal grape-growing and wine-producing area in Oregon. As a river valley/watershed, the Willamette Valley (cool Region I) starts below Eugene in the south and extends northward to Portland, where the Willamette River merges with the Columbia River. The flat plain of the valley is rich agricultural land, but the vineyards are all in the hills on the west side of the Willamette River. The central section from Salem to the Chehalem Mountains (mainly Yamhill County) contains a dozen wineries. There are 400–500 acres in vines, and prime locations for more than 20,000 acres of vines exist. To the north, in the hilly portions of Washington County and in the foothills of the Coast Range Mountains, are 400 or more acres of vineyard and a half-dozen wineries. The vines in the Willamette Valley are planted on their own roots and enjoy adequate groundwater and rainfall. Chardonnay, White Riesling, and Pinot Noir are the main varieties of grapes grown.

WINERY LAKE VINEYARDS (Napa) Situated on a hilly site in the middle of the Carneros district is the sculpture-studded, baronial estate of art collector René Di Rosa. From these 100-plus acres, grapes go out to 14 wineries, many of whom put the vineyard name prominently on the label. One that does not, Robert Mondavi, derives much of its Pinot Noir from this property. Excellent wines bearing the Winery Lake designation include Chardonnay from Acacia, La Crema Vinera, Kistler, and Veedercrest.

YAKIMA VALLEY *Washington* A major agricultural region located in the south-central part of the state. The south-facing slope holds about 500 acres of vinifera vines with a capacity of up to 20,000 acres. The area is relatively dry and subject to temperature drops as low as 20° F. below zero. Chateau Ste. Michelle has a major winemaking facility here, and there are several new wineries.

YOLO COUNTY Lying west of Sacramento in an area that is technically part of the Central Valley, Yolo County vineyards (700 acres) experience cooler growing conditions because of fog intrusions from San Francisco Bay up the Sacramento River lowlands. The majority of vineyards are planted in the southern part of the county in the Delta region and are primarily Chenin Blanc (300 acres) and Petite Sirah (100 acres). The Chenin Blanc is reported to go primarily to big wineries that use it to supplement their own grapes.

YORK CREEK VINEYARD (Napa) High on Spring Mountain sits the 125-acre York Creek Vineyard, belonging to washing-machine heir Fritz Maytag. Best known for its Petite Sirah (from 10 acres) that yield brawny, tannic wines at Freemark Abbey and Ridge, it has also produced Cabernet Sauvignon (35 acres) and Zinfandel (30 acres) bottled by Ridge.

ROBERT YOUNG VINEYARDS *(Sonoma)* Located in the Alexander Valley, this property ranks alongside Winery Lake Vineyards as California's most widely heralded. Its name has appeared prominently on the labels of the unsurpassed late harvest Rieslings and the exceptional Chardonnays of Chateau St. Jean. The property has also yielded Cabernets for Smothers and Felton-Empire.

YOUNTVILLE (Napa) Lying just 6 miles north of the city of Napa, the little town of Yountville is the first major wine community that one encounters when entering the Napa

Valley. Surrounding Yountville are a variety of important growing areas and wineries. Lying to the south in relatively cold growing conditions are Chardonnay vineyards that supply Chateau Montelena, Trefethen, and Beringer. To the west lies the dramatic new home of Domaine Chandon, and the eastern side of the valley contains the small Stag's Leap microclimate that produces the superb Cabernets of Stag's Leap Wine Cellars and Clos du Val.

Wineries and Wines
in California

Location by county and date established is indicated in
italics within each winery entry.

ACACIA WINERY *Napa 1979* Primarily using Carneros-grown
grapes, the winery is concentrating on Chardonnay and
elegant, rich Pinot Noir (all with vineyard designations).
First wines, about 13,000 cases, were immediate successes
and have placed Acacia among the leaders for both varieties.

Chardonnay (Winery Lake): *Intense, oaky, fruity, rich,*
complex, powerful 🏵🏵
Chardonnay (other bottlings): *Fruity, toasty, balanced,*
well-focused wines identified as Napa Valley and
Carneros have been best; others less interesting 🍷/🏵🏵🏵
Pinot Noir: *Toasty, elegant, somewhat restrained sense*
of proportion, good varietal fruit 🏵/🏵🏵

ADLER FELS *Sonoma 1980* Situated on the Sonoma Valley side
of the Mayacamas Mountains, this compact winery produces 5,000 cases annually. Its name derives from the German for Eagle Rock, a local landmark—which perhaps ex-
plains the ominous, Teutonic-looking eagle on the label.
The three main varietals, Johannisberg Riesling, Gewurztraminer, and Cabernet, are made from purchased grapes.

ADOBE CELLARS Negociant label primarily focused on purchasing North Coast lots of Cabernet, Chardonnay, and Zinfandel. Quality has been modest.

AHERN WINERY *Los Angeles 1978* Using grapes from Santa Barbara and Amador counties, this 3500-case winery has done
a creditable job with its varietals. While its barrel-aged
Sauvignon Blanc and Zinfandels have tended to be high in

alcohol, the Chardonnay has been well balanced and quite appealing.

Chardonnay: *Toasty, ripe, full-bodied* ✿

AHLGREN VINEYARDS *Santa Cruz 1976* A 1,200-case winery offering several varietals made from purchased grapes. Quantity of each varies from 40 to 400 cases. Its red wines are particularly successful.

Zinfandel: *Blackberry jam aroma, intense* ✿

ALATERA VINEYARDS *Napa 1977* First wines appeared in 1979. Winery specializes in Pinot Noir, Cabernet Sauvignon, and Gewurztraminer from grapes grown in partner's vineyards (70 acres) near Yountville. Efforts to date have been unexciting save for an exceptional, intense, honeylike late harvest Johannisberg Riesling. Current wine production is 3,000 cases.

ALEXANDER VALLEY VINEYARDS *Sonoma 1975* Family-run 120-acre vineyard is among the best in the Alexander Valley region. The winery has approached maximum output of 20,000 cases, mostly of white varietals. Cabernet blended with Merlot and Pinot Noir are the only reds. Enjoys a good reputation for the whites, with Chardonnay being the most consistent. All wines are made from its own vineyards. Reasonably priced.

Cabernet Sauvignon: *Herbaceous, soft, some oak* ♥
Chardonnay: *Ripe, moderate oak, balanced* ♥/✿
Johannisberg Riesling: *Flowery, delicate flavors, slightly sweet* ♥/✿
Pinot Noir: *Varietal fruit, slightly earthy, balanced, light oak* ♥/✿

ALMADÉN VINEYARDS *Santa Clara 1852* The third largest U.S. winery now sells 13.4 million cases and is still expanding. The company operates 5 facilities to offer some 60 wines under its labels. It owns 6,700 acres of vineyards, including large holdings in Monterey and San Benito counties. Both appellations appear on its vintage-dated varietals, most of which struggle to attain average-quality status. A high percentage of Almadén's production is in jug wines (generics and varietals), and the generic whites are not keeping pace with the competition. Yet Almadén is one of the largest champagne producers under its own and the Le Domaine labels, and a few of the Almadén sparkling-wine offerings are above average. The line is rounded out by numerous dessert wines headed by popular sherries. (See Charles Le Franc for review of Almadén's other label.)

Blanc de Blancs Champagne: *Fruity, yeasty, slightly sweet* ♥/❁
Burgundy: *Light, dull* ♥/δ
Cabernet Sauvignon: *Fruity, vegetal, soft, simple* ♥
Cabernet Sauvignon (Monterey): *Herbaceous, fruity, soft* ♥
Chablis: *Flat, overly chemical* δ
Eye of the Partridge Champagne: *Fresh, fruity, soft, slightly sweet* ♥/❁
Flor Fino Sherry: *Yeasty, thin, sharp* ♥
Gewurztraminer: *Spicy, sometimes flat, slightly sweet* ♥/❁
Merlot: *Herbs and spice, firm, light but fruity, slightly astringent* ♥
Zinfandel: *Light, fruity, vinous* ♥

ALTA VINEYARD CELLAR *Napa 1979* A Chardonnay-only producer operating in a refurbished winery constructed in 1878. Annual production is 2,000 cases, with some of the grapes grown in the winery's 10-acre hillside vineyard. The first wines have been inconsistent in quality.

AMADOR FOOTHILL WINERY *Amador 1980* Grew from 700 cases (White Zinfandel and Chenin Blanc) in 1980 to 2,000 cases in 1981. Made three vineyard-designated Zinfandels. Plans to add Sauvignon Blanc and Cabernet when its 8-acre vineyard matures. Optimum production will be 5,000 cases.

AMADOR WINERY *Amador 1967* The second oldest winery in Amador, offering 8 generic wines from purchased grapes. Low quality. 3,500 cases per year.

AMBASSADOR (PERELLI-MINETTI WINERY) A large line of vintage-dated, cork-finished varietals and generics, most of which are jug wine quality. Also included are vermouth, Marsala, and a good inexpensive bulk process *brut* champagne, finished slightly sweet. All wines are low-priced. Production is now at 75,000 cases total.

S. ANDERSON VINEYARD *Napa 1979* Champagne and Chardonnay are the products of this ambitious weekend winery venture of a Los Angeles dentist. The plan is to produce approximately 500 cases per year of sparkling wine, and the first cuvée was laid down in 1979. The Blanc de Blancs is made from Chardonnay, while a Blanc de Noirs is produced from purchased Pinot Noir grapes. In addition, 2,500 cases of varietal table wine are made from the winery's 36 acres of Chardonnay vines.

ANDERSON WINE CELLARS *Tulare 1980* Family winery using local grapes to make 800 cases of Chenin Blanc and the same amount of Ruby Cabernet. Output will remain under 2,000 cases. A 20-acre vineyard is being converted from table grapes to wine grapes.

ANDRÉ (E. & J. GALLO) Made by bulk process, this is likely the largest selling line of U.S. champagne. Ranges from slightly sweet to very sweet, including even those labeled dry. Inexpensive, but often bland in flavor and low in acidity.

ARGONAUT WINERY *Amador 1976* This 2,000-case winery makes Amador Zinfandel and Barbera. Over the first few vintages, it made them in an overripe, high-alcohol style.

ARROYO SONOMA WINERY *Sonoma 1937* Formerly a private label offering wines of erratic quality, the operation evolved into a winery when it rebuilt the Bandiera facility in 1980 into a modern plant capable of producing 100,000 cases per year. 379 acres of vineyards are farmed in Potter Valley, Dry Creek Valley, and the Chiles Valley. Pinot Noir and Chardonnay are purchased from a vineyard in Schellville. 3,500 cases of Chardonnay, Cabernet, Zinfandel, and Pinot Noir are produced for the Arroyo Sonoma label. A broad variety of whites, including Chardonnay, appear under the Potter Valley label.

Cabernet Sauvignon: *Ripe, brawny, full-bodied* ❦/❂

ARROYO WINERY The early name for the winery now known as Pendleton. Wine was offered under Arroyo through the 1977 vintage.

ASSUMPTION ABBEY (BROOKSIDE CELLARS) Assumption Abbey is the top line offered in Brookside's tasting rooms. Some varietals now carry vintage dates and Temecula or Sonoma appellations. Emerald Riesling and Petite Sirah are best sellers of a fairly full line. Quality has never been high.

BACIGALUPI A label for Chardonnay only that appeared first with the 1979 vintage. It is part of the Belvedere Wine Co. marketing program. Bacigalupi is a grower with 40 acres in the West Healdsburg area. His first bottling was unusual in character, but still a ❂ effort.

BALDINELLI VINEYARDS *Amador 1979* In 1972 Ed Baldinelli bought 70 acres of vineyard in the Shenandoah Valley region, including many acres of Zinfandel that were at least 40 years old. By 1979, he made 5,000 cases total of Zinfandel in a regular, white, and rosé style, plus a small amount of Cabernet Sauvignon. The regular Zin was typical of Amador—very warm and tannic.

BALE MILL CELLARS (CHARLES SHAW WINERY) A one-time-only label used for Zinfandel made by conventional fermentation. The quality suggested once was enough.

BALLARD CANYON WINERY *Santa Barbara 1978* 6,000-case production from the winery's 39 acres is expected to reach 10,000 cases when vines mature. Cabernet Sauvignon (23 acres), Johannisberg Riesling (16 acres), and Sauvignon Blanc will be offered.

BALVERNE VINEYARDS *Sonoma 1979* Located 2 miles south of Healdsburg along the foothills to the east are this new winery and its 175-acre vineyard. It produces 7 varietals (5 whites, 2 reds) and a blended white wine. The plan is to work toward 7 vineyard-designated varietals. Production hit 20,000 cases in 1981; 40,000 cases is optimum. The first whites were light in intensity, but include promising, oak-aged Chardonnay and Sauvignon Blanc. Debutante Cabernet scheduled for 1985. Ambitious owners.

BANDIERA WINES (ARROYO SONOMA WINERY) The old Bandiera Winery (formed 1937) has been converted into a modern facility for Arroyo Sonoma and the name is now used as a second label for an inexpensive line of wines either produced by the winery or purchased in bulk and packaged.

BARENGO VINEYARDS *San Joaquin 1934* Old-time large-scale (over 300,000-case) Central Valley producer in the Lodi area. Run by Dino Barengo until early 1970s, then sold twice and now controlled by Lost Hills Vineyards interests. Line has concentrated on jug wines and locally grown varietals, with purchases of North Coast wines filling out the line as demand allows. Production of Central Coast wines has now ended. Production techniques have changed to reflect modern technology, but the wines have not always kept pace. The latest ownership change will shift the emphasis back toward jug wines including Lost Hills label. A related product, Barengo's strong, pungent wine vinegar, is very highly regarded.

BARGETTO WINERY *Santa Cruz 1933* A broad line of varietals and fortified wines (30,000 cases in all) is offered. The winery owns no vineyards, so wines are from purchased grapes. Quality has varied widely over the years but took a turn for the positive in late 1970s as emphasis shifted to modern production techniques and better grapes. Bargetto is also well known for fruit and berry wines (10,000 cases).

Chardonnay (Santa Barbara): *Fruity, crisp, slightly floral, light oak* 🍷/🍇
Johannisberg Riesling: *Made in a variety of styles depending on the grapes. Slightly sweet offerings have been delicate, fruity, smelling of fresh peaches and honey* 🍇/🍇🍇; *late harvest bottlings are rich, intense, perfumed.* 🍇🍇

BEAULIEU VINEYARDS *Napa 1900* Once the proudest Napa Valley name, this fabled winery has more than quintupled its output (to 550,000 cases) since its acquisition by Heublein in 1969. Its most important wines—Cabernet Sauvignon, Pinot Noir, and Burgundy—have not maintained their earlier depth and richness. Except for the whites noted below, much of the rest is only of average quality. The winery offers a broad line including dessert wines, champagne, and an expanding proportion of generic wines in magnums.

Burgundy: *Fruity blend made in drinkable style* 🍷
Cabernet Sauvignon/Private Reserve: *Generous, ripe style, fairly tannic, oaky* 🍇/🍇🍇🍇 *with good to great depth until 1970;* 🍷/🍇 *thereafter.*
Cabernet Sauvignon (Rutherford): *Medium-bodied, moderately tannic, forthright, slightly oaky, clean* 🍷/🍇
⚘ **Cabernet Sauvignon (Beau Tour):** *Light and drinkable style, modest varietal, low tannin, worth the price in good years* 🍷
Chardonnay: *Crisp, fruity, moderate oakiness* 🍷/🍇
Johannisberg Riesling: *Medium sweet, fruity* 🍷/🍇
Pinot Noir: *Simple, fruity, some oak and tannin* 🍷
Pinot Noir (Carneros): *From BV's best Pinot Noir vineyard, rich and full in good years, thin in others* 🍷/🍇

BEAU VAL WINES *Amador 1979* Zinfandel and Sauvignon Blanc are the two main wines from this 2,500-case producer. Small amounts of Barbera and Zinfandel Blanc also appear. Vineyards consist of 7 1/2 acres total for the three varieties.

BEL ARBRES (FETZER VINEYARDS) A fast-growing second label now over the 50,000-case-per-year mark. It consists of an assortment of red and white table wines, some "produced by" and others "cellared by" Fetzer. Its appellations also vary from Mendocino to California. Most reds are fruity and simple; the whites, highly variable. The best seller is the Blanc de Blancs. All offerings are low-priced.

BELL CANYON CELLARS (BURGESS CELLARS) Its second label, used for small lots of wine purchased from other producers and bottled at the winery. The quality has varied widely and often failed to keep pace with price.

BELLEROSE VINEYARD *Sonoma 1980* With a 52-acre vineyard located in the southern end of the Dry Creek Valley, this winery intends to specialize in Cabernet. The vineyard consists of the traditional Bordeaux grapes—Cabernet, Merlot, Cabernet Franc, Malbec, and Petit Verdot. The first wine offered was an unusual rosé made from Johannisberg Riesling and Merlot. Initial Cabernet release (1979) bodes well for future success. Maximum production target is 10,000 cases.

BELVEDERE WINE COMPANY The parent company for several varietals which feature the grower or vineyard on the label, with Belvedere appearing in the fine print. The vineyard-designated varietals offered include Bacigalupi for Chardonnay, Robert Young for Cabernet Sauvignon, and Winery Lake for Pinot Noir. The early vintages were made at Sonoma Vineyards before a winery was built in the Healdsburg area. Belvedere markets 6,000 cases total.

BERINGER VINEYARDS *Napa 1876* This historic winery was completely restored and returned to current tourist appeal by Nestlé, which functions as its landlord but technically does not own the wines. The old winery, with aging cellars and reception center, is a showcase. All wines are made in a large, modern facility across the highway. Beringer's vineyard holdings have grown to 1,400 acres in various Napa locations, and 400 acres in Sonoma's Knight's Valley. Its major emphasis is on varietals, currently reaching 250,000 cases per year. Since 1975 this brand has registered steady quality improvement. Most whites represent good value; the reds are of standard quality in general. It bottles 4 Cabernets and 3 Chardonnays each year and tries (perhaps too hard) to make ❀❀❀ versions, while its best score is a ❀ Private Reserve Cabernet. The company's line of jug wines is now all under its Los Hermanos label.

Cabernet Sauvignon: *Modest varietal, light tannin* ♥
Chardonnay: *Appley, medium varietal, light oak* ♥

Chenin Blanc: *Aromatic, fruity flavors, medium sweet* ♥/❀
Fumé Blanc: *Varietal, crisp, fruity, light oak* ♥/❀
Johannisberg Riesling: *Fragrant, lively, medium sweet* ❀

BERKELEY WINE CELLARS (WINE AND THE PEOPLE) The low-volume (1,200-case) premium label of this wine supply and home brew specialist. Zinfandel from the Dry Creek area is the major offering, although Pinot Noir, Chardonnay, and a few small lots appear also.

BLUE HERON WINERY *Sonoma 1979* Working out of a tiny warehouse in Healdsburg, this producer wants to make Chardonnay only. The grapes come from two adjoining vineyards in the Russian River region and contribute to an annual production of 2,000 cases.

BOEGER WINERY *El Dorado 1973* As part of a small-scale wine revival in the Sierra foothills, the Boegers planted 20 acres, now make around 8,000 cases per year. Cabernets and Zinfandels are noteworthy. They also make blended reds and whites called Hangtown Red and Sierra Blanc, and in 1979 added Chardonnay and Sauvignon Blanc to their varietal program. Emphasis is on dry wines, wood aged. Successes to date have been with reds.

Cabernet Sauvignon: *Spicy, rich, complex* ❀
Zinfandel: *Berryish, woody, rough* ♥

BOGLE VINEYARDS *Yolo 1979* Growers selling mainly to big wineries (including Wente) now use small proportion of their own grapes to produce enjoyable Chenin Blanc and easygoing Petite Sirah. Production nears 15,000 cases.

BOISSET VINEYARD Burgundian wine-producer Jean-Claude Boisset purchased a 56-acre vineyard in the Napa Valley near Rutherford with the intention of starting a California branch of the business. In 1980 and 1981, Boisset crushed Cabernet and a little Chardonnay at the Conn Creek winery for debut in early 1983. A 40,000-case Napa Valley winery is anticipated in time for the 1983 crush.

JACQUES BONET Over a million cases of sweet, insipid, bulk process sparkling wines appear under this Heublein label.

BORRA'S CELLAR *San Joaquin 1975* Small (500-case) winery in Lodi specializing in Barbera. It uses about 5% of the production from its 30 acres, and ages Barbera for over 2 years in barrel. The style is ripe, and very heavy. Added small amount of Carignane to its line in 1978.

BOUNTY VINEYARDS A privately owned label for generics and varietals made at the Growers Winery. No discernible difference between Bounty wines and the Growers products.

BRANDER VINEYARD *Santa Barbara 1980* From his 40-acre vineyard, C. Frederick Brander (who is also the winemaker and part-owner of the Santa Ynez Valley Winery) makes up to 5,000 cases of Sauvignon Blanc and a Cabernet Sauvignon/Merlot/Cabernet Franc blended red. His Sauvignon Blanc, about 80% of total production, is blended heavily with Semillon.

BRAREN-PAULI WINERY *Mendocino 1980* This partnership farms 75 acres of vineyards divided between the Potter and Redwood Valleys. Initial production of 600 cases is expected to jump to 2,000 cases with the focus on Sauvignon Blanc, Chardonnay, and Zinfandel.

BRECKENRIDGE CELLARS (GIUMARRA VINEYARDS) Line of inexpensive, uninteresting varietals offered east of the Rockies since 1976. Sales at the 50,000-case level.

BROOKSIDE CELLARS *San Bernardino 1832* This large winery is a division of Chesapeake Industries of Newport Beach. The Brookside label appears on a broad range of specialty wines, generics, dessert wines, champagne, and brandy, all cheap. Brookside farms 3,000 acres and produces approximately 650,000 cases. Its top-priced labels are E. Vache and Assumption Abbey, sold primarily through the winery's chain of 34 tasting rooms. These are located mostly in California, with a few in Nevada, Arizona, and Illinois.

DAVID BRUCE WINERY *Santa Cruz 1964* Well known for heavyweight, wood-aged wines. Dr. Bruce was one of the first to espouse the minimum-handling concept of letting the wine make itself. His late 1960s late harvest Zinfandels were among the first and best. Bruce has always proclaimed himself a Burgundian and devotes his attention first to Chardonnay and Pinot Noir. Some Chardonnays have been superb; some simply big and dull. Other wines have been variable. 25 acres grow next to the winery in the Santa Cruz Mountains; in addition, grapes are purchased from San Luis Obispo, Mendocino, and Sierra Foothills vineyards for the remainder of its 18,000-case production.

Chardonnay: *Oaky, full-bodied, ripe* ❦/❀❀
Pinot Noir: *Oaky, sometimes rich, often thin* ❦/❀
Zinfandel: *Usually intense, often exotic and heavy* ❦/❀❀

BUEHLER VINEYARDS *Napa 1978* Quality-minded growers with 60 acres in eastern Napa hills who are now beginning to ease into winemaking. First vintage of Cabernet, Sauvignon Blanc, and Zinfandel totaled 1,000 cases. Production has reached 8,500 cases, including small amounts of Pinot Blanc and Muscat Blanc.

Zinfandel: *Ripe fruit, warm, tannic* ❀/❀❀

BUENA VISTA WINERY *Sonoma 1857* This historic property, established by the flamboyant Count Agoston Haraszthy, sat vacant for four decades until being returned to winemaking in the early 1940s. Drawing on its own vineyards nestled against the hills backing up to the city of Sonoma, Buena Vista produced hearty reds and usually uninspiring whites for 30 years. In 1968 the winery was sold to new owners with plans for change. 700 acres of vineyard were planted in the cooler Carneros district and a new, up-to-date winemaking facility was built alongside. Production is now in the 100,000-case range. Whites are showing improvement. In 1979 the winery was sold to German interests who are continuing progress and directing efforts toward "Special Selection" varietals grown in the Carneros area.

Cabernet Sauvignon: *Muted varietal, medium light* ❦
Chardonnay: *Modest varietal, light oak, lemony* ❦
Zinfandel: *Berryish, moderately tannic, a bit lacking in vigor* ❦/❀

BURGESS CELLARS *Napa 1972* Fairly modern winery occupying a site used for wine growing since 1880 and located in the hills east of the Napa Valley floor. The first Souverain winery structure, built here in the 1940s, was purchased by former airline pilot Tom Burgess in 1972 when Souverain moved. Production is now 30,000 cases, versus 14,000 in 1972. Most grapes are purchases, usually from the leading vineyards in the Napa Valley, but are no longer vineyard-identified on the label. Burgess is now developing 50 acres of his own in the Yountville area. Wines are high-quality and priced accordingly.

Cabernet Sauvignon: *Hard, moderately tannic, not always intense* ❦/❀
Cabernet Vintage Selection: *Rich, hard, ripe, weedy, fairly tannic, ages well* ❀/❀❀❀

Chardonnay: *Fruity, good varietal, big, crisp, oaky* ✪
Chenin Blanc: *Dry, fruity, lots of oak* ✪/✪✪
Zinfandel: *Fairly refined, fruity with good varietal and oak tastes* ✪/✪✪

DAVIS BYNUM WINERY *Sonoma 1975* Bynum ran a storefront winery near Berkeley from 1965 until moving to the present Russian River location. Most varietal offerings are made from grapes grown locally. The 20,000-case production leans toward the reds. Though there is a hit-or-miss quality record, the hits are generally with red wines.

Chardonnay: *Very oaky, fairly big, variable* ♟
Fumé Blanc: *Assertively varietal, strong flavors* ♟/✪
Pinot Noir: *Complex, ripe fruit, high acid* ♟/✪
Zinfandel: *Ripe, oaky, tannic* ♟

CADENASSO WINERY *Solano 1906* Much of the output (50,000 cases) is sold in bulk to others; some is available at the winery—the best of which is Zinfandel. Winemaking follows the "overlong aging in too old tanks" school.

CADLOLO WINERY *San Joaquin 1913* 5 acres and substantial amounts of purchased grapes yield the standard generic table wines and dessert wines. They are enjoyed mainly by local patrons.

CAIN CELLARS Producing 2,000 cases of Sauvignon Blanc for the moment in leased space, Cain will build a winery on Spring Mountain, Napa Valley, circa 1983 utilizing Cabernet Sauvignon from its own vineyard. By then we should know if Cain is able.

CAKEBREAD CELLARS *Napa 1973* Vineyard owner's 22 acres of wine, along with Cabernet from Steltzner vineyards and Zinfandel from hills, contribute to the winery's 12,000-case output. Wines to date, made in big barrel-aged style, have possessed admirable intensity, and have shown steady improvement over recent vintages.

Cabernet Sauvignon: *Good fruit and varietal, tannic* ♟/✪
Chardonnay: *Oaky, spicy, earthy, good acid balance, fairly big in the mouth* ♟/✪
Sauvignon Blanc: *Big, dry, oaky, ripe flavors* ♟/✪

CALAFIA CELLARS Wines from this Napa label are made at Stag's Leap Vineyard, whose winemaker is part-owner of Calafia. A total of 1,500 cases are spread out over several varietals. The quality of the initial offerings was mixed.

CALERA WINE *San Benito 1976* Established by Josh Jensen, whose aspirations to make great Pinot Noir are the driving force behind the winery. Latest efforts with this variety (using grapes grown adjacent to the winery at the 2,200-foot level in the Gavelan Mountains) have met with great critical success. Zinfandel, from purchased grapes, has varied both in style—rich, balanced to overripe—and also in quality. 6,000 cases.

CALISTOGA VINEYARDS (CUVAISON) Currently a second label used for Cabernet and Chardonnay, made from lots that were not used for Cuvaison's bottlings. Over recent vintages the Chardonnay, though coarse, has been the better value.

CALLAWAY VINEYARD & WINERY *Riverside 1974* As Southern California's first well-financed new winery, it initially attracted considerable interest. After the first few vintages the wines met with mixed acceptance. The white varietals, though low in intensity, were better than the reds, and now represent 90% of the annual 70,000-case output. About 65% of its sales is in restaurants today. A late harvest Chenin Blanc is occasionally offered under the Sweet Nancy name. The winery and its 140 acres of vineyards were sold in 1981 to Hiram Walker, Inc., which intends to expand production to 250,000 cases within a few years.

Chenin Blanc: *Fruity, simple, soft, slightly sweet* ♥
Fumé Blanc: *Grassy, round, soft, some wood* ♥/❀
Zinfandel: *Ripe, pruney, heavy, warm* ☰/♥

CAMBIASO VINEYARDS *Sonoma 1934* An old jug winery modernized by a new corporate owner, the Thai-owned Four Seas Corporation. Most of its 60,000-case sales are in generics, but a small varietal line has been added. Uses 1852 House as another generic brand. Owns 62 acres. Buys some grapes and still sells to other wineries. Most varietals are weak. The slightly tanky Burgundy is barely acceptable for the price.

CAPARONE WINERY *San Luis Obispo 1980* Small (3,500 cases), quality conscious, red wine producer oriented 80% to Cabernet Sauvignon from Tepusquet Vineyards with Merlot making up the remainder. The winery is experimenting with Nebbiolo in its own 8-acre vineyard but does not expect commercial quantities for many years.

CAREY CELLARS *Santa Barbara 1978* 43 acres of Cabernet Sauvignon, Merlot, Chardonnay, and Sauvignon Blanc provide grapes for the production of 4,000 cases. The most successful wines have been the Sauvignon Blanc and a tart, fruity Cabernet Sauvignon Blanc.

RICHARD CAREY WINERY *Alameda 1977* Biology-professor-turned-winemaker Richard Carey produces 35,000 cases of wine. The wide range of average-quality varietals sells at moderate prices, but an occasional special bottling costs more. Quality has varied widely with success centered on reds, generic blends, and the special bottlings. The winery has folded; the wines linger on.

✓ **Zinfandel (Amador):** *Ripe, fruity, moderately tannic* ❀
Blanc Fumé: *Grassy, lightly fragrant, oaky* 🍷

CARMEL BAY WINERY *Monterey 1977* Small, hobbyist winery (500 cases) producing Zinfandel and other red wines, primarily from Central Coast grapes.

CARNEROS CREEK WINERY *Napa 1972* Small (15,000-case) winery making high-quality varietals. Chardonnay and Pinot Noir are Carneros-area grown. Cabernet from 1977 vintage onward has come from Fay vineyard in the Stag's Leap area. Zinfandel is being phased out in favor of Merlot and Sauvignon Blanc. A small experimental plot of Pinot Noir grows next to the winery. Prices are generally reasonable.

Chardonnay: *Dry, crisp, oaky, sometimes needing greater intensity* 🍷/❀
✓ **Merlot:** *Soft, fruity, eminently drinkable* 🍷/❀
Pinot Noir: *Rich, intense varietal and oak, good depth* ❀/❀❀❀
✓ **Zinfandel:** *Occasionally late harvest, typically ripe-tasting, usually very tannic, diminishing quality in recent vintages* ♁/❀

CARTLIDGE & BROWNE Winemakers without a winery of their own, this partnership produces about 1,200 cases of Chardonnay from grapes purchased from the Oak Knoll area of the Napa Valley. First wines were successful and plans call for doubling production by the mid-1980s and adding other varietals.

CASA NUESTRA WINERY *Napa 1980* Located on the Silverado Trail, this tiny (500-case) winery opened with a dry Chenin Blanc. It added 300 cases of a blended red made from Zinfandel and Gamay. The winery owns 11 acres of Chenin Blanc, Zinfandel, and Gamay. The Chenin Blanc is of average quality.

CASSAYRE-FORNI CELLARS *Napa 1977* Small winery (7,000 cases) operated by full-time engineering consultants. Their Cabernet is a blend of 2 vineyards—one near the winery in Rutherford and the other across the valley near the Silverado Trail. Chenin Blanc is from Yountville. Zinfandel is from Dry Creek. A new production facility is under construction which will allow the winery to reach its goal of 12,000 cases by 1985.

Cabernet Sauvignon: *Medium weight, oak-aged, moderately tannic* ♥/❀
Chenin Blanc: *Dry to slightly sweet depending on the vintage; fruity, balanced style, light oak* ♥/❀

CAYMUS VINEYARDS *Napa 1972* The transition from growers to winemakers was distinguished by the production of superb-quality Cabernet and by a pioneering Blanc de Noirs labeled Oeil de Perdrix. Drawing from a 70-acre vineyard in Rutherford and some purchased grapes, Caymus makes close to 15,000 cases and sells another 5,000 under the Liberty School label. Recently added a Reserve Cabernet and Reserve Pinot Noir and expanded the line of varietals to include Chardonnay and Petite Sirah. High-quality varietals at reasonable prices; reds generally more exciting than whites.

⚕ **Cabernet Sauvignon:** *Minty, complex, tannic* ❀/❀❀❀
Pinot Noir: *Ripe, fruity, tannic, woody* ❀
Sauvignon Blanc: *Oaky, medium–full-bodied, varietal, usually fruity, dry* ♥/❀
⚕ **Zinfandel:** *Berrylike, rich, moderately tannic* ❀/❀❀❀

CC VINEYARDS (JFJ WINERY) A secondary label used by JFJ for generic wines sold in large containers at inexpensive prices. A sparkling wine is also offered. The wines are identical to those under the JFJ label and share their sweet-edged, jug-wine flavors.

CEDAR RIDGE Private label originally created by a San Francisco-based distributor to furnish restaurant house wines, but now selling 40,000 cases a year in general distribution. Wines are purchased at various large wineries.

CHALONE VINEYARD *Monterey 1960* A small, much-revered winery located high in the hills east of the Salinas Valley. Famous for ripe, oak-aged wines of the highest quality. Early success with Pinot Noir, Chardonnay, Chenin Blanc, and Pinot Blanc inspired other wineries to emulate the Chalone style—and often to exceed it in quality. Still, demand for Chalone wines remains high because their best continues to be superb. Production has expanded substantially to 12,000 cases as winery's 110 acres (including 50% Chardonnay, 25% Pinot Noir) come into full bearing.

Chardonnay: *Ripe, oily, very oaky; intense, great depth* ♥/✿✿✿
Pinot Blanc: *Usually ripe, powerful, balanced, oaky; occasionally flawed* ♥/✿✿✿
Pinot Noir: *Often intense and complex, always oaky, sometimes thin* ♥/✿✿✿

CHAMISAL VINEYARD *San Luis Obispo 1979* This operation's 52 acres of Chardonnay and 5 acres of Cabernet were the first vineyards planted in the Edna Valley. A small winery was completed in 1980 for a production level targeted at 2,000 cases. Initial Chardonnay was fairly big and oaky and the opposite of the crisp, high-acid style for which the winery wants to become noted. Grapes have been purchased for a Sauvignon Blanc.

CHANDON *Napa 1973* French-owned (Moët-Hennessy of Moët & Chandon champagnes and Hennessy cognac) champagne label produced at the architecturally sparkling new winery called Domaine Chandon. Two-thirds of the 250,000-case, sparkling-wine output is labeled Brut, a blend of Pinot Noir (60%), Chardonnay (30%), and Pinot Blanc (10%). The other major offering, Blanc de Noirs, is 100% Pinot Noir. Both are aged up to 2 years on the yeast *(en tirage)*. A third sparkling wine, Special Reserve Brut, is the Brut cuveé held 3 1/2 years on the yeast in magnum-sized bottles. The winery owns 500 acres of vineyards, mostly in the Carneros area.

※ **Blanc de Noirs:** *Same dry-tasting balance as Brut, a bit more body, slight onion-skin color* ✿/✿✿
※ **Brut:** *High acid balanced by slight sweetness, tight, hard fruit* ✿/✿✿
Special Reserve Brut: *Fuller bodied, more complex than the Brut* ✿✿/✿✿✿

CHAPARRAL A private label owned by a group of Southern California retailers. The wines, Pinot Noir and Chardonnay, are produced by Chalone from grapes grown in the Edna Valley.

CHAPPELLET VINEYARDS *Napa 1969* From 100 acres located on the eastern side of the Napa Valley, Chappellet is making Chardonnay, Chenin Blanc, Riesling, and Cabernet. The quality of Cabernet varies widely. Recent vintages of

Johannisberg Riesling are slightly sweet, but the Chenin Blanc remains dry. Production has reached the maximum 25,000 cases, which include an occasional bottling of Merlot. Gamay production ceased after 1979 vintage.

Cabernet Sauvignon: *Ripe, hard, slow ager* ♥/❀❀
Chardonnay: *Average varietal, firm, oaky* ♥/❀
Chenin Blanc: *Fruity, full-crisp, some oak* ❀
Johannisberg Riesling: *Floral, delicate, balanced* ♥/❀

CHATEAU BOUCHAINE *Napa 1981* Housed in a large facility located in the Carneros district, this winery made only 1,300 cases for its own label initially, but its 250,000-case capacity was used to make wines for other labels and wineries. The owners have a 70-acre vineyard near Santa Rosa and planted 30 acres in Carneros to Chardonnay and Pinot Noir, two varietals it intends to emphasize. By 1983 output under the Bouchaine label is expected to reach 100,000 cases of varietals.

CHATEAU CHEVRE *Napa 1979* First production from this winery's 10 acres of Merlot yielded 300 cases in 1979. Annual volume is expected to rise to 2,000 cases of Merlot. Sauvignon Blanc will be added when 9 new acres of vines come into bearing.

CHATEAU CHEVALIER *Napa 1972* This old (1891) estate on Spring Mountain was revived in 1969 when 60 acres of hillside vineyards were planted primarily to Cabernet and Chardonnay. By 1980, when production reached 10,000 cases, the owner had to buy Chardonnay and Pinot Noir from Edna Valley because of problems with his own vineyard. The winery occasionally offers Johannisberg Riesling, along with tiny amounts of Merlot and Pinot Noir. So far prices are in advance of quality, with exception of recent Reserve Cabernet. Mountainside Vineyard, once an important second label, is being phased out.

Cabernet Sauvignon: *Dark, ripe, very tannic* ♥/❀
Chardonnay (Napa): *Modest intensity and flavor* ♥

CHATEAU DIANA This negociant label is a stablemate of the Adobe Cellars brand and offers essentially the same wines in a different package.

CHATEAU D'IVRESSE *Riverside 1980* Until its 80-acre vineyard at the 5,200-foot level of Mt. San Jacinto (near Palm Springs) is planted and produces fruit, the winery buys grapes from the Rancho California area and makes a few hundred cases of Cabernet Sauvignon.

CHATEAU MONTELENA *Napa 1972* Noted from its outset as one of California's premier Chardonnay producers, Montelena gained worldwide fame in 1976 when its wine was chosen best among 12 leading California and French offerings by a highly regarded French tasting panel. Now producing approximately 25,000 cases per year, the winery has headed toward 50% Cabernet Sauvignon, about 35% Chardonnay, and 15% Zinfandel. Two Cabernets, one from Sonoma and one from estate-grown Napa grapes, are offered. In spite of critical success with Johannisberg Riesling, it has all but dropped that variety.

Cabernet Sauvignon: *Elegant, moderately tannic, balanced wines, good fruity qualities* ❸/❸❸
Chardonnay (Napa): *Among the best. Rich oak and deep fruit, superb balance* ❸/❸❸❸
Chardonnay (California): *Usually contains Central Coast grapes, often tastes simpler than Napa wine, sometimes grassy* ❶/❸❸❸

CHATEAU NOUVEAU A label devoted entirely to Gamay Beaujolais made 100% by carbonic maceration. The first offering from 1980 (330 cases) was finished inadvertently slightly sweet. The 1981 (700 cases) was dry and drinkable. Both vintages were made at Shown & Sons.

CHATEAU ST. JEAN *Sonoma 1973* This white wine specialist (97% of its 90,000-case production) has established solid credentials for highest-quality wines often produced from single vineyards. Over 50% of production is in Chardonnay, with smaller amounts in Johannisberg Riesling, Sauvignon Blanc, Gewurztraminer, and Pinot Blanc. The past array of red wines has been reduced to a single bottling of Cabernet Sauvignon. Chateau St. Jean has had extraordinary success with late harvest Johannisberg Riesling and Gewurztraminer. Among the Chardonnays, those labeled Robert Young Vineyard, Belle Terre, and Gauer Ranch are our favorites. Also in the works (scheduled to debut in 1983) is *méthode champenoise* sparkling wine.

Chardonnay (vineyard designated): *Fruity, oaky, fairly full-bodied style; quality varies among bottlings, but is usually high* ❶/❸❸❸
Chardonnay (Sonoma): *This high volume offering has been consistently fruity, fresh, drinkable* ❸

Johannisberg Riesling: *Late harvest bottlings are usually clean, honeyed wines. The most expensive reach 23–28% sugar in the finished wines and are remarkable achievements on an international scale. Regular bottlings are usually medium sweet, very clean, and fruity ♥/✿✿ for regular bottlings; ✿/✿✿ for most late harvest; ✿✿/✿✿✿ for the supreme efforts.*

Sauvignon Blanc (Fumé Blanc): *Small-lot St. Jean Vineyard, La Petite Etoile, and Crimmons bottlings are intense, fresh, fruity, and varietal with light oakiness and noticeable grassiness (especially Crimmins) ✿/✿✿✿; the other bottlings, both vineyard-designated and single-county-designated have usually been less attractive versions ♥/✿✿*

Pinot Blanc: *Typical varietal fruit, good balance, oaky ✿*

CHATEAU SONOMA Label owned by S. S. Pierce for red, rosé, and white tables wines made from Sonoma grapes at Souverain Cellars. About 2,500 cases annually. Light-style wines.

L. CHERPIN WINERY *San Bernardino 1934* Old firm continuing to sell its generics at the winery and local restaurants.

CHISPA CELLARS *Calaveras 1976* First new winery to materialize in Calaveras since Prohibition. Without vineyards, it buys Ruby Cabernet and Zinfandel from Amador and El Dorado counties. 2,500 cases is optimum production.

CHRISTIAN BROTHERS *Napa 1882* This venerable producer offers a full line of wines and brandies. It has 1,600 acres and 3 facilities in Napa, where it makes table wines and champagnes. Dessert wines and brandies are produced in the Central Valley. The wines total 2 million cases, consisting of the proprietary La Salle bottlings and the top-line Napa Valley varietals. Though vintage-dated wines are increasing, most wines are non-vintage blends. The white varietals are consistent and nicely priced; the reds tend to be light and overaged. Expanding production of generic wines in magnums.

Cabernet Sauvignon: *Light varietal, modest and mature ♥*

✤ **Chardonnay (non-vintage):** *Appley, medium-bodied, clean, crisp ♥/✿*

✤ **Chenin Blanc:** *Fresh and fruity, medium sweet ✿*

Fumé Blanc: *Herbal, light wood, flavorful ♥/✿*

Gamay Noir: *Tired, mature, woody ♥*

Zinfandel: *Vague fruit, thin, simple ♥*

CILURZO VINEYARD *Riverside 1978* An 8,000-case Temecula winery producing Cabernet, Petite Sirah, Gamay Beaujolais, Fumé Blanc, and dry Chenin Blanc from grapes grown in the Rancho California area of Riverside County.

CIRIACO BORELLI WINERY *San Joaquin 1979* Three generic wines are produced from purchased grapes. 1,000 cases per year.

CLOS DU BOIS *Sonoma 1976* Several partners own 1,200 acres in the Dry Creek and Alexander Valley regions. Through 1980 the Clos du Bois wines were made at Souverain and aged at the partners' facility in the Dry Creek area. By 1980 that winery crushed a high percentage of the total 45,000-case output. After early success with Gewurztraminer and Johannisberg Riesling, its white varietals are generally of average quality. Its emphasis is now on vineyard-designated wines—Briarcrest Cabernet, Cherry Hill Pinot Noir—and a proprietary blend of Cabernet and Merlot called Marlstone. The names are imaginative, but the quality lags behind price.

Cabernet Sauvignon (Alexander Valley): *Cherry-candylike fruit, soft, supple* ♥
Chardonnay: *Appley, light oak, monochromatic* ♥
Gewurztraminer: *Intensely varietal, slightly sweet* ❀/❀ ❀ *through 1978. "Early harvest" versions since are citric and light* ♥/❀

CLOS DU VAL *Napa 1973* The winemaker is French, and the winery's emphasis is on a Bordeaux-style Cabernet-Merlot blend. About 70% of the 22,000-case output is Cabernet. The remainder is divided equally among Zinfandel, Merlot, and Chardonnay. There are 120 acres planted near the winery plus a new 170-acre parcel in the Carneros district that is to be planted primarily to Chardonnay and will raise that variety's level from 2,000 cases to 15,000 cases. A small amount of Pinot Noir is also expected to be put in.

Cabernet Sauvignon: *Weedy, hard, tannic, ages well* ♥/❀❀
Chardonnay: *Has improved steadily; 1978 was best effort to date; crisp, rich with oak* ♥/❀
Merlot: *Fruity, rich, oaky, moderately tannic, inviting* ❀/❀❀
Zinfandel: *Complex, minty, firm, tannic* ❀❀/❀❀❀

CLOUDSTONE VINEYARDS *Santa Clara 1981* Small (400 cases) winery producing Chardonnay, Cabernet Sauvignon, and Zinfandel from purchased grapes grown in Lake County.

COAST RANGE Negociant's label for wines purchased ready-made and bottled at various wineries. The annual offerings are subject to what is available. Volume has been close to 3,000 cases.

COLOMA CELLARS *San Joaquin 1974* This old Gold Country label is now applied to a range of generic, dessert, champagne, and specialty wines. All are made from purchased wines. Offer 7,500 cases.

COLONY *1887* Founded at Asti in northern Sonoma County under the name Italian Swiss Colony, the winery eventually found its way into increasingly larger wine conglomerates until it was purchased a decade ago by Heublein. As recently as 10 years ago, ISC wines bore various North Coast appellations. Now most of the wine is produced and bottled at plants in the Central Valley. All the wines, including the reds, have noticeable sweetness. New packaging featuring cork-finished bottles (no more screw caps), drier blends is intended to make Colony competitive with Taylor, Inglenook, and Almadén rather than Gallo or Franzia. Sales exceed 4,000,000 cases annually.

> **Cabernet Sauvignon:** *Relatively clean, slightly sweet, low varietal, jug wine* ♥
> **Chenin Blanc:** *Medium sweet, soft, low-alcohol style* ♥
> ♦ **Zinfandel:** *Born again after years of being sweet nothing, new version is full, fleshy and hints at varietal* ♥

COLUMBIA CELLARS *Tuolumne 1974* The only winery crushing in this county. Its 2,000-case output consists of an Amador Zinfandel and several generics.

COMPASS BAY Distributor's private label for lots of wine purchased in bulk and packaged primarily for East Coast distribution. Approximately 10,000 cases a year.

CONCANNON VINEYARDS *Alameda 1887* Medium-sized producer (75,000 cases) in the Livermore Valley offering a broad line of vintage-dated varietals grown primarily on 250 acres of immediately adjacent estate-owned vineyards. Winery's staid image is changing due to improved winemaking technology. Concannon offered the first varietally labeled Petite Sirah in the mid-1960s, is the only California winery to offer varietal Rkatsiteli, and initiated trend-setting Muscat Blanc. Production is 70% white wine, but Petite Sirah is its leading seller. New ownership and new distribution channels will bring further changes, including increased emphasis on estate-bottled and vine-yard-designated wines.

☙ **Muscat Blanc:** *Perfumed, floral and spice, medium sweet to sweet* ❸/❸❸
Petite Sirah: *Clean, fruity, slightly ripe, moderately tannic; less brawny than most competitors* ♥/❸
☙ **Sauvignon Blanc:** *Dry, fruity, elegant style* ♥/❸❸
☙ **Zinfandel Rosé:** *Slightly sweet, intensely fruity, one of the best* ♥/❸

CONGRESS SPRINGS VINEYARDS *Santa Clara 1976* Winery located on historic vineyard and building site in the Santa Cruz Mountains. Current production is 5,000 cases. The quality has been mixed, with greatest success in Pinot Blanc, Sauvignon Blanc, and Zinfandel.

Pinot Blanc: *Floral, fruity, flavorful* ♥/❸❸
Sauvignon Blanc: *Dry style, labeled fumé, is weedy, spicy, strong;* ❸ *slightly sweet, called Sauvignon Blanc, is fruity, pungent* ♥/❸
Zinfandel: *ripe, spicy, vanilla oakiness* ❸/❸❸

CONN CREEK WINERY *Napa 1974* With construction of its new winery now comfortably accomplished and grape sources assured through the 150 acres owned by partners in the venture (including the Château La Mission Haut-Brion interests of Bordeaux), Conn Creek has settled down to the production of 20,000 cases of Cabernet, Chardonnay, and Zinfandel only. The Cabernet has been the star to date, with the other wines showing less well only by comparison.

Cabernet Sauvignon: *Complex, curranty aroma, rich, tannic* ♥/❸❸
Chardonnay: *Oaky, ripe, medium–full bodied* ♥/❸
Zinfandel: *Brawny, full-bodied, improving in recent vintages, sometimes overripe* ♥

CONROTTO WINERY *Santa Clara 1933* Old-time generic wine producer selling to local restaurants and stores. An occasional varietal is offered.

CONTI ROYALE Viewed by its owner, East-Side, as the premium label, it encompasses a range of varietals, generics, and brandies. The red varietals sometimes offer good value. Ports and sherries are among the best of the inexpensive California offerings. Conti Royale 10-year-old brandy is extremely good.

COOK'S CHAMPAGNE   This historic label has been resurrected in California by the Guild cooperative for a line of inexpensive, bulk process sparkling wine.

R & J COOK WINERY *Yolo 1979*   After several wineries, notably Grand Cru, produced excellent Chenin Blanc from their vineyards, the Cooks entered winemaking. They now produce 40,000 cases from their 130-acre vineyard in the Clarksburg region, while continuing to sell grapes to numerous producers. Their primary wine is Chenin Blanc made in three styles—Extra Dry (barrel fermented), Very Dry (oak aged), and Semi-Dry (no oak and slightly sweet). Petite Sirah and a host of blended table wines round out the line.

CORDTZ BROTHERS *Sonoma 1980*   From its 50 acres and purchased grapes, Cordtz made 7,000 cases of varietals in 1981. Chardonnay, Sauvignon Blanc, Gewurztraminer, Zinfandel, and Cabernet Sauvignon are the main varietals in this winery's roster. Optimum production will be 20,000 cases. Reception to first wines was lukewarm.

CORTI BROTHERS   A private label owned by a Sacramento delicatessen/wine store operation. From 1968 to 1975, it bottled Amador Zinfandel made at Sutter Home Winery. The label reappeared on a 1979 Amador Zinfandel made at Santino Vineyards. Total output: 600 cases.

H. COTURRI & SONS *Sonoma 1979*   Buying grapes from Sonoma Valley growers, this Glen Ellen winery is among the latest to go with traditional, semi-primitive winemaking methods. Its wines ferment on the wild yeasts, and temperatures are not controlled by refrigeration systems. The wines are clarified naturally. Its first wines included a cloudy, unstable Chardonnay, a raisined Zinfandel, and awful Pinot Noir and Cabernet. Collectively, they made a dramatic statement favoring scientific know-how and precision.

COWBOY WINE   Trying to catch the wave of popularity for Western fashions, a San Francisco distributor created this label in 1981. Red and white are offered. The white is a French Colombard and Chenin Blanc blend made by Souverain.

CRESCINI WINERY *Santa Cruz 1980*   Three varietals—Cabernet Sauvignon, Petite Sirah, and Chenin Blanc—are made from grapes purchased in Napa and Monterey counties. 400-case production with a goal of 1,200.

CRESTA BLANCA WINERY *Mendocino 1971* A famous brand established in 1880 in Livermore. Underwent several changes in ownership until acquired by the Guild cooperative, which reestablished it in Ukiah. The winery has been expanded and has a storage capacity of 2.3 million gallons, although the label itself covers only one-tenth of that amount. Most of the table wines carry vintage dates, and a few bear a Mendocino County appellation. Recently, several varietals have been made from Central Coast grapes. The quality to date is inconsistent. The white wines are generally thin and low on character; the reds, including the top-selling Zinfandel, are variable. The brand's most consistent good-quality wines are the sherries, which are made at other facilities.

Chenin Blanc: *Weak varietal, rough, medium sweet* ☼/♀

Triple Cream Sherry: *Aromatic, full-bodied, very sweet, award winner* ♀/✿

♉ **Zinfandel:** *A nonvintage bottling, slightly berrylike and balanced* ♀

CRIBARI WINES This historic name is now a label owned by the Guild cooperative. It covers a large line of inexpensive, sweet-finished, flat-tasting table and dessert wines as well as a few varietals and sweet, bulk process sparkling wine. Quality ranges from dull to dismal.

CRONIN VINEYARDS *San Mateo 1980* Small lots of four varietals are produced from a number of high-quality vineyard sources. Approximately half of the 500 cases per year is barrel-fermented Chardonnay.

CUCAMONGA VINEYARD *San Bernardino 1870* This million-case producer is California's Bonded Winery No. 1 and proud of it. Its major labels are Cuvee d'Or and Bonded Winery No. 1. The bulk process champagne is fairly interesting for the price. Much of the production is sold to other wineries. Recent sale of the winery promises more aggressive marketing efforts. Whether the overall quality will improve is still open to question.

CULBERTSON CHAMPAGNE CELLARS *San Diego 1981* Small (2,000-case) producer of Blancs de Blancs and Blanc de Noirs Champagnes. Both are made by the *méthode champenoise.* The owner uses grapes from his own 6-acre vineyard and buys the rest from Temecula growers. Schramsberg's winemaker serves as the consulting enologist.

CUVAISON *Napa 1970* Medium-sized (20,000-case) producer of quality-oriented, full-bodied varietals. Offers only Chardonnay, Cabernet Sauvignon, and Zinfandel, made from purchased grapes. Hillside vineyards are preferred, except for Winery Lake Chardonnay. Acquired in 1979 by a Swiss banking family which is currently developing a 150-acre vineyard in the Carneros region.

Cabernet Sauvignon: *Medium–full-bodied, tannic, oak-aged style* ♥/❀
Chardonnay: *Oaky, good varietal, sometimes low on intensity, ages well.* ♥/❀
Zinfandel: *Ripe, brawny style* ♥/❀❀

CYGNET CELLARS *San Benito 1977* 3,000-case winery offering mainly late harvest style, high alcohol wines from purchased grapes. Quality of offerings has ranged from flawed to uninteresting.

D'AGOSTINI WINERY *Amador 1856* The oldest and largest producer in Amador, this winery has been family-owned since 1911. The 125-acre vineyard is mixed—Zinfandel and Mission mostly. The wines are old-style generics, Zinfandel being the one varietal. The generics are inexpensive; the Zinfandel is an overaged, tanky blend of vintages. It is not modern Amador fare. Production averages 80,000 cases per year.

DEER PARK WINERY *Napa 1979* The current owners acquired a historic winery site and its 48-acre estate. They began planting 6 acres to Sauvignon Blanc and Zinfandel. Both varieties will be about equally represented in the expected maximum production of 6,000 cases. Early winemaking effort did not impress.

DEHLINGER WINERY *Sonoma 1976* One of our favorites for quality and price. It has 14 acres and buys grapes from hillside vineyards in Sonoma. Production is 6,000 cases limited to 4 varietals. Crushed its first Pinot Noir in 1977. Its performance over the first several vintages places it among the best of the new Sonoma wineries.

Cabernet Sauvignon: *Dark, ripe, flavorful, stylish* ❀/❀❀
Chardonnay: *Varietal, medium full, light oak* ♥/❀❀
Zinfandel: *Briary, rich, woody, ages well* ❀/❀❀

DELICATO VINEYARDS *San Joaquin 1935* A large (22-million-gallon capacity) winery selling wines to other brands, but beginning to expand its own line of generics and varietals rapidly. Recently added Light Chablis is for those who count calories, not flavors. All wines are low-priced, but not bargains.

DE LOACH VINEYARDS *Sonoma 1979* Grower turned winemaker converted 140 acres to grapes and made a highly successful debut with first vintages. White Zinfandel and Zinfandel table wine lead list of offerings from 18,000-case production. Other varieties—Sauvignon Blanc, Pinot Noir, Chardonnay, and Gewurztraminer—are all highly rated in initial vintages.

- ⚕ **Chardonnay:** *Ripe, fruity, slightly blossomy style* ✿✿
- ⚕ **Gewurztraminer:** *Intense, slightly sweet, ripe fruit flavors* ✿
- ⚕ **White Zinfandel:** *Fresh, zesty, soft, inviting* ✿
- ⚕ **Zinfandel:** *Ripe, berryish, slight briary* ♥/✿

DEVLIN WINE CELLARS *Santa Cruz 1979* A 2,000-case winery, with a capacity for 5,000 cases, offering 4 varietals from purchased grapes. Releases have included an attractive Zinfandel from San Luis Obispo County, but quality of most offerings still shows room for improvement.

DIABLO VISTA WINERY *Solano 1977* The partners buy grapes from the Dry Creek area and make 600 cases of Cabernet Sauvignon, Zinfandel, and Merlot.

DIAMOND CREEK VINEYARDS *Napa 1972* A Cabernet-only winery offering 3 distinct bottlings each vintage. Its 20-acre vineyards are situated in 3 adjoining sites, each of which exhibits significant differences in soil composition and exposure. The separate bottlings carry the vineyard names: Gravelly Meadows, Red Rock Terrace, and Volcanic Hill. However, all three share a dark color, ripe flavors, and extremely tannic character. About 2,500 cases are produced per year.

Cabernet Sauvignon: *Ripe, rough, sometimes complex, tannic* ♥/✿✿

DIAMOND OAKS VINEYARD *Napa 1979* For now, a label attached to 15,000 cases of varietals. The 1979s are from Lake County; the 1980s from assorted places, all made at Souverain. With over 200 acres in Napa, the owners, now searching for a winery site, will make 35,000 cases of Cabernet, Sauvignon Blanc, and Chardonnay.

DOLAN VINEYARD *Mendocino 1980* Paul Dolan, Fetzer's wine-maker, produces Mendocino Cabernet and Chardonnay in his own tiny winery. Each varietal is vineyard-designated on the label. Average annual output is 1,400 cases total.

DOMAINE LAURIER *Sonoma 1978* Small winery using its 30-acre vineyard in Forestville to supply most of the grapes for its five varietal wines. Production is 5,000 cases each year. The winery has been particularly successful with Chardonnay.

Chardonnay: *Tart, citrusy, lively flavors* ❁

DONATONI WINERY *Los Angeles 1980* When pilot Hank Donatoni isn't flying, he makes Cabernet Sauvignon and Chardonnay at his small (less than 1,000 cases) winery located on the flight approach to Los Angeles airport. The Cabernet grapes come from the Nepenthe Vineyard near Santa Maria.

DONNA MARIA VINEYARD *Sonoma 1980* A San Francisco attorney acquired a 580-acre estate northeast of Windsor and planted 180 acres to vines in an area along Chalk Hill. The major emphasis is on Chardonnay followed by Gewurztraminer. Pinot Noir, Cabernet, and Sauvignon Blanc will contribute to an eventual 10,000-case annual output. Production could expand quickly as vineyards mature.

DRY CREEK VINEYARDS *Sonoma 1972* This 40,000-case winery has advanced the cause for both the Dry Creek region and for Fumé Blanc wines. It was also among the first new, small wineries to settle in Sonoma. Although noted more for the whites, the quality of all varietals is above average. The current mix is 80% white and 20% red wine. About 25% of its grapes come from 50 acres surrounding the winery.

Cabernet Sauvignon: *Modest varietal, fruity, soft* ♥
Chardonnay: *Medium intense, lemony, oaky, crisp* ♥/❁
Chenin Blanc: *Fruity, crisp, but slightly sweet* ♥/❁
Fumé Blanc: *Assertive varietal, medium-bodied, balanced* ♥/❁❁
Zinfandel: *Spicy, berryish, tannic, sometimes overripe* ♥/❁❁

GEORGES DU BOEUF & SON Well-known producer/shipper of French Beaujolais decided in 1980 to replicate the wine in California. The early effort, labeled Red Table Wine, was a blend of three red varieties. Subsequent vintages have been made from Gamay Beaujolais only. Produced at

Souverain and made partially by carbonic maceration, the wines have achieved modest critical acclaim. Current output is 12,000 cases.

DUCKHORN VINEYARDS *Napa 1978* Crushed only Merlot and Cabernet Sauvignon (3,000 cases) in first vintages with superb results. Planned expansion will enable the production of white wines, Sauvignon Blanc and Chardonnay. Gradual growth to 12,000 cases is planned.

Cabernet Sauvignon: *Tight, hard, long-aging wine with potential for balance, elegance* ❀/❀❀
Merlot: *Rich, balanced, oaky, accessible flavor, good potential* ❀/❀❀❀

DURNEY VINEYARDS *Monterey 1976* From 120 acres located in the Carmel Valley, Durney produces close to 14,000 cases, which will climb to 25,000 when all of the vines mature. Half of the production is in Cabernet, with secondary emphasis given to Chenin Blanc, Johannisberg Riesling, and Gamay Beaujolais. The 1982 harvest marks the winery's introduction of Chardonnay to its line. Showing annual quality improvement.

Cabernet Sauvignon: *Ripe varietal, full, round, well-balanced, moderately tannic* ❀/❀❀

DUTCHER CREEK CELLARS A negociant label slowly evolving into a winery. Table wines will continue to be purchased for resale with on-site production limited to a few thousand cases of champagne. Initial offerings have been fairly priced for their quality.

EDMEADES VINEYARDS *Mendocino 1972* After a rough beginning Edmeades is now making good red varietals in better vintages and light-style whites. From 35 acres in the Anderson Valley and purchased grapes it produces about 22,000 cases. Also offers blended proprietary wines— Rain Wine (white), Opal (Blanc de Noirs), and Mendocino Red.

Cabernet Sauvignon: *Herbaceous, earthy, thin to balanced* ❦/❀
Gewurztraminer: *Light varietal, delicate, slightly sweet* ❦/❀
Zinfandel: *Berrylike, variable depth and tannin* ❦/❀❀

EDNA VALLEY VINEYARD *San Luis Obispo 1980* A 50,000-gallon winery operated as a joint venture by Chalone Vineyard and a local grower. After making limited quantities in 1979 and 1980 in borrowed space, the completed winery began operation in 1981. Production consisted of 80% Chardonnay, 16% Pinot Noir, and 4% Vin Gris (a dry, crisp, light pink wine from Pinot Noir). Although quality has generally varied in early vintages, the best efforts with Pinot Noir and Chardonnay have received ✿ ratings.

EMILE'S CAVALCADE (EMILIO GUGLIELMO WINERY) Label for good-sized (30,000-case) line of jug wines. Mostly inexpensive generics in a heavy style.

Burgundy: *Vinous, full-bodied, aged flavors* ♚

ENZ VINEYARDS *San Benito 1973* Offers Zinfandel, Fumé Blanc, Pinot St. George, and French Colombard of modest to less-than-average quality. Production is 3,500 cases. Owns 30 acres.

ESTRELLA RIVER WINERY *San Luis Obispo 1977* Originally the owners of this large (500-acre) vineyard and winery intended to use only a small percentage of their own grapes for wines under the Estrella River label. By the time the vineyards reached full production, the owners were not able to find enough wineries interested in buying their excess grapes, so were forced to produce much more wine than they were able to sell. The result is that many wines under this label are growing old. Its two most significant varietals are Chardonnay and Cabernet. The brand's reputation may be saved by its French Syrah, which shows considerable promise. The current production is close to 100,000 cases, double its once-anticipated goal.

Cabernet Sauvignon: *Spicy, herbaceous, moderate tannins* ♚/✿
Chardonnay: *Grassy, light fruit flavors, some oak* ♚
Sauvignon Blanc: *Vague varietal, a little flat, light oak* ♚
Syrah: *Fruity, slightly minty flavors, some oak* ♚

EVANS WINE COMPANY *Napa 1980* Australian wine writer Len Evans and his associates are producing Chardonnay, Cabernet Sauvignon, and Merlot intended primarily for export to Australia. The first wines were produced at Souverain from purchased grapes, but a 14-acre vineyard has been purchased in the Napa Valley and a new 20,000-case winery is expected to be ready for the 1982 crush.

EVENSEN WINERY *Napa 1979* The Evensens make 1,000 cases or so of Gewurztraminer from their own 20-acre vineyard near Oakville. Early efforts have been pleasant.

FALCON CREST Second label used by Spring Mountain Vineyards where many scenes have been shot for the television soap opera of that name. Initial wines were of more interest than the program.

FARNESI WINERY *Fresno 1936* Grape growers who turn out limited quantities of a red generic sold in gallon jugs only at the winery.

FAR NIENTE WINERY *Napa 1979* A historic Napa Valley name brought back to life on the century-old premises near Oakville. Until restoration is completed in time for 1982 crush, grapes are pressed at Markham Winery and juice is transported to temporary facilities for fermentation—half in barrels, half in stainless-steel tanks. Production is now 9,000 cases of Chardonnay and 2,000 cases of Cabernet Sauvignon.

Chardonnay: *Big, ripe, oaky, more powerful than elegant* ✿

FARVIEW FARM *San Luis Obispo 1979* Primarily a vineyard operation with 36 acres of Zinfandel and 14 acres of Merlot. The partners are slowly edging toward construction of a winery. Meanwhile, about 7,000 cases are produced annually at other wineries. Quality has been inconsistent.

FELTON-EMPIRE VINEYARDS *Santa Cruz 1976* About 65% of the 18,000-case output consists of Johannisberg Riesling from different regions made in a variety of styles, and a full 85% of production is in white wine. Winemaker prefers Rieslings either in a low-alcohol style and/or from Botrytis-affected grapes. Efforts with Cabernet and Zinfandel attract less attention. The winery farms 62 acres. It also offers popular non-alcoholic grape juice from wine grape varieties.

White (Johannisberg) Riesling: *Fruity, fresh, soft, medium sweet to sweet finish* ♀/✿✿

FENESTRA WINERY *Alameda 1976* Smallish producer (1,500 cases) located in Livermore. Most offerings are produced from Central Coast grapes. A few very good wines but most have been average or worse. Called Ventana Winery until 1978.

Chenin Blanc: *Dry, green apple aroma, clean* ♀
Zinfandel: *Ripe, slightly earthy, rich* ♀

FENTON ACRES WINERY A label belonging to a longtime Sonoma grower with 100 acres west of Healdsburg. Using leased space in a neighboring winery, he bottles 2,000 cases total of his own Chardonnay and Pinor Noir.

FETZER VINEYARDS *Mendocino 1968* This family-owned winery first built a reputation for sturdy red varietals, but has recently become one of the great growth stories of California. Its current production is about 400,000 cases, with a 50-50 split in reds and whites. Its reputation still rests on the reds—Petit Syrah Reserve, vineyard-designated Zinfandels, and an occasional vintage of Estate Bottled Cabernet. It owns 400 acres in Mendocino, including recently acquired 200-acre Sundial Ranch, targeted in 1981 for sparkling-wine production. The white varietals are clean and reliable at best, headed by Pinot Blanc. Lake County Cabernet and Zinfandel are popular sellers, as are the red, white, and rosé table wines. Bel Arbres is its second label.

Cabernet Sauvignon (Lake County): *Light, fruity, simple, vinous* ♥

Cabernet Sauvignon (Mendocino): *Ripe, fruity, oaky, tannic* ♥/❀

Chardonnay: *Low varietal, fairly oaky, little excitement* ♥

Gewurztraminer: *Spicy, medium light, slightly sweet* ♥/❀

Petite Syrah: *Peppery, medium full, rough, tannic* ♥/❀❀

Pinot Blanc: *Appley, medium-bodied, firm, some oak* ♥/❀

Zinfandel: *Spicy, ripe berries, woody* ♥/❀❀

FICKLIN VINEYARDS *Madera 1946* The first port specialist and still highly regarded. Follows a long-aging policy and releases over 5,000 cases annually. The nonvintage port improves with age.

Tinto Port: *Dark, rough, complex, warm* ♥

JAMES ARTHUR FIELD *Alameda 1975* San Francisco advertising executive Field dropped into the wine business. At his Emeryville bottling facilities, Field blends dry, mainly coastal-county wines into tasty jug blends, Chablis and Burgundy. Sales reach 40,000 cases, in California exclusively.

FIELD STONE WINERY *Sonoma 1966* A 12,000-case winery drawing from its 140 acres of vineyards in the Alexander Valley region. All grapes were sold until the winery was completed in 1977. Its white varietals and rosés (subtitled

Spring wines) are field crushed and pressed. The red wines, headed by Petite Sirah from an old parcel, are conventionally handled. Cabernet Sauvignon and Gewurztraminer complete the list below.

Chenin Blanc: *Fresh, citrusy, spritzy, medium sweet* ♀/✿
Johannisberg Riesling: *Intensely fruity, light, medium sweet* ✿
Petite Sirah: *Forwardly fruity, good varietal, medium tannins* ✿

FILIPPI VINTAGE COMPANY *Riverside 1934* Under Chateau Filippi and J. Filippi primary labels, it sells a range of table wines, dessert wines, and bulk process champagnes. Virtually all of its annual 150,000-case sales are at the company's 8 tasting rooms in Southern California. Part of the production for the 36 different wines comes from 322 acres under lease.

FIRESTONE VINEYARD *Santa Barbara 1974* This dynamic venture is owned by members of the Firestone tire family, and a one-third interest belongs to Suntory of Japan. It has 300 acres planted in the Santa Ynez Valley and has achieved its 65,000-case maximum level. Over the first few vintages, Firestone had better success with white varietals than reds, although its Pinot Noir has become one of California's best.

Chardonnay: *Ripe, sometimes grassy, medium full, oaky* ♀/✿
Gewurztraminer: *Spicy, firm, balanced* ♀/✿
✤ **Johannisberg Riesling:** *Complex aroma, balanced, slightly sweet* ✿
Merlot: *Low-priced but too assertively herbaceous* ☉/♀
✤ **Pinot Noir:** *Good fruit, herbal, oaky, fat in good years* ♀/✿✿

FILSINGER VINEYARDS *Riverside 1980* Half of the production of this 4,000-case, 27-acre Temecula area winery is Fumé Blanc, while the remainder consists of small quantities of Chardonnay, Zinfandel, Petite Sirah, and Emerald Riesling. In addition, a late harvest White Riesling was produced in 1981 from purchased grapes.

FISHER VINEYARDS *Sonoma 1979* Located high in the Mayacamas Mountains adjacent to its 18-acre vineyard (8 of Cabernet, 10 of Chardonnay), this 5,000-case winery will focus mainly on Chardonnay. Its harvest will be supplemented by purchases until a 50-acre vineyard on the Napa Valley floor along the Silverado Trail is converted to Chardonnay. Pleasant first wines.

FLORA SPRINGS WINES *Napa 1979* Set on the west side of the Napa Valley on property that was once the homestead of the late Louis M. Martini and contained the Martini sherry solera. With grapes from 90 acres at the winery, 60 acres across the valley floor on Zinfandel Lane, and 100 acres in Oakville, the winery is specializing in Chardonnay, Sauvignon Blanc, and yet-to-be released Cabernet Sauvignon. Production is in the 10,000-case range.

Chardonnay: *Fruity, crisp, oaky* ✪/✪✪

FOPPIANO VINEYARDS *Sonoma 1896* This family-run 200,000-case winery located south of Healdsburg is gradually sloughing off its jug wine image. It offers 9 varietals and 4 generics, heavily oriented toward red wines in both types. Wines from its 200-acre vineyard carry a Russian River Valley appellation. New stainless steel tanks and small casks have resulted in cleaner and better varietals of late. Average-quality wines with reasonable prices.

Cabernet Sauvignon: *Vinous, medium-bodied, vague* ♥
⚕ **Petite Sirah:** *Good fruit, medium weight and tannins* ♥/✪
Sonoma Fumé: *Modest varietal, simple, crisp* ♥
Zinfandel: *Vaguely varietal, dull* ♥

FORTINO WINERY *Santa Clara 1948* Produces a wide variety of table wines in the low-priced end. The reds are heavy and coarse and often represent good values. Much of its 10,000-case production is sold at the winery.

⚕ **Zinfandel:** *Berryish, rough, woody* ♥/✪

FOUNTAIN GROVE (MARTINI & PRATI) Famous late 19th- and 20th-century winery closed in 1951. The label occasionally shows up on not-so-famous wines bottled by bulk-wine-producer Martini & Prati.

FRANCISCAN VINEYARDS *Napa 1973* A West German firm acquired the winery in 1979 and became its fifth owner since it opened. The vineyards involved consist of 450 acres, 200 acres in Oakville and 250 in the Alexander Valley. The major variety grown is Cabernet Sauvignon, and the winery bottles one from Napa, one from the Alexander Valley, and one under a Reserve designation. Several other varietals and a few generics are offered by Franciscan. It has been making Champagne by the *méthode champenoise,* but the early efforts failed to achieve average quality rankings. The current total production is about 100,000 cases, but the maximum will be three times that by the mid-1980s.

✓ **Burgundy:** *Mature and flavorful, balanced* 🍷
Cabernet Sauvignon (Alexander Valley): *Light weedy varietal, fruity, simple* 🍷
Cabernet Sauvignon (Napa Valley): *Herbaceous, sometimes too ripe, medium-bodied, slightly tannic* 🍷
Chardonnay: *Appley, medium-bodied, crisp* 🍷/❁
Johannisberg Riesling: *Modest varietal, fruity, slightly sweet* 🍷

FRANZIA BROTHERS *San Joaquin 1906* Giant winery (13-million-case storage capacity; 4,000 acres of vineyards) producing large quantities (350,000 cases) of inexpensive sparkling wines, jug wines, and limited amounts of locally grown, mass-produced varietals. Most of its production is sold in bulk or appears under a host of secondary labels usually adorning very uninspiring wines. Franzia products can be identified by the Ripon, California, bottling location. Winery was purchased in 1973 by Coca-Cola of New York.

Champagne: *Sweet, cooked flavors* δ/🍷
Chenin Blanc: *Medium sweet, clean, light flavors* 🍷
French Colombard: *Slightly sweet, dull* 🍷
Robust Burgundy: *Lightweight but clean, flirtation with Gallo Hearty Burgundy* 🍷
Zinfandel: *Clean, but hot and dull* 🍷

FRED'S FRIENDS (CHANDON) Second label of this champagne producer used for a still wine, called Blanc Nature, made from the second pressing of white grapes used in its sparkling wines. 4,000 cases.

FREEMARK ABBEY *Napa 1967* In 1967, the historic Freemark Abbey site was modernized into a new winery (25,000 cases) by a consortium of 7 partners, including Charles Carpy (whose grandfather was partner in the now defunct Uncle Sam Cellars, 1887–1916), noted vineyardist Laurie Wood, and oenologist Brad Webb. Winery and partners hold substantial vineyard acreage that supplies greatest part of winery crush. Very successful Petite Sirah is from the York Creek Vineyard.

Cabernet Bosché: *From a select vineyard in Rutherford; good depth, some complexity; 1970 was superb* ❁❁❁; later vintages rate 🍷/❁

Cabernet Sauvignon: *Pleasant, medium intensity, but lacking depth* ♥

Chardonnay: *Intense varietal and oak-aged style, classic dimensions in great years* ✿✿/✿✿✿

Edelwein: *Late harvest Johannisberg Riesling with richness, depth, and complexity* ✿/✿✿✿

Johannisberg Riesling: *Fruity, slightly spicy, slight to medium sweet* ♥/✿

Petite Sirah: *Brawny, tannic, distinct black-pepper spiciness* ♥/✿✿

FRETTER WINE CELLARS *Alameda 1977* Tiny (500-case) producer of good-quality wines owned by wine seller Travis Fretter. Cabernet Sauvignon and Chardonnay bottled on a single-vineyard basis are the rule.

FREY VINEYARDS *Mendocino 1979* Cabernet Sauvignon and Grey Riesling are estate-produced from a mature 30-acre vineyard in the Redwood Valley. Initial production is at the 2,000-case level, and grapes have been purchased for the Chardonnay and French Colombard that complete the current line.

FRICK WINERY *Santa Cruz 1977* Barrel-fermented Chardonnay and Pinot Noir are the focus of this small (2,000-case) winery with high ambitions. Its first release, however, was a not very interesting Chenin Blanc.

FRITZ CELLARS *Sonoma 1979* First crushed in new winery home in 1981, making 7,500 cases, close to optimum. Its three main varietals—Chardonnay, Sauvignon Blanc, and Zinfandel—come from 45 acres, half of which are in the Cloverdale area, the rest in Dry Creek Valley.

GALLEANO WINERY *Fresno 1933* Makes generic and dessert wines of all types and a Zinfandel. All sales are from the tasting room.

E. & J. GALLO WINERY *Stanislaus 1933* This could well be the world's largest winery. Headquartered in Modesto, it has 4 facilities with a total storage capacity of over 250 million gallons. Though it owns 4,000 acres, it must purchase 95% of its grapes crushed. Predominantly a producer of generic wines bottled with screw caps, in 1975 it started a line of varietals with cork closures. Over recent years, it has been using grapes from cooler regions, particularly the North and Central coasts. A massive underground aging cellar is now finished to provide longer aging and also to augment the varietal offerings. Its Chardonnay was the first wood-aged varietal to appear, a limited edition (40,000 cases) that was made at a Gallo winery in the Dry Creek Valley. Champagnes are bottled under both Gallo and André labels. Table and dessert wines are sold under numerous labels. All Gallo labels combined represent one-third of California wine sales. The white wines often represent good value.

Chablis Blanc: *Fruity, simple, light, medium sweet* ☻
Chardonnay: *Light varietal, but a bit thin and short in the finish* ☻
Chenin Blanc: *Clean varietal, fresh, slightly sweet* ☻
French Colombard: *Modest, fruity, medium sweet* ☻
Gewurztraminer: *Sometimes varietal, sometimes not; always slightly sweet* ☻
Hearty Burgundy: *Vinous, medium full, medium sweet* ☻
Johannisberg Riesling: *Fruity, simple, light, slightly sweet* ☻
✦ **Sauvignon Blanc:** *Light grassy aroma and flavor, simple* ☻
Zinfandel: *Vinous, light, balanced* ☻

GAVILAN VINEYARDS (CHALONE) A label used for French Colombard made from purchased grapes. Output is close to 2,000 cases, but the 1981 vintage is destined to be the last.

GEMELLO WINERY *Santa Clara 1934* Known for hearty, long-aged, and long-lived reds from nearby vineyards. While the winery stopped producing wine after 1978, it continues to bottle and distribute from its inventory.

Zinfandel: *Fruity, woody, rough, astringent* ☻

GEYSER PEAK WINERY *Sonoma 1972* A longtime producer of bulk wines acquired by Schlitz of Milwaukee in 1972. It has since been modernized and expanded, producing close to 200,000 cases today under this label. The first several vintages were made from purchased grapes, and the wines with California appellations were of marginal quality. Many varietals now come from Sonoma County, where the winery owns 600 acres. With few exceptions, notably a Chardonnay and soft Johannisberg Riesling both from the Kiser Ranch, the quality level has yet to rise above average. The whites are simple, sometimes thin. Most reds are fruity, sometimes tanky. Summit Wines is a second label for generic wines sold in large bottles and the bag-in-the-box container. Much of the winery's 2-million-case output goes under the Summit label.

Cabernet Sauvignon (California): *Slightly fruity, simple herbaceous flavors* ♥
Chardonnay (Sonoma): *Light fruit, round, dull* ♥; *the Kiser bottling offers richer fruit and better balance* ♥
Fumé Blanc: *Light fruit, soft, clean* ♥
Gewurtztraminer: *Slightly spicy, muscatty* ♥/❸

GIBSON WINE COMPANY *Fresno 1934* A large winery specializing in fruit and berry wines. It offers a range of generic, dessert, and sparkling wines that have not attracted much interest.

GIRARD WINERY *Napa 1980* Located along the Silverado Trail on the Oakville side, the winery, finished in 1980, has the capacity to make 12,000 cases. The now-mature 44-acre vineyard consists of Chardonnay, Cabernet Sauvignon, and Chenin Blanc in descending order. It uses Stephens as a second label for Alexander Valley–grown Chardonnay. The Chenin Blanc is dry, oaky, and warm.

GIUMARRA VINEYARDS *Kern 1975* A large (12-million-gallon capacity) winery owned by a family active in the bulk wine business since 1946. First attempt with a line of varietals and generics failed; a second attempt in 1979 was based on blending Central Coast wines with wines from the family-owned Central Valley vineyards. Prices are low; quality is still inconsistent. Annual sales of close to 500,000 cases.

GLENDALE RANCH With 1,800 acres located on Napa's Silverado Trail just north of the Phelps winery, the owners of this label began with 3,000 cases of Sauvignon Blanc and Cabernet Sauvignon. Production is expected to grow slowly through 1983, leading in time to a winery.

GLEN ELLEN WINERY Scheduled for completion in time for the 1982 crush, winery is expected to produce up to 10,000 cases of Cabernet Sauvignon and 4,000 cases of Sauvignon Blanc. Through 1981, limited amounts of Cabernet were crushed by Chalone. The home vineyard is located high in the Mayacamas Mountains on the east side of the Sonoma Valley.

GOLD MINE WINERY *San Joaquin 1974* This label is part of Coloma Cellars and is used for generic wines and several flavored table wines, including one called Columbian Gold.

GRAND CRU VINEYARDS *Sonoma 1970* Over its first decade, this winery made several varietal wines and earned some critical recognition along the way, mainly for its slightly sweet whites. It was best known for Gewurztraminer. Now under new ownership, its annual production has doubled to 40,000 cases, 80% of which is white wines. Its primary emphasis is on Chenin Blanc and Sauvignon Blanc. Two Cabernets, one from the Delta area and the other from Alexander Valley, are the featured reds.

Chenin Blanc: *Fruity, soft, slightly sweet* ♥/❁
Gewurztraminer: *Spicy, rich flavors; round, medium sweet* ❁/❁❁❁

GRAND PACIFIC VINEYARDS *Marin 1974* Small (8,000 cases) winery that buys all grapes from Sonoma and Santa Barbara counties. Most of the output is in Chardonnay and Merlot, both of which have failed to achieve any distinction. It also offers a Fumé Blanc and a Blanc de Noirs from Merlot.

GRANITE SPRINGS WINERY *El Dorado 1980* 23 acres are newly planted and when mature will supply about half of this 7,500-case winery's annual output. Chenin Blanc, Zinfandel, and Cabernet are offered as varietals.

GRANVAL (CLOS DU VAL) This label first appeared on second-quality wine. It has reappeared for 2 vintages of 100% Cabernet Sauvignon, a style deviating from Clos du Val's usual Cabernet-Merlot blends. Both—1975 and 1977—were good Cabernets. Also appeared recently on a flurry of Chardonnays, 1975 to 1977.

GREEN & RED VINEYARD *Napa 1977* Small (2,000-case) winery producing Zinfandel from a vineyard in the Chiles Valley. Quality has been inconsistent to date.

GREENWOOD RIDGE VINEYARDS *Mendocino 1980* In 1972 8 acres were planted to Cabernet Sauvignon, Johannisberg Riesling, and Merlot in the Anderson Valley area near Philo. The first wine, a Johannisberg (White) Riesling, was excellent, if very delicate. The 1980 Cabernet (blended with Merlot) is set for a 1983 debut. Maximum combined production is 2,000 cases.

GRGICH HILLS CELLARS *Napa 1977* Winemaker Grgich built a reputation with Chateau Montelena and then started his own winery with coffeeman Austin Hills. Hills owns 140 acres in Napa that over time will go toward this winery's

15,000-case production. The varietal lineup includes regular and late harvest Johannisberg Rieslings, Chardonnay, Fumé Blanc, Zinfandel, and Cabernet Sauvignon.

Chardonnay: *Medium ripe, oaky, fat* ❀
Johannisberg Riesling: *Medium varietal, fruity, medium sweet* ❦/❀❀
Zinfandel: *Ripe, warm, complex, tannic* ❀/❀❀❀

GROVER GULCH WINERY *Santa Cruz 1979* A small (600-case) red wine producer offering Petite Sirah, Zinfandel, Cabernet, and Carignane made from grapes grown in the Hecker Pass/Gilroy area.

GROWERS BRAND *Tulare 1936* A highly visible, broad line of wines and brandies are produced at a large (19-million-gallon capacity) facility called California Growers Winery. Other labels used by this winery include Setrakian Vineyards, L. Le Blanc Vineyards, and Bounty Vineyards. Most Growers table wines are of low, jug wine quality. Its varietals are light and thin at best; most often they are dull and occasionally flawed.

GUASTI (PERELLI-MINETTI) WINERY Historical label revived recently by the parent winery. It covers a line of table wines, champagne, vermouth, and brandies. The table wines are vintage dated with California appellations. Most are blends of Central Valley and Central Coast grapes. Annual production is 150,000 cases, and most wines are simple, fruity, and inexpensive. The most noteworthy of them are a medium sweet French Colombard, a light, vinous Zinfandel, and a fruity, deeply colored rosé.

GUENOC RANCH *Lake 1981* On the site of actress Lily Langtry's turn-of-the-century Lake County retreat, 255 acres of new vines have been planted and a winery constructed. Prior to 1981 limited amounts of Guenoc wines were crushed under contract at Raymond in the Napa Valley. Production will escalate from 15,000 cases to 75,000 cases or more by the mid-to-late-1980s.

EMILIO GUGLIELMO WINERY *Santa Clara 1925* Longtime producer of relatively high quality jug wines under the Emile's Cavalcade label. Also offers 10,000 cases of low-priced, vintage-dated varietals, of which 80% is Petite Sirah, Zinfandel, and Cabernet Sauvignon, all made in a rough, hearty style under E. Guglielmo. 150 vineyard acres are devoted primarily to the varietal program.

Petite Sirah: *Medium-bodied, vinous, dull* ❦

GUNDLACH-BUNDSCHU WINERY *Sonoma 1973* 125 years of grape-growing and 50 years of pre-Prohibition winemaking preceded the reopening of this family-owned winery. Half of the crop from the 350 acres is used in the winery. Production, now 24,000 cases, is split evenly between red and white wines. So far the reds seem to be of better quality.

Cabernet Sauvignon: *Full-bodied in good years, ripe flavors, some oak* ♥/❀
Chardonnay: *Fruity, round, oaky* ♥/❀
Merlot: *Varies from varietal with ripe fruit to excessively tannic and hot* ♥/❀
Zinfandel: *Ripe flavors in big years, often brawny* ♥/❀

HACIENDA WINE CELLARS *Sonoma 1972* Located in the Sonoma Valley, the winery now makes 20,000 cases of varietals per year. It uses grapes from the adjacent 50-acre vineyard that once belonged to Buena Vista. Recent Zinfandels come from a partner's 60-acre vineyard in Cloverdale, although a small amount of Amador grapes are to be included in the mix. The Chenin Blanc is made from Delta grapes. The winery is at its best with Gewurztraminer and has also succeeded fairly well across its entire line of offerings. A Reserve Chardonnay that is barrel-fermented has recently been added.

Cabernet Sauvignon: *Minty, medium-bodied, tannic* ♥/❀
Chardonnay: *Medium intensity, balanced, oaky* ♥/❀
⚘ **Chenin Blanc:** *Lively, slightly sweet, balanced, good depth* ❀
Gewurztraminer: *Spicy-floral, balanced, slightly sweet* ❀/❀❀

HAGAFEN CELLARS Who said that Kosher wines had to taste like grape jelly? The owners of this label make theirs out of Johannisberg Riesling in a light, fruity, medium-sweet style. Not surprisingly, new vintages are released just in time for Passover.

HANZELL VINEYARDS *Sonoma 1956* The original showcase winery designed by the late Ambassador James D. Zellerbach, who modeled it after a French chateau. It was among the first to produce Chardonnay in a ripe, balanced, oak-aged style. The Pinot Noirs are less consistent, but the finest are often big, fat, complex, and high in alcohol. After several ownership changes, it continues to offer exceptional wines. Production from its 34-acre vineyard is about 3,000 cases annually. Plans to add Cabernet Sauvignon in a few years. Its wines carry Sonoma Valley appellations. ·

Chardonnay: *Ripe, supple, oaky, slow ager* ✿/✿✿
Pinot Noir: *Dark, complex, herbal, ripe, tannic* ✿/✿✿

J. J. HARASZTHY & SON *Sonoma 1978* Run by direct descendants of Agoston Haraszthy, founder of Buena Vista, this winery offers a fairly broad line of Sonoma-grown varietals headed by Zinfandel, which makes up 60% of the volume (10,000 cases). A majority of wine is vinified for Haraszthy by other Sonoma Valley producers (including Kenwood and Haywood) and then bottled at its Glen Ellen facility.

HARBOR WINERY *Sacramento 1972* In his amateur days in the late 1960s, Harbor's winemaker discovered Amador Zinfandel. Today he makes Amador Cabernet, Zinfandel, Mission del Sol, and Napa Chardonnay. Total production is under 1,000 cases, sold only in California.

Chardonnay: *Fruity, flavorful, complex* ♥
Zinfandel: *Ripe fruit, medium-bodied, tannic, but
recently variable* ♥/ᶗ

HART WINERY *Riverside 1980* Former home winemaker Joseph Hart planted 9 acres in the Temecula area in the early 1970s. Now using his own grapes and buying from neighbors, he makes under 2,000 cases per year. Mostly red varietals with a small amount of Sauvignon Blanc have appeared.

HAVELOCK GORDON A negociant's label for wines purchased in bulk from various wineries and packaged for national distribution. The volume in 1981 was 12,000 cases; mainly Cabernet, Chardonnay, and Zinfandel. The wines have been sound but not outstanding.

HAWK CREST (STAG'S LEAP WINE CELLARS) Label often used for sweet-finished, fragrant Johannisberg Riesling and occasionally for light, early-maturing Cabernet and slightly sweet Gewurztraminer.

HAYWOOD WINERY *Sonoma 1980* Owners acquired 100 acres south of town of Sonoma and made 5,000 cases in 1980. First wines well-received; plans are for 12,000 cases, mostly Chardonnay, Cabernet, Zinfandel, and Riesling.

HECKER PASS WINERY *Santa Clara 1972* Red varietals and dessert wines are made by this 3,000-case winery. The prices are low, the quality variable. Sales are mainly at the winery.

HEITZ CELLARS *Napa 1961* Moderately sized winery (approximately 30,000 cases) of high repute. Makes superb and expensive Cabernet from Martha's Vineyard. Other Cabernets include Fay vineyard and Bella Oaks vineyard. However, look for Fay to be phased out of the line after the 1980 vintage appears. Also well known for Chardonnay and for estate-grown Grignolino rosé. Many lesser wines are purchased in bulk, aged, and blended. Others (sparkling and dessert wines) are bottled especially for Heitz. Colorful, outspoken, often irascible owner.

Cabernet Martha's Vineyard: *Always distinctively minty with deep, rich, black currant; ages well; 1968 and 1974 are classic; 1969, 1970, 1972, 1973, 1975 not far behind* ✿/✿✿✿
Chardonnay: *Fragrant, sometimes spicy, oily texture, good depth* ♥/✿
Grignolino Rosé: *Tart, fruity, nice for its type* ♥
Johannisberg Riesling: *Dry, fruity, acceptable but not outstanding for type* ♥

WILLIAM HILL WINERY A label owned by investors and vineyard developers who have established 400 acres of vineyards in sites along Mount Veeder in Napa and are in the process of purchasing and developing some 1,000-plus acres across the valley in the Atlas Peak area over the next decade. Most of the current acreage is planted to Cabernet and Chardonnay, as the new property will be. Production of the 2 varietals is split into 5,000 cases of Cabernet, 2,500 cases of Chardonnay. A winery is planned for 1982.

HOFFMAN MOUNTAIN RANCH *San Luis Obispo 1972* After weathering financial problems in 1981, this winery is expanding its production toward 50,000 cases per year and 125 acres of new vines are being added to 58 acres of mature vines. The vineyard is favorably situated on a mountainous site with soils rich in chalk and limestone. The winemaking style emphasizes ripe grapes and traditional fermentations—barrel fermentation for Chardonnay and inclusion of stems during red wine fermentation. To date, its Chardonnays are variable; Pinot Noirs are usually good. The other varietals are of average quality. Prices tend to be high for all wines.

Chardonnay: *Ripe, toasty, medium full, complex, oaky* ♥/✿
Pinot Noir: *Ripe, herbal, good depth, sometimes raisiny, heavy, oaky* ♥/✿✿
Zinfandel: *Fruity, round, oaked, lacks depth* ♥

HOP KILN WINERY *Sonoma 1975* The winery is an enchanting refurbished hop kiln that is now a state historical landmark. It is surrounded by a 65-acre vineyard that supplies the grapes for the winery's current 6,500-case production. Most wines, varietals and proprietary blends, carry the Russian River Valley appellation. Its successes have been with very ripe Petite Sirahs and Zinfandels. All white wines are finished dry with an oak-aged Colombard as the most interesting.

Gewurztraminer: *Always dry; at best the aroma is fruity and muscatty; firm, sometimes bitter* ♥
Petite Sirah: *Heavy, astringent, low or overripe fruit* ♥
Zinfandel: *Ripe, briary, and complex, fairly oaky, tannic* ♥/❊

HORIZON WINERY *Sonoma 1977* Tiny (under 2,000-case) winery making only Zinfandel from vineyards in Healdsburg and Dry Creek areas in fruity, ripe, moderately tannic style.

HUGO'S CELLARS *Riverside 1979* A home winemaking operation grew into hobbyist-scale commercial operation. Production is pegged at 500–800 cases.

HULTGREN & SAMPERTON *Sonoma 1978* Production is expected to reach the 10,000-case level in the early 1980s, with Chardonnay and Cabernet sharing top billing. All wines are made from purchased grapes, and offerings include Petite Sirah and Gamay.

HUSCH VINEYARDS *Mendocino 1968* No longer owned by the Husch family, it remains the oldest winery in the Anderson Valley. It consists of 23 acres in the vicinity of the winery plus another 12 located in the warmer Talmage area owned by current proprietors before acquiring the winery in 1979. Quality has varied over the years, but Husch has offered some of the best wines from the Anderson Valley.

Chardonnay: *Floral, appley, tart with vanilla overtones* ♥/❊
Gewurztraminer: *Spicy, high acid* ♥
Pinot Noir: *Cherry-like aroma, medium bodied, balanced* ♥/❊
Sauvignon Blanc: *Spicy and herbaceous, firm, complex flavors, light oak* ♥/❊

INGLENOOK VINEYARDS *Napa and Central valleys 1879* Inglenook labels now appear on wines from every part of the state and in every price range. In total, Inglenook sales are in the 1-million-case range. The top of the line, loosely labeled Estate Bottled, consists of vintage-dated Napa Valley wines whose sales are about 250,000 cases annually. Inglenook also offers 2 lines of jug wines that are neither produced nor bottled in the Napa Valley. The so-called Vintage lines consists of average-quality, lower-priced wines. The Navalle wines (not related to Napa Valley) are the high-volume, jug wine end of the line. In 1969, Inglenook was purchased by corporate giant Heublein, owner of Beaulieu Vineyard and Italian Swiss Colony.

ESTATE BOTTLED

Cabernet Cask Bottling: *Ripe, medium-full-bodied, some tannin* ♥/✺

Cabernet Sauvignon: *Medium body, some varietal, moderate tannin* ♥

Chardonnay: *Good varietal, never intense, light oak* ♥/✺

Chenin Blanc: *Medium sweet, fruity, moderate varietal* ♥

NAVALLE

French Colombard: *Medium sweet, somewhat floral* ♥

Ruby Cabernet: *Vinous, clean jug wine* ♥

IRON HORSE VINEYARDS *Sonoma 1978* The 110-acre vineyard adjacent to this winery in the Sebastopol area is planted to Chardonnay and Pinot Noir. Another vineyard (26 acres) is located in the warmer Alexander Valley area and contains Sauvignon Blanc, Cabernet, and Zinfandel. Current production has reached 14,000 cases, including 2,000 cases of Brut Sparkling Wine by the *méthode champenoise*. Its Chardonnay is consistently successful. Plans growth to about 20,000 cases.

Chardonnay: *Appley, fruity, medium intense, light oak* ♥/✺✺

Fumé Blanc: *Light fruit, medium full, modest varietal* ♥

ITALIAN SWISS COLONY The century-old name belonging to a winery in Asti (northern Sonoma County) that is now owned by Heublein. The winery still exists, but the wines are now called simply Colony and are not necessarily bottled at Asti.

JACARE This inexpensive stuff comes in a frosted bottle with a label suggesting mystery and romance. However, in spite of the "lifestyle" packaging, it is just average quality, sweet jug wine. The offerings are titled Petite Rouge, Classique Rosé, Crystal Blanc, and White Rosé.

JEKEL VINEYARDS *Monterey 1978* Using primarily grapes from its 140 acres in Greenfield, Jekel is nearing its projected peak production of 40,000 cases. Johannisberg Riesling and Chardonnay head the list of offerings and account for almost two-thirds of the annual output. Pinot Blanc, Cabernet Sauvignon, and Pinot Noir fill out the roster. Reserve bottlings of Chardonnay and Cabernet debuted in spring 1982. First late harvest Riesling was superb.

Chardonnay: *Ripe, grassy, medium full, balanced, oaky* ✪
Johannisberg Riesling: *Floral, delicate, balanced, medium sweet* ✪/✪✪✪
Pinot Blanc: *Fruity, crisp, slightly blossomy, light oak* ✪

JFJ WINERY *Stanislaus 1973* When their fathers sold Franzia Brothers to Coca-Cola of New York in the early 1970s, the cousins Franzia started their own winery just down the road. After spending a half dozen years buying wine in bulk from others, the brothers installed crushing and fermenting equipment and now make their own. About 60% of their multimillion-case production is bottled under the JFJ or CC labels; the other 40% is sold to a variety of producers. All JFJ wines carry generic identifications and are sold either in carafes, big bottles, or bag-in-boxes. Sparkling wines also appear under the JFJ moniker. Low price keys the marketing strategy.

JOHNSON'S WINES *Sonoma 1975* An affable family of growers removed pears and prunes and planted 70 acres of wine varieties. They make 10,000 cases annually from their Alexander Valley grapes. So far they've been totally erratic with most varietals. All whites tend to lack fresh fruitiness, while the reds have been low on varietal character. A dry-styled Rosé of Pinot Noir is the only consistent wine, and a slightly sweet late harvest Zinfandel is the most unusual.

JOHNSON-TURNBULL VINEYARDS *Napa 1979* A Cabernet-only winery drawing grapes from its 20 acres just north of Oakville. First release totaled 800 cases. Maximum output will reach 1,500 by 1983.

JORDAN VINEYARD *Sonoma 1976* Instead of buying a French château, a Denver geologist built a handsome estate in the Alexander Valley and established a 275-acre vineyard on the valley floor. Wanting to make one wine only, he planted Cabernet Sauvignon and Merlot in hopes of replicating a Bordeaux wine, but since then has added considerable Chardonnay acreage. The first Cabernets were widely heralded and showed promise of greater excitement from Jordan as vineyards mature. Chardonnay was first crushed in 1979. Production for the two varietals will reach 65,000 cases.

Cabernet Sauvignon: *Herbaceous, refined, supple, balanced* ♥/✿
Chardonnay: *Fruity, slightly blossomy, oaky* ✿

KALIN CELLARS *Marin 1976* High-energy experimenter with small lots of wine. Reds are oak-aged, handled for refinement. Track record is good, though ambition occasionally exceeds success. 3,000 cases.

KARLY WINES *Amador 1979* Small (1,100-case) Shenandoah Valley winery with 18 acres planted. Its vineyard—12 acres of Sauvignon Blanc, 4 of Zinfandel, and 2 of Petite Sirah—is just reaching productivity. Early wines include an Amador Zinfandel and Santa Barbara Chardonnay. Output will reach 6,000 cases with vineyard maturity, half of it Sauvignon Blanc.

KEENAN WINERY *Napa 1977* Atop Spring Mountain, this 7,000-case producer offers Chardonnay and Cabernet Sauvignon from its young 45-acre vineyard. The vines are not yet mature, however, so the same varieties are purchased. A ripe, massively scaled Merlot has been dropped from the line.

Cabernet Sauvignon: *Inky, tannic, ripe, deep, needs a decade or more to age out* ✿
Chardonnay: *Oaky, oily, lemony, good varietal* ♥/✿✿✿

KATHRYN KENNEDY WINES *Santa Clara 1979* Small winery producing Cabernet Sauvignon from 8-acre vineyard in the hills of Saratoga, near Mount Eden Vineyard, and Pinot Noir from purchased grapes. First release was offered under the Saratoga Cellars label. 2,000 cases per year.

KENWOOD VINEYARDS *Sonoma 1906* This former jug-wine-only facility was refurbished and modernized when the new owners took over in 1970 and began emphasizing varietals. Its Zinfandels first attracted attention and remain among its best wines. Current emphasis is being placed on the Cabernet Sauvignons and other varietals with a Sonoma Valley appellation. The current output (about 40,000 cases) is fairly evenly divided between red and white wines. The majority of wines are made from Sonoma County grapes, except for a very popular Chenin Blanc from the Delta region. The quality is reliable. The prices for most wines are average.

Cabernet Sauvignon: *Herbaceous, fruity, soft, woody* ♥/❈

Cabernet Sauvignon (Artist Series): *Ripe varietal, rich, often tannic* ❈

Chardonnay: *Medium fruit, oaky, blanced* ♥

Chenin Blanc: *Fruity, light, well-balanced, slightly sweet* ♥/❈

Red Table Wine: *Soft, fruity, ready to drink* ♥

Sauvignon Blanc: *Intense varietal, firm, light oak, crisp* ♥

Zinfandel: *Ripe, full, warm, tannic* ♥/❈❈

KENWORTHY VINEYARDS *Amador 1980* Presently a 1,000-case producer offering Amador Zinfandel and El Dorado Cabernet. The winery has planted 5 acres of Zinfandel and 2 of Cabernet. It has offered small quantities of barrel-fermented Monterey Chardonnay. Production will peak at 2,000 cases after its vineyards reach maturity.

KIRIGIN CELLARS *Santa Clara 1976* The old Bonesio Uvas Brand winery was purchased by the Kirigins in 1976 and now produces a broad range of varietals and generics. Total production nears 15,000 cases from its 50-acre vineyard. Wines are priced low but are not bargains.

French Colombard: *Clean, light fruit* ♥

KISTLER VINEYARDS *Sonoma 1979* From isolated site high in Mayacamas Mountains, debuted with 3 excellent Chardonnays from purchased grapes. Second vintage results were far less favorable, partially reflecting the difficulties of high-ripeness 1980 Chardonnays, but do not dim the prospect that Kistler will be a leading name in the full-bodied school of winemaking. First reds, also powerhouses, showed mixed results. Own 40-acre vineyard has Cabernet Sauvignon and Pinot Noir. Production is expected to reach 8,000 cases. Prices are high.

KONOCTI CELLARS *Lake 1975* After 4 years of selling grapes and making small amounts of wine from their 400 acres, the 27 growers in the Lake County Vintners cooperative built a winery in 1979. Current production is 20,000 cases, with Cabernet Blanc and Cabernet as the mainstays. They also have small acreage of white varieties and Zinfandel. Production could grow to 150,000 cases, but growth depends on the acceptance of Lake County Cabernet.

KORBEL *Sonoma 1862* The largest (over 500,000 cases) producer of *méthode champenoise* Champagne in the U.S. Korbel has 600 acres located in cooler parts of Sonoma County and buys a high percentage of grapes. Its sales are strong, but of late the quality of its popular Champagnes seems to have been sacrificed to growth. Most Champagnes are reliable, if unexceptional. Korbel also sells over 400,000 cases of brandy per year.

Blanc de Blancs: *Fruity, slightly yeasty, simple, dry* ♥/
✿

Blanc de Noirs: *Yeasty with a weedy note, light, a bit coarse.* ♥/✿

Brut: *Fairly fruity, sweeter than the natural* ♥

Demi-Sec: *Sweet taste, but low on elegance* ♥

Natural: *Yeasty, austere style, very slightly sweet* ♥

HANNS KORNELL CHAMPAGNE CELLARS *Napa 1952* Specializing in champagnes. It makes 7 types, all by the *méthode champenoise,* and sales average 100,000 cases per year. The driest style is the house specialty, Sehr Trocken, but most others are on the sweet side. Except for the muscat wine, the cuvées often hint of Johannisberg Riesling. The style in general is light in body with a softness and excellent effervescence. The quality ranges from average to ✿. The top seller is the Extra Dry.

Brut Champagne: *Vinous, soft, slightly sweet* ♥

Extra Dry Champagne: *Fruity and yeasty, crisp, medium sweet* ♥

Muscat of Alexandria: *Strong muscatty aroma, medium sweet* ♥

CHARLES KRUG WINERY *Napa 1861* Founded by immigrant Charles Krug, who ran it until the 1890s; winery then experienced 50 years of instability until purchased by Cesare Mondavi in the 1940s. Sales are in the 2-million-case range, including jug wines under the C. K. Mondavi label and varietal and generic wines under Charles Krug. Winery is now run by Peter Mondavi. Red varietals are of middling quality; whites sometimes better. Chenin Blanc was first to have sweetness. Reasonably priced.

Blanc Fumé: *Light, simple flavors, low-key varietal character* ♥

Cabernet Sauvignon: *Medium body, flavors lack depth* ♥

Cabernet Vintage Select: *Somewhat ripe, distinct varietal, medium tannins when young; best vintages age*

10–15 years; price has escalated along with the best but quality has not gained equally ♥/✿

Chardonnay: *Fruity, but often with disturbing grassy or vegetal notes* ♥

Chenin Blanc: *Medium sweet, fruity, fresh, reliable* ♥/✿

Johannisberg Riesling: *Floral, fragrant, medium intensity* ♥/✿

THOMAS KRUSE WINERY *Santa Clara 1971* Enthusiasm exceeds the quality of wines, which all too often exhibit the consequences of winemaking peccadilloes. 2,500 cases.

RONALD LAMB WINERY *Santa Clara 1976* Small lots of Gamay Beaujolais, Pinot Noir, Cabernet Sauvignon, and Zinfandel are produced by this fledgling winery aiming for 2,500-case production level. Early experimentation has been with Gamay Beaujolais and Zinfandel in different types of oak barrels. Quality has varied from pleasant to dull.

LA CREMA VINERA *Sonoma 1979* Focus is on Chardonnay, Pinot Noir, and Cabernet Sauvignon, with each wine bearing vineyard identification. A favorable first impression was made with Chardonnays from Winery Lake and Ventana vineyards. Production has climbed to 7,000 cases.

LAKESPRING WINERY *Napa 1980* A new 15,000-case winery with high expectations. Will make five varieties headed by Chardonnay and Cabernet Sauvignon from its own 7-acre vineyard and from purchased Napa Valley and San Luis Obispo grapes. First results are interesting, not exciting.

LA MARQUE Label created in 1981 by a winemaker in order to market occasional lots of barrel-fermented Chardonnay independently.

LAMBERT BRIDGE *Sonoma 1975* Located in the Dry Creek region, this efficient, well-financed winery makes only Cabernet and Chardonnay. With 78 acres, it is building toward a 10,000-case limit. The quality has been quite erratic, though aging often brings improvements.

Chardonnay: *Medium intensity, variable, oaky* ♥/✿

M. LA MONT WINERY *Kern 1966* This former, large, growers' cooperative experienced lean years and was sold to a Canadian corporation in 1978. It ranks as the sixth largest U.S. producer, and sells 2.5 million cases under its own labels and many private labels. Grapes come from neighboring vineyards in this hot area. The varietals are the usual Central Valley fare, joined in the market by a range of dessert and generic wines. The most difficulty was experienced with white wines, which were poorly made. But all current table wines are of low quality. Its other labels used for cheap generics are Mountain Gold and Mountain Peak, sold cheaply in supermarkets.

LA MONTANA (MARTIN RAY VINEYARDS) A label occasionally used for wines purchased and finished by this winery.

LANDMARK VINEYARDS *Sonoma 1974* The present emphasis in this 15,000-case winery is on Chardonnay and Cabernet Sauvignon. These 2 varietals account for 75% of its production. The owners have 80 acres in Sonoma County. Limited amounts of Chenin Blanc and Johannisberg Riesling are made from purchased grapes. Steady quality progress has been shown by its Chardonnays.

Cabernet Sauvignon: *Weedy, lightly oaked, moderate tannins* ☻
Chardonnay (Alexander Valley): *Grassy varietal, medium bodied, light oak* ☻
Chardonnay (Sonoma-Cutrer): *Appley, fruity, citric flavors, light oak, balanced* ☻/☻
Chardonnay (Sonoma County): *Ripe fruit, full-bodied, complex* ☻/☻☻
Chenin Blanc: *Fruity, medium to thin, dry* ☻
Pinot Noir: *Fruity, somewhat complex, rich oak* ☻/☻

LA QUESTA VINEYARD (WOODSIDE VINEYARDS) Cabernet Sauvignon, grown in the historic La Questa Vineyard in the Santa Cruz Mountain foothills near Palo Alto, is vinified by Woodside Vineyards. Although the wine is now being bottled under the Woodside name, La Questa wines live on in many cellars.

LAS TABLAS WINERY *San Luis Obispo 1890* This old facility in the Templeton Hills, known until recently as Rotta Winery, is under new ownership that changed the name but not the reputation for hearty jug-styled wines of more weight than elegance. Most sales are at the winery.

LAUREL GLEN VINEYARDS *Sonoma 1980* From 25 acres of hillside vineyard on the west side of the Sonoma Valley, Laurel Glen will produce 5–6,000 cases of Cabernet Sauvignon.

LAWRENCE WINERY *San Luis Obispo 1979* The first large-sized (350,000-case-capacity) winery in the county, Lawrence has been producing about 200,000 cases under its own label. It offers an assortment of varietals, several rosés, and a trio of table wines. Most wines are given minimal aging, and marketed early. The white varietals have been low on varietal character and freshness. Some reds offer lively fruitiness, but often without varietal distinction. All are relatively high-priced, and have not been well-received. The brand was acquired by Glenmore Distillers in late 1981.

LA ZACA VINEYARDS The owners have 100 acres in the Santa Ynez Valley of Santa Barbara County, and make wines from them by contracting with nearby wineries. Currently marketing about 10,000 cases in all of Cabernet, Chardonnay, and Johannisberg Riesling.

LAZY CREEK VINEYARDS *Mendocino 1979* An Anderson Valley winery that has grown slowly over the first vintages to its present 3,500-case production. All wines come from the adjacent 20-acre vineyard, which consists of 12 acres of Chardonnay, 4 of Pinot Noir, and 4 of Gewurztraminer.

LE BAY CELLARS *Sonoma 1980* 7,500 cases of Zinfandel, Sirah, and Fumé Blanc are planned from 58 acres of vineyards. Chardonnay and Chenin Blanc are from purchased grapes. First Chardonnay was attractive, Chenin Blanc less so.

LE DOMAINE (ALMADÉN VINEYARDS) Almadén's second-quality champagnes. Both Brut and Extra Dry are made by the transfer method. Once fine values, they have become flat, oversweetened wines geared to the mass market.

LEEWARD WINERY *Ventura 1979* Small winery (3,500 cases) producing Chardonnay from San Luis Obispo and Monterey counties and Zinfandel from Amador County. First Chardonnays were very impressive; first Zinfandel less so.

LE FLEURON (JOSEPH PHELPS VINEYARD) Second label used primarily for wines from young vineyards or for an occasional surplus wine. To date, the quality has been quite adequate for the $5–7 price tags of its mixed bag of issuances.

CHARLES LE FRANC (ALMADÉN VINEYARDS) This line, introduced in 1978, represents Almadén's foray into the world of limited-production, higher-priced wines. It consists of well-known varietals along with some specialty wines such as Pinot St. George and late harvest style white varietals. Also there are 2 blended wines—Maison Blanc and Rouge

—both high-priced. All are improvements over Almadén's regular offerings.

Chardonnay: *Light fruit and oak, dry* 🍷
Pinot St. George: *Slightly spicy, medium-bodied, soft with light tannins* 🍷

LEJON A label belonging to Heublein (owners of Inglenook and Colony) and used for low-quality champagnes and brandies. It is now also attached to a new line of soft table wines. The Burgundy, Chablis, and Rosé are sweet, low in alcohol, and low in character. Slightly more interesting is the "soft" line of varietals—Chenin Blanc, French Colombard, and Gamay Beaujolais.

LELAND STANFORD CHAMPAGNE (WEIBEL) Inexpensive, too sweet, bulk process sparkling wine named for Leland Stanford, governor, senator, and university founder. He also established the original winery at Warm Springs in Alameda County that is now Weibel.

LIBERTY SCHOOL VINEYARDS (CAYMUS VINEYARDS) A second label used primarily for nonvintage Cabernets purchased and aged. Identified by lot numbers, they offered good value through Lot #8. The label now includes Chardonnay on a regular basis. Other wines are offered depending on the availability of surplus grapes and wine. Combined sales now reach 5,000 cases per year.

⚘ **Cabernet Sauvignon:** *Fruity, varietal flavors, light oak* 🍷

LIVE OAKS WINERY *Santa Clara 1912* Produces 16,000 cases of generic table wines, an occasional varietal, and wine vinegar. Except on rare occasions, the vinegar is the better product. Winery sales are the rule.

LIVERMORE VALLEY VINEYARDS *Alameda 1978* Longtime grower turned winemaker, taking advantage of well-developed 34-acre vineyard. Vines are a potpourri of varieties including French Colombard, Golden Chasselas, Grey Riesling, and 10 acres of mixed whites consisting of equal parts Chenin Blanc, Pinot Blanc, and Chardonnay. All wines are fermented to dryness in stainless-steel, temperature-controlled tanks and then aged in small oak barrels. 4,000-case production is distributed in California only.

LLORDS & ELWOOD WINERY This operation owns neither vineyards nor winery. Aging and blending are performed in leased space at Weibel and in San Jose. Sales have reportedly reached 25,000 to 30,000 cases, but the varietals may be slipping, since new technology and technique have seemingly bypassed this winemaker. Sherries and ports are its most successful products.

J. LOHR WINERY *Santa Clara 1974* Partners developed 280 acres of vineyards in Greenfield and built a winery now operating at about 80,000 cases. Best known for white varietals with Monterey appellations. However, Chenin Blanc and Petite Sirah are purchased from the Delta region and Cabernet from Napa. Production is 80% white wine.

Chardonnay: *Grassy varietal, crisp, balanced, light oak* ♥

Fumé Blanc: *Pungent, bell pepper varietal character* ♥

Johannisberg Riesling: *Floral, delicate, citrusy, slightly sweet* ♥/✿

LONG VINEYARDS *Napa 1977* Small winery (2,000-case maximum) owned, in part, by Simi's winemaker. The 14-acre mountainside vineyard (Chardonnay and Johannisberg Riesling) supplied Mount Veeder's excellent Chardonnays in previous vintages. The quality has been exceptional and prices high.

Chardonnay: *Rich varietal aroma, balanced, oaky* ✿✿/✿✿✿

Johannisberg Riesling: *Floral, sweet, well-balanced* ✿/✿✿

LOS ALAMOS VINEYARDS *Santa Barbara 1974* Mainly a vineyard operation, grapes unsold from its 350 acres are made into varietal wines and marketed under this label. Current production is in the range of 3,500 cases, mostly Cabernet.

LOS HERMANOS (BERINGER VINEYARDS) Fast-growing, unpretentious, and inexpensive line of generics and varietals. Production is about 1 million cases per year. The line is made from purchased grapes and bulk wine from the North Coast and Central Valley, all under the California appellation. Generally, they are light, clean, and palatable wines; the white generics are medium sweet. The Light Chablis and Light Rosé enjoyed immediate sales success and account for 30% of total production.

Chenin Blanc: *Low fruit, heavy, medium sweet* ♥

Zinfandel: *Varietal fruit, light, simple* ♥

LOST HILLS VINEYARDS A label belonging to a group of agricultural investors who own 1,500 acres of vineyards in Kern County. The California appellation wines, mostly jugs and totaling about 100,000 cases, are produced at Barengo, which is, in fact, now owned by the Lost Hills principals. An occasional varietal from any source including Argentina (true!) is also offered. The California varietals and generics made from Kern County grapes are generally low in price, but weak in quality.

LOS VINEROS WINERY *Santa Barbara 1981* 15,000 case production emphasizes Cabernet Sauvignon in red and Blanc de Noirs versions. Chenin Blanc in slightly sweet, soft style and Chardonnay in firm, high acid presentation are the leading white varieties. Most grapes are purchased from partners' vineyards in Santa Maria and Santa Ynez Valley areas. The winery occupied its own facility for the 1981 harvest after spending its first vintage in borrowed space.

LOWER LAKE WINERY *Lake 1977* First Lake County winery since Prohibition. All grapes are purchased from local growers. Opened with a White Cabernet (900 cases) in 1978 and is specializing in Cabernet under specific vineyard designations. Current production is about 4,000 cases. Early vintages of its two primary varietals, Cabernet and Sauvignon Blanc, leave plenty of room for improvement.

LUCAS WINERY *San Joaquin 1978* This label belongs to Lodi growers (15 acres of Zinfandel and 15 of Tokay) supplying grapes to home winemakers across the country. It makes 700 cases of Zinfandel.

LYTTON SPRINGS WINERY *Sonoma 1975* A well-known Zinfandel vineyard in the area, once selling to Ridge, has become a real winery. The 50-acre vineyard averages 80 years of age and contains a smattering of Petite Sirah. The winery's first vintage was 1976. Production now reaches 10,000 cases of Zinfandel only. Hard to find a better example of ripe Sonoma County-style Zinfandel.

Zinfandel: *Ripe, spicy, complex flavors, oaky* ❀/❀❀

MADRONA VINEYARDS *El Dorado 1980* Emphasizing the El Dorado appellation, this winery makes 5,500 cases of varietals from its 35-acre vineyard. The output is 60% red wine, but because the vineyards are located at the cooler 3,000 foot level, they contain Chardonnay, Riesling, and a small percentage of Gewurztraminer. Zinfandel and Cabernet (blended with Merlot) are the top items. 10,000 cases annually is viewed as maximum.

MARIETTA CELLARS *Sonoma 1980* Approximately 5,000 cases of Cabernet and Zinfandel are produced from vineyards in

Healdsburg and the Dry Creek Valley and aged in used French oak barrels. A proprietary red is also made from 70-year-old Carignane and Petite Sirah vines. First efforts were sound but lacked distinction.

M. MARION A private label owned by negotiant M. Dennis Marion, who buys wine from several sources and has it bottled to his specifications. To date the wines have been fairly priced with an occasional bargain popping up.

MARKHAM WINERY *Napa 1978* A well-financed, large (over 1-million-gallon capacity) winery owning 300 acres and using only a small portion of its premises and vineyards for Markham wines. Production, now at 18,000 cases, is two-thirds white and one-third red. Line includes a broad range of medium to expensive varietals. Wine quality has generally been above average.

Chardonnay: *Ripe, oaky style, good acid balance* ♥/❁

MARNITON VINEYARDS (SAN MARTIN WINERY) Second label created in 1981 to market generic wines.

LOUIS M. MARTINI WINERY *Napa 1922* Well-known winery noted for its inexpensive line of varietals and generics. Close to 75% of the annual 400,000-case output consists of red wines. The family owns 800 acres, half in Sonoma County and 350 acres in the Carneros district. All wines carry a California appellation including the occasional bottling with a vineyard designation. The family phillosphy is to age red wines primarily in large cooperage and to finish the white varietals on the dry side. Most wines are light, fruity, simple, and intended for early consumption. The exceptions among the reds are the Barbera and occasionally special bottling type Cabernet. The best white wines are Gewurztraminer and Johannisberg Riesling, both often rising above average quality. Recent Chardonnay vintages reflect quality improvements and the more aggressive attitude toward change brought about by a younger generation's influence on the winery's direction.

⚘ **Barbera:** *Ripe berry character, powerful, ages well* ♥/❁
Cabernet Sauvignon: *Simple varietal, light-bodied* ♥
⚘ **Gewurztraminer:** *Spicy aroma and flavor, firm, dry* ♥/❁
Moscato Amabile: *Fruity, fragrant, sweet, slightly effervescent, fresh and enticing. Available mainly at the winery* ❁
Johannisberg Riesling: *Floral, spicy, balanced, dry* ♥/❁
Zinfandel: *Vinous, medium-bodied, fruity* ♥

MARTINI & PRATI WINES *Sonoma 1951* An old, large (2 1/2-million-gallon capacity) winery that sells 90% of its wines in bulk to various large wineries. It bottles 20,000 cases under its label, both varietals and generics. All are low-priced; most are tanky and unappealing.

PAUL MASSON VINEYARDS *Santa Clara 1852* One of the oldest and one of the biggest. Sales of this Seagrams-owned winery approach 7 million cases, covering almost every possible wine type. Most wines are nonvintage, fairly low priced, and aimed at the broadest levels of acceptance. Limited quantities of vintage-dated varietals, champagnes, and fortified wines have managed to reach somewhat higher quality levels. Masson owns 4,500 acres of vineyard in Monterey County.

⚥ **Brut Champagne:** *Dry, crisp, clean, lightly fruity* ♟/❸
   Cabernet Sauvignon: *Soft, dull, vegetal* ☾/♟
   Chardonnay: *Vintage versions are fruity, citric, oaky, but thin* ♟ ; *nonvintage wine is heavy and less interesting* ♟
   Chenin Blanc: *Medium sweet, fruity, simple* ♟
⚥ **Emerald Dry:** *Medium sweet, good acid, clean* ♟
   Fumé Blanc, Pinnacles: *Very grassy, well-balanced, noticeable oak* ♟/❸
⚥ **Rare Souzao Port:** *Rich, fruity, powerful* ♟/❸❸
   Zinfandel: *Light, soft, low varietal* ♟

MASTANTUONO WINERY *San Luis Obispo 1977* A Zinfandel-only winery, making 2,000 cases from its 11-acre vineyard and from the nearby Dusi Vineyard. The house style is full-bodied, oak-laden, rich, and somewhat earthy.

MATANZAS CREEK WINERY *Sonoma 1978* Located in the Bennett Valley, adjacent to the Sonoma Valley, this winery has 22 acres of vineyard which contribute to its 4,000-case output. The primary wine is Chardonnay, followed by Cabernet Sauvignon. Over the first years, however, it also made small quantities of other varietals—Gewurztraminer, Semillon, Pinot Blanc, and Pinot Noir—and they all were quite successful. A tiny amount (140 cases) of Champagne has also been made on an experimental basis. Production will remain at 4,000 cases over the next few years.

Chardonnay: *Ripe fruit, lots of depth, complex* ❸/❸❸❸

MAYACAMAS VINEYARDS *Napa 1941* Consistent, high-quality Cabernet and Chardonnay have been offered by this Mount Veeder producer. It has 50 acres on hillsides and purchases some grapes to supplement its production. Both Cabernet and Chardonnay require long cellaring. Although most of its 5,000-case output consists of these varietals, it also makes small lots of Zinfandel, Pinot Noir, and Sauvignon Blanc.

Cabernet Sauvignon: *Ripe, powerful, tannic* ✿/✿✿
Chardonnay: *Rich, complex, oily, and oaky* ✿/✿✿✿

MCDOWELL VALLEY VINEYARDS *Mendocino 1979* Success of other wineries with McDowell Valley grapes encouraged this large vineyard operation to open its own winery. 8 varietals are being produced totalling 40,000 cases. The wines have been clean, fruity, and on the simple side. The red Grenache is one of the few in California and easily its best.

Fumé Blanc: *Somewhat lean, direct style* 🍷
Zinfandel: *Berryish, clear, simple, likable* 🍷

MCHENRY VINEYARDS *Santa Cruz 1980* Chardonnay and Pinot Noir are produced from a 5-acre vineyard. Initial crush was 300 cases, which will increase to 500 when all the vines reach maturity.

MCKENZIE CREEK (ROUDON SMITH VINEYARDS) Second label used initially for an odd-lot blend of Zinfandels.

MCLESTER WINERY *Los Angeles 1980* A 1,200-case winery sits within an old warehouse located close to the Los Angeles airport. Both of its varietals—Cabernet Sauvignon and Zinfandel—have been made from San Luis Obispo County grapes. The first versions of each were in a nouveau style, both of decent quality.

MENDOCINO VINEYARDS A label revived by the Guild Cooperative in 1981 to market yet another line of modest-quality jug wines.

MESA VERDE VINEYARDS *Riverside 1980* Owned by a Texan with big plans to develop a complex of 11 wineries, of which Mesa Verde is one. He owns 140 acres of vineyards and manages 700 additional acres in the general vicinity. So far, fewer than 3,000 cases of varietals have appeared under this label.

MEV (MOUNT EDEN VINEYARDS) A second label used for wines produced from purchased grapes (the main label being reserved for estate-grown wines). The quality is often very high and the prices somewhat less shocking than those charged for the main label. In recent years, only Chardonnay purchased from Ventana Vineyards has appeared under the MEV label. 3,000 cases.

Chardonnay: *Oaky, fat, rich, lots of depth* ♀/❀❀

MILANO WINERY *Mendocino 1977* Attractive new winery in a refurbished hop kiln. The near-term goal is 12,000 cases composed of small-lot production from low-tonnage, hillside vineyards. Zinfandel and Petite Sirah come from a Talmage-area vineyard.

Zinfandel (Pacini Vineyard): *Big, mouth-filling, rich flavors* ❀/❀❀

MILL CREEK VINEYARDS *Sonoma 1976* After planting a 70-acre vineyard in 1965, the owners completed a winery in 1975. Current offerings are Cabernet, Chardonnay, Pinot Noir, Merlot, and Blanc de Noirs. Most have achieved average-quality status to date. Production is close to 12,000 cases.

Cabernet Sauvignon: *Herbaceous, soft, fruity* ♀/❀
Chardonnay: *Ripe appley, medium flavors and oak* ♀/❀
Merlot: *Spicy with varietal fruit, ample oak* ♀/❀

MIRASSOU VINEYARDS *Santa Clara 1966* Family winery involved for decades in the bulk wine business, and now producing over 350,000 cases per annum. It owns over 1,000 acres in northern Monterey County, and close to 400 in Santa Clara County. Its Monterey grapes are machine-harvested and field-crushed. Through the 1977 vintage the white wines (about 60% of total output) were fruity and slightly sweet. Since then, they have become rather bland when dry-finished and too sweet otherwise. Mirassou's red varietals are plagued by an overly vegetative character which extends even to those labeled "Unfiltered" and "Harvest Selection," their counterpart to Reserve. This brand's reputation and sales derive from personal efforts which would be better used if directed toward quality improvement. Champagnes by the *méthode champenoise* have grown to 25,000 cases.

Cabernet Sauvignon: *Lightly herbaceous, sometimes vegetative and thin* ♀/ŏ
Chardonnay: *Grassy varietal, average flavors at best, crisp* ♀
Chenin Blanc: *Recent vintages are only modestly fruity; slightly sweet* ♀
Johannisberg Riesling: *Light floral, light-bodied, medium-sweet* ♀

Monterey Riesling: *Popular wine, but simple, fruity character in a light-bodied, medium-sweet style* ♟
Zinfandel: *Berryish fruit in a good year; often vegetative and short generally* ♟

C. K. MONDAVI WINES (CHARLES KRUG WINERY) A label covering a variety of jug generics and a Zinfandel. The C. K. Mondavi wines represent about two-thirds of Krug's annual 2-million-case sales. Although still popular, the wines now trail most competitors on a quality basis.

ROBERT MONDAVI WINERY *Napa 1966* Robert Mondavi left the Charles Krug Winery to make wines in his own style. The winery is without equal in design and equipment and now makes 300,000 cases of generally high-quality wines. It owns 1,000 acres and buys high-quality grapes at high prices. Mondavi pioneered slightly sweet Chenin Blanc with Krug and dry, balanced Fumé Blanc more recently at Mondavi. Highly innovative, the Mondavi family buys small oak barrels from numerous regions and continues experimenting with different theories of barrel aging and vinification. The popular Table Wines, about 1 million cases total, are made at a winery in Lodi. Oakville Vineyards is a second label.

Cabernet Reserve: *Complex, lush, long-ager* ✪/✪✪✪
Cabernet Sauvignon: *Elegant, supple, appealing, a bit less intense in recent vintages* ♟/✪
Chardonnay: *Medium ripe, balanced, lightly oaky* ♟/✪✪
Chardonnay Reserve: *Appley and spicy, toasty oak flavors, balanced, needs aging* ✪/✪✪
Fumé Blanc: *Herbal, smooth, stylish, light oak* ✪/✪✪
Chenin Blanc: *Lively fruit, fresh flavors, slightly sweet* ♟/✪
Gamay: *Dark, ripe fruit, rough, tart* ♟/✪
Gamay Rosé: *Fresh, candy-like fruit, spritzy, slightly sweet, best of type* ♟
Johannisberg Riesling: *Fragrant, delicate, medium sweet* ✪/✪✪✪
Red Table Wine: *Juglike, fruit, balanced* ♟

MONDAVI-ROTHSCHILD *Napa 1979* The likely label for a Cabernet-type wine produced in concert by the owners of Robert Mondavi Winery and of Château Mouton-Rothschild. The Cabernet Sauvignon and Cabernet Franc blend will be given a proprietary name. First crush was in 1979 at the Mondavi winery, with the first wine scheduled to be released in 1983. Maximum production is 5,000 cases.

MONTCLAIR WINERY *Alameda 1975* Small (1,200-case) winery operated on a part-time basis. Buys grapes from leading vineyards with focus on Zinfandel (50% of production), its best efforts to date. Small-lot experiments with Petite Sirah are under way

French Colombard: *Dry, oak-aged, fairly big style* ♥/✿
Zinfandel (Dry Creek): *Oaky, ripe, berryish, sometimes late harvest* ♥/✿

MONTEREY CELLARS (MONTEREY PENINSULA WINERY) Second label used mostly for generics made from press wine and for less expensive varietals (Ruby Cabernet and Emerald Riesling) the winery feels are of lower quality.

MONTEREY PENINSULA WINERY *Monterey 1974* A try-anything attitude prevails at this 17,000-case-per-year winery. It buys all grapes and prefers to make red varietals, mainly Cabernet and Zinfandel, usually from very ripe grapes. The major emphasis is on Zinfandels from Amador County and the Central Coast region. This winery was among the first to offer good quality Monterey-grown Cabernet Sauvignon. The Chardonnays, though once erratic, have been improving steadily in quality. The maximum output is 20,000 cases.

Cabernet Sauvignon: *Pungent and peppery, sometimes complex; sometimes tart* ♥/✿
Zinfandel (California): *Spicy, full-bodied, soft* ♥
Zinfandel (Shenandoah): *Ripe berry character, big style, oaky, rough* ♥/✿
Zinfandel (Late Harvest): *Finished slightly to medium-sweet, the best are concentrated, berry-like, and balanced* ♥/✿✿

MONTEREY VINEYARD *Monterey 1973* A 2-million-gallon capacity winery that began with high aspirations for Monterey County varietals only to find the going rough. Now owned by Coca-Cola of Atlanta, it has no vineyards, but offers close to 150,000 cases under its own label as well as contributing another million gallons or so to the Taylor California Cellars (also owned by Coke) line of generics and varietals. Production will likely grow rapidly over the next few years. Although in flux, it has made better whites than reds, consistent with the experience of others in northern Monterey. Prices have been kept reasonably low for coastal wines and offer good value in top vintages.

☆ **Chardonnay:** *Fruity, slight citrusy, direct, light oak* ♥/✿
☆ **Classic Red:** *Fruity, slightly vegetal, medium–full-bodied* ♥

Johannisberg Riesling: *Floral, citric, fruity, slightly sweet* 🍷

MONTEVIÑA VINEYARDS *Amador* 1973 A well-regarded winery best known for its Zinfandels and its experimental batches of other varietals. The Zinfandels, including those made in nouveau and white styles, are often among the best. Occasionally, some of its wines go unchecked in intensity and alcohol. The current output is 45,000 cases, made almost entirely from its 160-acre vineyards. The production of Sauvignon Blanc is expanding significantly. So far, the small-scale experiments with Barbera and Ruby Cabernet have been the most interesting.

Cabernet Sauvignon: *Ripe, powerful, tannic* 🍷/❀
Sauvignon Blanc: *Intense, big, harsh, unrestrained alcohol* 🍷/❀
Zinfandel: *Complex, spicy, ripe berries, unrestrained tannins* ❀/❀❀
Zinfandel Nuevo: *Jamlike, delicious, best of type* ❀

MONTICELLO CELLARS *Napa* 1980 This grower's 125 acres of Chardonnay, Gewurztraminer, and Sauvignon Blanc have supplied grapes to several prestigious Napa Valley wineries. After two small crushes at other facilities, a winery was completed in 1982 designed to operate at a 12–20,000 case capacity. The name comes from a replica, also built in 1982, of Thomas Jefferson's home at Monticello, which houses the winery's offices.

MONT ST. JOHN CELLARS *Napa* 1979 Owned by a Napa family active in the vineyard and wine business since 1934. After the family sold Oakville Vineyards in 1971, it purchased 160 acres in the Carneros district and established large plantings of Chardonnay, Pinot Noir, and Johannisberg Riesling. These 3 varietals represent a high percentage of the current 8,000-case output. By the mid-1980s it expects to be at its full capacity of 25,000 cases.

J. W. MORRIS WINERIES *Contra Costa* 1975 Started as a specialist in port, the winery rapidly has become oriented to table wines that now account for 92% of its current 50,000-case output. Grapes are purchased under long-term contract from 120-acre La Reina Vineyard in Monterey (60 acres each of Pinot Noir and Chardonnay), 100-acre Black Mountain Vineyard in Sonoma County (mostly Zinfandel, Chardonnay, and Sauvignon Blanc), and 30-acre St. Amant Vineyard in Amador. Chardonnay comprises 40% of production, Pinot Noir 25%, and Zinfandel about 20%. An occasional late harvest white is also produced.

Chardonnay (La Reina): *Crisp, almost sticky fruit, toasty oak* ♥/✿

Chardonnay (Black Mountain): *Fuller style, rich, almost fat, good fruit* ✿

Sauvignon Blanc: *Slightly grassy, crisp fruity edge, oaky* ♥/✿

Vintage Port: *Ripe grape nose, good fruit, complex, among best of California offerings* ✿/✿✿

Zinfandel (Sonoma): *Heavy, ripe, berryish, tannic* ♥/✿

Zinfandel (St. Amant): *Somewhat lighter color and style, tries for early drinkability* ♥

MOUNTAIN HOUSE WINERY *Mendocino 1980* Quality-minded 2,500-case winery producing Chardonnay, Cabernet, and late harvest style Zinfandel from purchased grapes. New winery facility planned for the 1982 crush. Five acres of vines.

MOUNTAINSIDE VINEYARDS (CHATEAU CHEVALIER) Second-label wines usually made from purchased grapes. The first few vintages were produced from the winery's young vineyards. Chardonnays have recently been weak, whereas the Cabernet Sauvignons are average-quality. This label will be discontinued if and when a 1979 Pinot Noir sells out.

MOUNTAIN VIEW WINERY *Santa Clara 1980* Small (400-case) winery producing barrel-fermented Chardonnay from Rutherford-grown grapes and Zinfandel from the Dry Creek area. A Cabernet is being added, and the wines will be sold directly through a mailing list.

MOUNT EDEN VINEYARDS *Santa Clara 1972* A prestigious, high-quality producer located on an isolated hilltop in the Santa Cruz Mountains. 2,000 cases of estate-bottled wines are produced from the 22 acres of vineyard (10 Cabernet Sauvignon; 8 Pinot Noir; 4 Chardonnay) surrounding the winery. The second label, MEV, is used for wines made from grapes grown elsewhere. Prices are never modest for Mount Eden wines.

Cabernet Sauvignon: *Complex, oaky, herbal, ripe, tannic, occasionally lacking refinement* ✿/✿✿✿

Chardonnay: *Fat, mouth-filling, oaky, spicy, intense* ♥/✿✿

Pinot Noir: *Oaky, rich, good varietal, often superb depth and balance* ♥/✿✿

MOUNT PALOMAR WINERY *Riverside 1975* Located in the Temecula region, where it has 150 acres planted, this winery sells most of its current 12,000 cases either in its tasting room/gift store or through Southern California outlets. Its top sellers are a Chenin Blanc, Johannisberg Riesling, and a sweet-finished Cabernet Sauvignon. The winery has developed a sherry *solera* and offers 3 sherries.

MOUNT VEEDER WINERY *Napa 1972* Small winery (4,500 cases) located high on Mount Veeder in the Mayacamas Mountains west of Napa. Brawny reds are made from own vineyard and until 1978 from a variety of other sources. Chenin Blanc is home grown.

Cabernet Sauvignon (Estate): *Brawny, tannic, deeply colored, weedy and currants flavors* 🍷/❀❀
Chenin Blanc: *Dry, intensely fruity, sometimes lemony and crisp* ❀/❀❀❀

J. MUELLER CELLARS A private label for limited amounts (400 cases) of white wines produced in leased space at Parducci by consulting engineer Mueller. The two whites (Chardonnay and Chenin Blanc) are light, fragrant, and fruity.

NAPA CREEK WINERY *Napa 1980* The owner converted a former meat-packing plant into a winery with an 18,000-case capacity. Its first wines—Gewurztraminer, Johannisberg Riesling, and Chardonnay—lacked distinction and were no bargains. Additional wines offered include Cabernet, Sauvignon Blanc, and Chenin Blanc. Present production is about 14,000 cases.

NAPA WINE CELLARS *Napa 1975* Located north of Yountville, this winery is surrounded by 3 acres of Chardonnay. It makes several varietals, mostly from purchased grapes, in a style that emphasizes very ripe grapes, and high alcohol. Zinfandel, late harvest and regular styles, is its most successful varietal. The Chardonnays are well oaked; the other wines are of average quality to date, with the hope for improvement under new management. Production has grown to 12,000 cases.

Chardonnay: *Fruity, round, oaky* 🍷/❀
Zinfandel: *Ripe berries, full-bodied, variable style* 🍷/❀

NAVARRO VINEYARDS *Mendocino 1975* This 4,000-case winery focuses on Gewurztraminer grown on 30 of its 33 planted acres. It also has 3 acres of Pinot Noir and purchases grapes for Cabernet, Riesling, and Chardonnay. Most wines are average-quality for type.

NEPENTHE CELLARS From 1967 to 1977, this was a winery located in Santa Cruz. Now it is a label which the owner keeps alive, more or less, by having small quantities of Chardonnay or Riesling made for him.

NEVADA CITY WINERY *Nevada 1980* A winery organized mainly by local investors determined to revive wine production in this Sierra Foothills area. The winery has 20 acres newly planted and has encouraged other growers to plant 42 acres. 1,500 cases are produced from five varieties purchased outside of the county until local vines mature.

NEWTON VINEYARD *Napa 1979* Former Sterling executives went off on their own, planted 60 acres on lovely, terraced Spring Mountain sites, and built a winery. First crush consisted of 2,000 cases of Merlot only. Over next vintages the output grew to 8,000 cases with the addition of Cabernet Sauvignon (blended with Merlot and Cabernet Franc), a Sauvignon Blanc/Semillon blend, and Chardonnay from the Rutherford area.

NEYERS WINERY *Napa 1980* Bruce Neyers works at Joseph Phelps in marketing and promoting and has now ventured into winemaking. He concentrates on barrel-fermented Chardonnay and Cabernet Sauvignon (blended with Merlot and Cabernet Franc) made predominantly from Napa grapes. The Cabernet Sauvignon is from the Eisele Vineyard. Total production is steady at 3,000 cases.

NICHELINI VINEYARDS *Napa 1890* Located in the Chiles Valley, away from the main wine road, this old winery relies on faithful customers or tourists on their way to Lake Berryessa. It makes 6,000 cases of varietals, including a Sauvignon Vert. The wines are low-priced, but the quality (oxidized whites and poorly handled reds) prevents them from being bargains.

NIEBAUM-COPPOLA ESTATES *Napa 1978* Movie director Francis Ford Coppola acquired the historic Niebaum mansion (long associated with Inglenook's founder) and the adjacent 90-acre vineyard. Only Cabernet (blended with Cabernet Franc, Merlot, and Malbec) and Chardonnay are being produced. Initial output was about 5,000 cases total. By the mid-1980s production could grow to 25,000 cases, unless persistent rumors of financial troubles prove reliable and delay yet another plan for a big production.

A. NONINI WINERY *Fresno 1935* This family-owned winery makes a variety of generics along with a Barbera and a

Zinfandel from its own 200-acre vineyard. Retail sales are through the quaint tasting room.

NORTH COAST CELLARS A private label for varietal wines made, like many others, at Souverain, except that these are made from grapes owned by many of the winery's partners-growers. All wines are nonvintage, and carry "North Coast" origins. All are inexpensive. The whites are simple, if low on varietal personality; the reds, Cabernet and Zinfandel in particular, represent good value. Sales have reached 40,000 cases.

NOVITIATE WINES *Santa Clara 1888* This historic winery began to phase out operation in 1980 after undergoing modernization in the late 1970s. Only its well-regarded Black Muscat was produced in 1981. Existing inventory continues to be marketed, including some good-quality dessert wines.

Black Muscat: *Strong muscat character, full-bodied, sweet* ❦

N.V. (NAPA VINTNERS) *Napa 1975* There has been wine under this label for several years, but it was not until 1978 that the owners formed their own winery. The label also appeared in 1979, but latest releases are now called D.C. Ross Winery.

Sauvignon Blanc: *Dry, fruity, good varietal, noticeable oak* ✿

OAK BARREL WINERY *Alameda 1960* Produces 2,000 cases of lackluster jug wines and varietals sold at low prices only at its Berkeley winery.

OAKVILLE VINEYARDS (ROBERT MONDAVI WINERY) After a winery by this name went out of business, Robert Mondavi acquired the trademark and aging inventory. The wines from that inventory have mercifully disappeared. But the label occasionally is seen on airlines or in a few remote regions where quality is not very important.

OBESTER WINERY *San Mateo 1977* Offers a broad range of varietals, all made from purchased grapes. First vintages evidenced good quality overall, the Sauvignon Blanc and Johannisberg Riesling being above average. Production is near 4,000 cases.

OLD CASTEEL VINEYARDS *San Luis Obispo 1980* In the rolling hills west of Paso Robles, this new winery is producing about 2,000 cases per year from its 20-acre, 50-year-old vineyard. Most of the production is Zinfandel, with smaller quantities offered of Grenache, Pinot Noir, and Carignane.

ORLEANS HILL *Yolo 1980* Produces 1,000 cases of Zinfandel and Sauvignon Blanc from vineyards in Amador County and the Lodi area. Winery was named after a vinicultural association that produced wine in Yolo County from the 1860s to the mid-1890s.

CHARLES ORTMAN The private label of a highly regarded consulting winemaker who finds time in his peripatetic rounds to offer wine under his own label—3,000 cases of Chardonnay and Sauvignon Blanc from Napa Valley and San Luis Obispo vineyards.

PACHECO RANCH WINERY *Marin 1976* In the northern end of this ultra-suburban county known for its hot tubs and mellow residents is this small (1,000-case) winery. It specializes in Cabernet Sauvignon grown on its 15-acre terraced vineyard planted in 1971. The production consists of an oak-aged Cabernet, a Rosé of Cabernet, and a Chardonnay from Sonoma County. Most wines are sold to the local, laid-back types.

PAGE MILL WINERY *Santa Clara 1976* Small winery producing big, oak-aged wines from purchased grapes, including Napa Valley Chardonnay and Zinfandel, San Luis Obispo Cabernet—all earning ✿ ratings in recent vintages.

PANACHE (CHANDON) Second label of this champagne producer used for a sweet, fortified wine from the second pressing of red grapes first devoted to sparkling-wine production. 2,000 cases.

PANNONIA WINERY *Napa 1979* In spite of the promise of small production and a limited line from grapes grown near the winery, only disappointment has been found in the bottle.

ANGELO PAPAGNI VINEYARDS *Madera 1973* Longtime grape grower Angelo Papagni had a better idea: Take the best of his several thousand acres of wine grapes, build a winery, and make limited amounts of wine. Benefiting from the latest technology, the wines have often turned out a beat above the usual Central Valley fare. In spite of the winery's capacity (1.2 million cases) sales of Angelo Papagni–labeled wines have been limited to date to 100,000 cases. Reds and a few whites are barrel aged. Some 20 wines are offered, including the only Alicante Bouschet in California. Attempts at making high-quality, bulk process sparkling wines have met limited success. Papagni Vineyards is a line of inexpensive but clean wines sold in 1–5 liter bottles.

Alicante Bouschet: *Vinous, tannic, clean* ♥
Chenin Blanc: *Fruity, slightly sweet, best when young* ♥
 ⚘ **Moscato d'Angelo:** *Very sweet, fragrant, easy to sip* ☻

PARDUCCI WINE CELLARS *Mendocino 1931* During the past decade Parducci converted from a bulk operation to a producer of quality wines at low prices. This early champion of Mendocino-grown grapes now has 350 acres in vineyards and produces about 300,000 cases, two-thirds in varietals and one-third in jugs annually. The winery's style is to emphasize fruit and to avoid excessive oak aging. Despite rapid expansion and an increased line, the overall quality level has continued to be reliable. Lots Parducci deems special are labeled Cellar Masters Selection.

Cabernet Sauvignon: *Medium varietal, fruity, balanced* ♥/☻
 ⚘ **Chardonnay:** *Appley, crisp, tart* ♥/☻
 ⚘ **Chenin Blanc:** *Fruity, lively, delicate, slightly sweet* ☻/☻☻
 ⚘ **Petite Sirah:** *Peppery, medium-bodied, tannic* ♥/☻
 ⚘ **Sauvignon Blanc:** *Fruity, slightly perfumed, well-balanced* ♥/☻
Zinfandel: *Fruity, round, light tannins* ♥

PARSONS CREEK WINERY *Mendocino 1979* The emphasis here is on white varietals finished with some sweetness. The winery contracts for all grapes and has them field crushed. Gewurztraminer is made in a sweet (4% sugar) style; the Johannisberg Riesling is in a slightly sweet style. Experiments with making Chardonnay with perceptible sweetness have been well-received. Good quality overall. Current output is 9,000 cases, with 12,000 set as maximum.

PASTORI WINES *Sonoma 1975* A pre-Prohibition name in the bulk wine business was revived and a small winery built. Its first wines, released in 1975, consisted of tired, tanky, purchased wines. It is now making wines from its 60-acre vineyard. The reds are overaged, and the whites are even less interesting. Production is close to 10,000 cases, mostly consisting of inexpensive generics.

PAULSEN VINEYARDS *Sonoma 1980* Former comedian and presidential candidate Pat Paulsen retreated to a 600-acre ranch near Cloverdale, planted 35 acres to wine grapes, and recently completed a winery of 25,000-case capacity. Made 1,600 cases of Sauvignon Blanc in 1980, with plans to offer Cabernet and Chardonnay by 1983. Prior to 1980 grapes went to Chateau St. Jean.

Sauvignon Blanc: *Strong varietal fruit, firm, crisp, light oak* ❸

ROBERT PECOTA WINERY *Napa 1978* 40 acres of vineyard surrounding the Calistoga winery provide 8,000 cases of wine per year. First releases were youthful, fruity wines. Still to come is a dry, oaky Sauvignon Blanc.

French Colombard: *Dry, fruity and somewhat oaky* ❸
Gamay Beaujolais: *Intense fruity nouveau style* ❷/❸

PEDREGAL (STAGS' LEAP VINEYARDS) Second label used for wines made from purchased grapes and wines not meeting the winery's prime-label standard. First three vintages of Cabernet Sauvignon appeared under this label.

PEDRIZZETTI WINERY *Santa Clara 1938* An old roadside winery modernized in 1976 after being reacquired by the family. New equipment and renewed effort are bringing quality closer to respectability. The winery tore out its vineyards in 1977 and has subsequently purchased all grapes for its 80,000-case production, which is primarily white wine. Only the Chardonnay and Cabernet Sauvignon spend time in small barrels, for the winery wants to minimize the character of wood in its wine.

Petite Sirah: *Hearty, robust, fairly tannic* ❷
Zinfandel: *Fruity, light-bodied, tart* ❷

PEDRONCELLI VINEYARDS *Sonoma 1904* A longtime bulk wine producer, it began bottling wines under its own label in the early 1960s. It has 135 acres under vine and purchases grapes in Sonoma County to reach its current 135,000 cases per year output. After gaining an early reputation for consistent quality and value, the winery ran into some quality problems in the mid-1970s, but has since solved them and returned to form. All wines, including popular jugs, carry Sonoma County appellation.

Cabernet Sauvignon: *Vague varietal, simple fruit* ❷
Chardonnay: *Appley, light varietal flavors, crisp* ❷/❸
Chenin Blanc: *Fruity, spritzy, clean, but sweetness lacks balance* ❷
Gewurztraminer: *Slightly spicy, firm, slightly sweet* ❷
Sonoma White Wine: *Fruity, light-bodied, good, slightly sweet jug* ❷

Zinfandel: *Fruity, simple* 🍷
Zinfandel Rosé: *Fruity, spritzy, slightly sweet* 🍷

PELLEGRINI VINEYARDS *San Mateo 1934* Distributors and growers (100 acres of Chardonnay and Pinot Noir), Pellegrini uses the Cambiaso plant to produce approximately 33,000 cases a year of varietal and vineyard-named wines. The main market is restaurants and the wines have been generally well-made.

PENDLETON WINERY Santa Clara 1976 Moved into a new, 6,000-case winery in 1979 and changed name from Arroyo. First 3 vintages were made elsewhere. Major emphasis is on Monterey-grown Chardonnay and Pinot Noir, with small amount of Chenin Blanc, Sauvignon Blanc, and Cabernet. Efforts with Chardonnay and Pinot Noir have resulted in above-average quality. Reasonable prices.

Chardonnay: *Ripe, buttery, oaky* ✪

ROBERT PEPI WINERY *Napa 1981* After selling grapes for 16 years, the Pepi family built a winery adjacent to their Oakville plantings. First year's output reached 4,000 cases, but the winery will grow quickly to the 15,000-case maximum. Sauvignon Blanc is the most prominent varietal, followed by Cabernet and Chardonnay.

PERELLI-MINETTI WINERY This old name in California wine is now a new label for a line of varietals. Although the winery is in Delano, the varietals are from grapes purchased in the North and Central coast regions. Production is 12,000 cases. Neither the reds nor the whites have been consistently well-made.

MARIO PERELLI-MINETTI WINES Private label (owned independently of the Perelli-Minetti Winery) for Cabernet Sauvignon and Chardonnay purchased ready-made. First vintages offered light varietal character in an early-drinking style.

PESENTI WINERY *San Luis Obispo 1934* A 30,000-case producer of inexpensive wines for consumers in the San Luis Obispo area, especially those at the local college.

Zinfandel Rosé: *Fruity, overly sweet* 🍷

PETRI WINES Label for fairly sweet, inexpensive, cooked-fruit-tasting jug wines bottled by Heublein (Inglenook, Colony). Below average in quality; 2 million cases sold annually.

JOSEPH PHELPS VINEYARD *Napa 1973* Handsome 50,000-case winery producing wines of very high quality. Its early reputation for success with Riesling and Gewurztraminer now extends to Cabernet Sauvignon, Zinfandel, Chardonnay, and almost every other varietal it has offered. Late harvest Riesling and Gewurztraminer always rate ❁❁ to ❁❁❁. The winery's own vineyards (220 acres) supply 80% of its needs.

Cabernet Sauvignon: *Fruity varietal, fairly full* ❦/❁❁
Chardonnay: *Oaky, medium-full-bodied, fat style* ❦/❁❁
Fumé Blanc: *Light, fruity, elegant, blended with Semillon* ❦/❁
Gewurztraminer: *Spicy, perfumed, balanced, slightly sweet* ❁❁
Insignia: *Winery's best blend from available Cabernet, Merlot, and Cabernet Franc; content varies each year, although wine maintains depth and charm* ❁/❁❁❁
Johannisberg Riesling: *Floral, good varietal, fruity, medium sweet* ❁/❁❁
Zinfandel: *Ripe, berryish, fairly tannic* ❦/❁❁

PINE RIDGE *Napa 1978* Using Napa grapes from vineyards in the Carneros, Stag's Leap, and Rutherford areas, this winery has grown into a 12,000-case producer specializing in Chardonnay, Carbernet, and Chenin Blanc. Results to date have been promising and prices refreshingly in line with quality.

❦ **Cabernet Sauvignon:** *Medium-intensity, good varietal, light oak* ❦/❁
Chardonnay: *Big, ripe, a touch hot, oaky* ❦

PIPER SONOMA VINEYARDS *Sonoma 1980* A joint venture specializing in sparkling wines. The grapes come from Sonoma, and the expertise from Piper-Heidsieck. First offering due in mid-1982 consists of 35,000 cases, mostly called Brut. Other styles planned are Blanc de Noirs and a Tête de Cuvée. In 1981, an $8 million facility was built, capable of producing 100,000 cases per year.

POINT LOMA *San Diego 1980* Produces 200 cases of reds from Southern California vineyards in San Diego and Riverside counties.

POMMERAIE VINEYARDS *Sonoma 1979* One of the most elegant new labels on the market belongs to Pommeraie, a 1,200-case winery targeted toward a maximum production of

2,000 cases divided between Chardonnay and Cabernet Sauvignon. Owners have high goals, although first release had technical flaws.

POPE VALLEY WINERY *Napa 1972* A family-run (12,000-case) winery that makes a variety of wines from a variety of regions. All grapes are purchased, and the annual offerings seem to depend on which grape varieties are available. The quality is inconsistent ranging from an occasional ✿ to below average. No logical reason is apparent for either its successes or failures.

PHILIP POSSON (SIERRA WINE COMPANY) The only label used by the gigantic (30-million-gallon capacity) Central Valley bulk wine producer. Dry Flor Sherry, made by the "submerged flor" technique, is the only retail offering. It is one of California's best. Under 5,000 cases annually.

Dry Flor Sherry: *Yeasty, flavorful, medium-bodied, dry* ✿

PRAGER PORT WORKS *Napa 1980* Despite the name, the output (3,000 cases) is 50% table wines. Chardonnay, Cabernet Sauvignon, and Zinfandel are Napa Valley in origin. The 1980 port is made entirely from Cabernet grown in the Knight's Valley. It comes in two lots, with the second receiving longer barrel aging. Subsequent blends for the port include Petite Sirah and Zinfandel.

PRESTON VINEYARDS *Sonoma 1975* From its 80 acres in the Dry Creek region, Preston has emphasized Fumé Blanc and Zinfandel in its 5,000-case annual output. After experimenting with other varietals, it has settled on Gamay and Chenin Blanc, finished dry, as regular offerings. Production will grow to a maximum of 12,000 cases.

Fumé Blanc: *Intense varietal, good fruit, dry* ♥/✿
Zinfandel: *Fruity, rough, tannic* ♥/✿

QUADY WINERY *Madera 1977* Quady is among the leaders in a new wave of interest in port wine production. Andrew Quady prefers to use only Zinfandel grown in Amador and to age the wine 2 years in American oak, making 2,500 cases of Vintage Port in his small winery. First vintages were appealing; the degree of improvement that long cellaring will produce remains to be seen. In addition, the winery makes 1,000 cases of a sweet dessert wine from Orange Muscat grapes offered under the name Essensia.

Essensia: *Orange perfume, sweet, distinctive* ✿

Vintage Port (Amador): *Rich, intense, moderately tannic* ✪/✪✪

QUAIL RIDGE WINERY *Napa 1978* Small producer aiming toward 4,000 cases in 1982, emphasizing Chardonnay with lesser amounts of Cabernet and barrel-fermented French Colombard. 20 acres of vineyard on Mount Veeder are planted to Chardonnay.

QUERCUS VINEYARDS A privately owned label for Lake County Cabernet Sauvignon. About 2,000 cases per year, made at Souverain Cellars. Variable quality in a light style.

A. RAFANELLI WINERY *Sonoma 1974* With 25 acres in Dry Creek, this 3,000-case winery offers only Gamay Beaujolais and Zinfandel. The first releases were vintage blends. The more recent vintage Zinfandels are good both for the type and region.

⚘ **Zinfandel:** *Dark, ripe berries, tannic, powerful* ✪

RANCHITA OAKS *San Luis Obispo 1979* 4,000-case production of Zinfandel, Cabernet Sauvignon, Petite Sirah, and Chardonnay are produced from the winery's 44-acre vineyards located in the hills near Shandon. Winery is seeking a tannic, long-aging style for its reds.

RANCHO DE PHILO *San Bernardino 1975* Cream sherry is produced through the solera method. Approximately 250 cases are offered each year, and the product is reported to be composed of wines averaging 16 years old.

RANCHO SISQUOC *Santa Barbara 1977* Small (2,000-case) winery located in the midst of a 38,000-acre diversified agricultural development. Close to 200 acres of vineyards are established, half of which are planted to Cabernet Sauvignon. Most grapes are sold. To date, the wines made have been uneven in quality. Sales have been primarily to winery visitors.

RANCHO YERBA BUENA A limited-production label associated with Papagni Vineyards. The wines, Cabernet Sauvignon and a few generics, carry modest price tags.

RAPAZZINI WINERY *Santa Clara 1962* Burned out by a fire in 1980 that destroyed both the winery and inventory, the Rapazzinis crushed enough grapes in 1981 at other wineries to produce 8,000 cases of about 10 varietals. A new winery was built in time for the 1982 crush.

RAVENSWOOD WINERY Winemaker and equipment are in leased space in Sonoma County. The emphasis is on Zinfandel and Cabernet Sauvignon made from grapes grown in El Dorado, Amador, and Napa counties, and from vineyards in the Dry Creek Valley. The Zinfandels are ripe and briary, but sometimes are overripe and too tannic. The Cabernets are made in the same vein, though are somewhat less powerful. Both varietals periodically succeed and have earned up to 🟢🟢 rankings. Production is currently at 7,000 cases total, with 10,000 viewed as optimum.

MARTIN RAY VINEYARDS *Santa Clara 1946* Established by the late Martin Ray after he sold his interest in Paul Masson. His son, a professor at Stanford, now oversees the winery's 5,000-case output. Chardonnay is the volume leader; Cabernet Sauvignon, Pinot Noir, Johannisberg Riesling, and sparkling wine are also offered. Prices are among the highest in California; quality has been erratic but seems to be improving.

Chardonnay: *Very oaky, fat, ripe, sometimes lovely, sometimes dirty and oxidized* 🔵/🟢🟢

RAYMOND VINEYARDS *Napa 1974* The Raymond family is directly related to the Beringer clan and was long involved with that winery. The Raymonds established an 80-acre vineyard in 1971 and completed their own winery in 1978, designed to make 20,000 to 25,000 cases. The early record was spotty, with a disappointment to match every major success. Recent attention was focused on Chardonnay and Cabernet and has brought about a more consistent quality performance.

Cabernet Sauvignon: *Herbaceous, oaky, and tannic* 🍷/🟢
Chardonnay: *Medium varietal, very oaky, round* 🍷/🟢🟢

REGE WINES (LE BAY CELLARS) Once popular jug wine label now phased out by the new owners of this renovated winery.

RICHERT CELLARS *Santa Clara 1954* Formerly a dessert wine specialist (sherries and ports), now devoting 60% of its 5,000-case production to table wine (including Cabernet, Chardonnay, and Johannisberg Riesling) and a line of attractive fruit and berry wines.

RIDGE VINEYARDS *Santa Clara 1962* Among the first wineries to demonstrate that Zinfandel can be made into a first-class wine. It did so by scurrying about to locate the finest hillside vineyards. Ridge red wines were once the biggest and brawniest; the style today is a bit more restrained. Current production is 40,000 cases, over half in Zinfandel and 40% in Cabernet Sauvignon. It buys Cabernet and Petite Sirah from York Creek in Napa. Monte Bello refers to several vineyards located along the ridge near the winery. Prices are ordinarily high, but the non-vineyard designated (San Luis and Amador) Zinfandels are often good values.

Cabernet Sauvignon, Monte Bello: *Earthy, oaky, tannic, recently variable* ✹/✿✿✿✿

Petite Sirah: *Briary, tannic, intense, hot* ✹/✿✿✿✿

✤ **Zinfandel (Amador):** *Forward, jammy* ✹/✿

Zinfandel (Geyserville): *Ripe, intense, powerful* ✿/✿✿✿✿

✤ **Zinfandel (San Luis):** *Berryish, earthy* ✹/✿

Zinfandel (York Creek): *Spicy and berrylike, brawny* ✹/✿✿✿✿

RITCHIE CREEK VINEYARDS *Napa 1974* This label represents a small trickle. 6 acres of Cabernet Sauvignon, along with a little plot of Chardonnay, are planted on Spring Mountain. Annual production is well under 1,000 cases. Cabernets from recent vintages have been medium-full-bodied with ample tannin, but far from harmonious.

RIVER BEND CELLARS (DAVIS BYNUM WINERY) A second label for lower-priced wines aged for shorter periods than the first label. Most offerings are simple and carry Sonoma County appellations. Quantity sold is a maximum of 5,000 cases annually.

RIVER OAKS VINEYARDS This label belongs to a limited partnership of growers and investors who own 600 acres of vineyards in the Alexander Valley. They have wines made at 4 different Sonoma County facilities. The line consists of inexpensive varietals and generics that at best offer fruity, straightforward character. A trio of table wines in the 1.5 liter magnum enjoys sales success and accounts for a high percentage of the annual 50,000-case production.

RIVER ROAD VINEYARDS *Sonoma 1978* Currently making 7,000 cases of varietals, the owners use only one-third of the production from their vineyards. They have 70 acres in Forestville and 45 acres south of Cloverdale. The wines have been made at Sonoma Vineyards. Chardonnay is the best and most plentiful. Fumé Blanc, Zinfandel, and Johannisberg Riesling fill out the line.

RIVER RUN VINEYARDS *Santa Cruz 1978* Orchard owner Will Hangen has started a small winery on his riverfront property. Output is limited (1,200 cases of red varietals), and grape sources tend to be Central Coast vineyards.

RIVERSIDE FARMS (LOUIS J. FOPPIANO WINERY) Newly devised second label used for generic wines.

RODDIS CELLARS *Napa 1978* It offers only a few hundred cases of Cabernet Sauvignon grown on its 4-acre Diamond Mountain vineyard.

ROMA A jug wine and inexpensive bulk process sparkling-wine label belonging to the Guild cooperative. Distribution is primarily in the northeastern U.S.

ROSENBLUM CELLARS *Alameda 1978* Small (1,500-case) producer of North Coast varietals. Prices are reasonable and make the successes good values.

D. C. ROSS WINERY *Napa 1978* The new name of the winery previously called Napa Vintners. Owner Ross will continue the winery's past emphasis on Lake County Sauvignon Blanc. Current production is 5,000 cases.

CARLO ROSSI VINEYARDS (E. & J. GALLO) This highly visible Gallo label now covers 4 generics in the inexpensive, jug wine end. It has recently been consolidated with the former Red Mountain Vineyards label. Carlo is really a cousin of the Gallos.

ROSS-KELLEREI *Santa Barbara 1980* The owners are horse breeders who have started a 3,000-case winery operation offering five varietals from purchased grapes. The literal translation of the name from German is "winery of the steed" and the wines may have to be faultless to avoid becoming the butt of rustic jokes.

ROUDON-SMITH VINEYARDS *Santa Cruz 1972* New winery for this 10,000-case producer was finished in 1979. It has settled on making Cabernet, Zinfandel, Petite Syrah, and barrel-fermented Chardonnay from purchased grapes. The wine-making style favors big, ripe, fairly alcoholic wines. Recent Chardonnays come from Monterey and Edna Valley; Cabernets from San Luis Obispo, Saratoga, and Sonoma; Zinfandels from Sonoma and San Luis Obispo.

Cabernet Sauvignon: *Complex, fruity, round, early-maturing* ♥/❀❀
Zinfandel (Old Hill): *Ripe berrylike fruit, good depth, fairly tannic* ♥/❀
Chardonnay: *Intense, oaky, ripe* ♥/❀

ROUND HILL VINEYARDS *Napa 1975* Began as a blender and bottler of purchased wines, now also produces 18,000 cases at its own winery, and at other wineries by contract. Some 50,000 cases are bought in bulk and finished by Round Hill. These are identified on the label as "cellared by" the winery. Many are inexpensive.

Cabernet Sauvignon: *Weedy varietal, soft, round* ♥
Chardonnay (Napa Valley): *Fruity, fresh, light oak* ♥/❸
Zinfandel (Napa Valley): *Berrylike, fruity* ♥

ROYAL HOST A primary label for wines and brandies made by Lodi's East-Side Winery. Its ports and sherries, particularly those finished sweet, win numerous awards. The label also appears on many inexpensive, low-quality generics and an excellent 6-year-old brandy.

RUBY HILL (STONY RIDGE WINERY) This second label has been used for some very modest, sometimes flawed wine.

CHANNING RUDD CELLARS *Alameda 1977* Label designer Rudd operates his 400-case winery part-time, emphasizing big reds, port, and occasionally offering barrel-aged whites. Although expensive, his Sonoma County Zinfandels have attracted a following for their intense, ripe berry style. A 55-acre vineyard site in Lake County near Middletown has been purchased and is being planted in anticipation of the winery's relocation there.

RUTHERFORD HILL WINERY *Napa 1976* This is a new label, although the winery was operated by Pillsbury as Souverain of Rutherford earlier. Several partners behind Freemark Abbey, who own large acreage in Napa, decided to acquire these premises instead of building a new winery. The first series of varietals released was of average quality (the reds were inherited in the transaction). By the 1978 vintage the white varietals were of above-average quality, and the reds had become more interesting also. Production has leveled off at 100,000 cases.

Cabernet Sauvignon: *Medium-bodied, some fruit, noticeable oak* ♥/❸
Chardonnay: *Fruity, round, oaky* ♥/❸
Johannisberg Riesling: *Flowery, balanced, slightly sweet* ♥/❸
Merlot: *Ripe, slightly heavy, deep, oaky* ❸/❸❸
Zinfandel: *From Atlas Peak east of Napa Valley; ripe, rich, often high in alcohol* ♥/❸

RUTHERFORD RANCH CELLARS (ROUND HILL CELLARS) From vineyards in the hills west of St. Helena, 1,200 cases of

Zinfandel, 1,700 cases of Cabernet, and 1,500 cases of Sauvignon Blanc are produced. 1,000 cases of Chardonnay from the Gamble Ranch (Napa Valley) round out this line of wines. The reds have been exceptional.

⚘ **Zinfandel:** *Ripe varietal, big, rich, and tannic* ❀/❀❀
⚘ **Cabernet Sauvignon:** *Complex aroma and flavors, tannic* ❀/❀❀

RUTHERFORD VINTNERS *Napa 1977* This compact winery with its 30 acres represents working retirement for former Louis Martini employee Bernard Skoda. Cabernet Sauvignon, Johannisberg Riesling, and Pinot Noir come from the adjacent vineyard; a sweet muscat is made from Fresno grapes, and a Chardonnay from the Alexander Valley. Production is at 15,000 cases with plans to double. The quality record to date shows a series of generally dull wines.

SAGE CANYON WINERY Starting with 1,200 cases of Chenin Blanc crushed at borrowed facilities in 1981, the plan is to double production, add Chardonnay, and build a Napa Valley winery. The goal is 8–10,000 cases.

ST. ANDREW'S WINERY *Napa 1980* 2,000 cases of Chardonnay are produced annually with about 20% of the grapes coming from the 65-acre vineyard surrounding the winery. Most of the harvest is sold to Chandon.

ST. CLEMENT VINEYARDS *Napa 1975* Small winery producing limited quantities (7,500 cases) of high-quality wines. Only Cabernet Sauvignon, Chardonnay, and Sauvignon Blanc are offered, all in oaky, long-aging style. Prices are high but not out of line for quality.

Cabernet Sauvignon: *Good varietal, oaky, fairly tannic style* ❀
Chardonnay: *Oaky, fat style with good varietal fruit* ❀/❀❀
Sauvignon Blanc: *Tight, weedy, oaky flavors* ❀

ST. FRANCIS WINERY *Sonoma 1979* New winery in Kenwood surrounded by 100 acres of vineyards containing 5 cool-climate varieties. Initial success was enjoyed practically across the board, and production grew to 12,000 cases with twice that amount anticipated by mid-decade.

Chardonnay: *Estate-grown, deeply fruity, well-balanced, oak-edged* ❀/❀❀
Gewurztraminer: *Slightly sweet, floral, attractive, varietal spice* ❀/❀❀

Merlot: *Ripe, curranty, somewhat broad plummy flavors, moderately tannic* ✣

SAN CARLOS DE JONATA (ROSS-KELLEREI) A second label used for generic white made from Chardonnay and Chenin Blanc and given the name "White Burgundy."

SANFORD & BENEDICT VINEYARDS *Santa Barbara 1970* Emphasizing barrel-fermented Chardonnay and Pinot Noir, the winery is now producing 10,000 cases a year. Its limited line of varietals also includes Merlot and Cabernet. Most grapes come from its 110-acre vineyard. After some early successes, the winery has become inconsistent in quality. Recent vintages have been victimized by poor winemaking.

Chardonnay: *Ripe, often oily and round, but flawed of late* 𝛿/✣
Pinot Noir: *Sometimes complex, recently dirty* 𝛿/✣

SAN MARTIN WINERY *Santa Clara 1908* Dramatically improved quality was registered in the late 1970s by this Norton Simon–owned 250,000-case winery. White wines represent close to 60% of the current total. Most are average to slightly above average in quality and are made in a fresh, fruity, simple style for immediate consumption. An Amador Zinfandel heads the red wine roster. Almost all other varietals come from purchased Central Coast grapes. This winery was instrumental in the production of soft, low-alcohol table wines and occasionaly offers a limited amount of late harvest Riesling with Botrytis. Very reasonable prices.

Cabernet Sauvignon: *Ripe, oaky, weedy* ❦/✣
Chardonnay: *Grassy varietal fruit, simple, balanced, light oak* ❦
Chenin Blanc: *Fruity, lively, spritzy, medium sweet* ❦/✣
✤ **Fumé Blanc:** *Herbaceous, round, fruity, light oak* ❦/✣
✤ **Johannisberg Riesling:** *Fragrant, citrusy, tart, slightly sweet* ❦
✤ **Zinfandel:** *Spicy, ripe flavors, woody, sharp* ❦/✣

SAN PASQUAL VINEYARDS *San Diego 1973* The first San Diego winery to produce quality varietals. It has 120 acres of vineyards near the winery and is close to a maximum output of 25,000 cases. The Fumé Blanc is emerging as its most successful wine, followed by Chenin Blanc. Gamay is made in a nouveau style and a very ripe version. It also offers both a dessert style and fortified Muscat Blanc. Sparkling wine has been added, using Gamay grapes and following the *méthode champenoise.*

Fumé Blanc: *Peppery, herbaceous flavors, lively, light oak* ♥/☸

SANTA BARBARA WINERY *Santa Barbara 1962* Jug wine bottler that has added a 42-acre vineyard operation and its own line of varietals. Production at 10,000 cases. Erratic results to date.

SANTA CRUZ CELLARS (BARGETTO WINERY) Line of inexpensive, fair-quality jug wines distributed primarily at the winery and to a few local retailers.

SANTA CRUZ MOUNTAIN VINEYARD *Santa Cruz 1975* A Pinot Noir specialist with 14 acres planted on mountainous terrain quickly learned that it is unwise to make only Pinot Noir. Pinot Noir now represents 40% of the winery's 3,000-case production, and a similar amount of Cabernet Sauvignon is produced from the Bates Ranch, Santa Cruz Mountains. The winery's third variety changes from year to year, although eventually a Chardonnay will be a regular, made from grapes grown at the winery.

Pinot Noir: *Aromatic, complex, rich, tannic* ☸/☸☸☸

SANTA YNEZ VALLEY WINERY *Santa Barbara 1976* About 10,000 cases are made in a refurbished dairy barn with grapes coming from the partners' 165 acres supplemented by purchased grapes, mainly Sauvignon Blanc, in response to demand. White wines represent 90% of the production and most of the winery's successes. The reds have generally been execrable failures to date, except for experimental batches of Cabernet Franc.

Sauvignon Blanc: *Strong varietal, good fruit flavor, hot* ☸
Chardonnay: *Lemony, crisp, slightly toasty* ♥/☸; *the occasional Reserve bottling earns up to* ☸☸.

SANTINO WINES *Amador 1979* Amador Zinfandels aged in French oak are the main focus. Sauvignon Blanc is also produced from both Amador and Russian River Valley grapes. All grapes are purchased, and the winery's near-term goal is 12,000 cases per year.

Zinfandel (Fiddletown): *Oaky, ripe, berryish* ♥/☸

SARAH'S VINEYARD *Santa Clara 1978* One of the first new, small, quality-minded wineries in the Hecker Pass area. It has 7 acres planted to Chardonnay. Its first few vintages from purchased grapes included some exceptional Chardonnays from a variety of vineyard sources. The remaining half of its 1,500 cases is composed of small lots of Zinfandel, Cabernet, Riesling, and Petite Sirah. Production is expected to double in 1983.

SARATOGA CELLARS (KATHRYN KENNEDY WINES) Markets wines from purchased grapes. A pleasant rosé was the first offering.

V. SATTUI WINERY *Napa 1975* This small, 8,000-case winery is attached to a tourist-oriented gift store and gourmet shop, both of which seem as important to the owners as wine production. In the last couple of years, wine output has increased in volume and, concomitantly, in quality. However, sales are limited to the winery and are directed as much to picnickers as they are to connoisseurs.

SAUSAL WINERY *Sonoma 1973* Primarily growers (owning 125 acres in the Alexander Valley) who wanted to make only bulk wine originally. By 1975 they decided to bottle some under their own label. Other wineries, notably Joseph Phelps, have produced excellent Zinfandel from Sausal grapes. Sausal's first Zinfandels were long-aged and about average in quality. A Chardonnay and a popular-priced blended white called Sausal Blanc have been added. The winery's capacity is 30,000 cases.

 ⚜ **Zinfandel:** *Mature, medium-full-bodied, slightly woody* 🍷/❦

SCHARFFENBERGER CELLARS *Mendocino 1981* This grower sells all grapes to Mendocino wineries and then buys from growers in the Anderson Valley to produce Champagnes. Initial production was 7,000 cases (4,500 of Brut, 2,500 of Cuvée de Pinot Noir), all by the *méthode champenoise.* The aging regime calls for three years in the bottle. About 1,000 cases of Chardonnay are made from grapes too ripe for Champagne.

SCHRAMSBERG VINEYARDS *Napa 1966* Only *méthode champenoise* sparkling wines, possibly the finest produced in California, are offered by this hillside winery reoccupying the 19th-century vineyard site and aging caves. The winery owns 40 acres of vineyards split between Chardonnay and Pinot Noir, but purchases most grapes that go into its 25,000 cases (an expansion program will double production to 50,000 cases by the mid-1980s). The best-selling Blanc de

Blancs, primarily Chardonnay with a little Pinot Blanc, is aged 2 years on the yeast *(en tirage).* Blanc de Noirs, about two-thirds Pinot Noir and one-third Chardonnay, is kept *en tirage* for over 4 years. A special, limited-edition Reserve bottling also receives long aging on the yeast.

Blanc de Blancs: *Crisp, fruity, slightly yeasty* ❁/❁❁
Blanc de Noirs: *Crisp, slightest hint of sweetness, aged yeasty champagne nose, deep and complex in best years* ❁/❁❁❁
Crémant: *Sweet, floral, inviting* ❁/❁❁
Cuvée de Pinot: *Pinkish color, somewhat fat style* ♥/❁

SCHUG CELLARS Another winemaker (Joseph Phelps Vineyards) who makes wine in his spare time. Initial emphasis is on Pinot Noir (1,700 cases) from Yountville-area grapes made at Storybook Mountain Vineyards.

SEAVIEW WINERY *Sonoma 1980* Located 3 1/2 miles from the Pacific Ocean, the winery enjoys a view of the sea. It has 10 acres total of Chardonnay and Pinot Noir in this cool region. Small amounts of Sauvignon Blanc and Zinfandel contribute to a 5,000-case output.

SEBASTIANI VINEYARDS *Sonoma 1889* Though enjoying a rustic image in the 1970s, this family-run winery grew quickly to 4 million cases per year. As it expanded into a full-range producer of table, sparkling, and dessert wines, its quality began to diminish, not only for the white wines but also for the reds, once its claim to wine fame. After his father's death, Sam Sebastiani took charge in early 1980 and began implementing numerous changes. The results of some were quickly felt, such as the introduction of a Light Country White, and a line of Country varietals and a rosé under the August Sebastiani logo. Others, such as the building of a separate facility for generic wines and modernization of the existing winery, along with supply contracts with well-known Sonoma Valley growers, have yet to take place. Meanwhile, the current batch of jug generics remain below average quality. The best tangible sign for the future is the improved quality of recent Proprietor's Reserve Barbera and Cabernet Sauvignon.

Barbera: *Berryish, mature, tart* ♥/❁
Mountain Burgundy: *Rough, coarse, heavy* ♥
Mountain Chablis: *Thin, medium sweet* ♥
Chardonnay: *Artificial, flat, dry* ☯/♥
Chenin Blanc: *Dull, flat, sweet* ☯/♥
Zinfandel: *Berryish, sometimes raisined; full-bodied* ♥

SEQUOIA CELLARS *Yolo 1977* 400-case production of this part-time effort is split among Amador County Zinfandel and Cabernet Sauvignon, Alexander Valley Gewurztraminer, and locally grown Carnelian.

SEQUOIA GROVE VINEYARDS *Napa 1980* On the outskirts of Oakville sits this 24-acre vineyard and small winery. It opened with two barrel-fermented Chardonnays, one from its own mature 9 acres and the second from Sonoma-Cutrer Vineyards. Cabernet (from 1980) will debut in 1983. Currently making 4,000 cases total.

ROBERT SETRAKIAN VINEYARDS (GROWERS WINERY) Though viewed as the company's top line, its table wines are no better or worse than those under the Growers label. However, Setrakian Brandy is of good quality, and the Solera Ports and Sherries are of average quality.

SHAFER VINEYARDS *Napa 1980* The first vintages, though made elsewhere, were impressive. A winery was finished by 1980, when 4,000 cases were made. Chardonnay, Cabernet, and Zinfandel come from its 40-acre vineyard in the Stag's Leap area. Production will grow to 10,000 cases.

CHARLES F. SHAW VINEYARD *Napa 1979* After purchasing an established 35-acre vineyard north of St. Helena, Shaw built a 5,000-case winery. The winery offers Napa Gamay, made by carbonic maceration. The wine, aged briefly in large oak casks, is made in a light, fruity style.

Gamay: *Good fruit, fresh, balanced* ❦

SHENANDOAH VINEYARDS *Amador 1977* Developing a 30-acre vineyard planted to Barbera, Cabernet, and Sauvignon Blanc. Vineyard includes experimental planting of Rhone and Portuguese varieties. However, the current production of 7,000 cases is almost entirely made from purchased grapes. The quality of the white varietals is uneven, but the Zinfandel has been among the best produced from Amador grapes. A rich Black Muscat dessert wine also deserves high marks.

Zinfandel: *Blackberry, spicy, rich* ✿/✿✿

SHERRILL CELLARS *San Mateo 1973* Settled into a new winery in 1979 and committed itself to buying only Central Coast grapes for its limited production line of varietals, totaling 4,000 cases annually. More successful with Petite Sirah and Zinfandel. 7 acres planted to Chardonnay.

SHOWN & SONS WINERY *Napa 1979* A fairly well-known grower, with 75 acres in Rutherford, built a winery on the Silverado Trail. About 15,000 cases are produced; predominantly Cabernet Sauvignon and smaller amounts of Johannisberg Riesling and Chenin Blanc. Initial offerings have been undistinguished.

SIERRA VISTA WINERY *El Dorado 1977* This winery makes 2,000 cases from its 12 acres and purchased grapes. It offers Fumé Blanc, Zinfandel, Chardonnay, and Cabernet. It has a few acres of French Syrah planted. The Zinfandels have been remarkably attractive both in quality and price.

⚘ **Zinfandel:** *Ripe, berrylike, tannic* ❦/❀❀

THE SILVERADO VINEYARDS *Napa 1981* Because it is jointly owned by the president of Disney Productions and Mrs. Walter Disney, this winery attracted immediate attention. It has 165 acres planted along the southern end of the Silverado Trail. The most prominent varieties are Sauvignon Blanc, Chardonnay, and Cabernet. Some 8,000 cases in all were made the first year. By 1985 the production will be at the maximum of 40,000 cases.

SILVER MOUNTAIN VINEYARDS *Santa Cruz 1979* Barrel-fermented Chardonnay is produced from Ventana Vineyard grapes. Zinfandel from varying sources. The current 1,200 cases a year will increase to 2,000 cases as the winery's 12 acres of Chardonnay reach maturity.

SILVER OAK CELLAR *Napa 19772* Using grapes from the Alexander Valley, this Cabernet-only winery makes 5,000 cases per year. Each vintage is aged 4 years prior to release, but such regal treatment is a bit inappropriate for the quality. Fairly high-priced.

Cabernet Sauvignon: *Herbaceous, oaky, simple* ❦/❀

SIMI WINERY *Sonoma 1867* A historic winery that has changed ownership and direction several times since the late 1960s. Its present owner, Moët-Hennessey of France, has rebuilt all but the shell of the old winery since 1979 and has refocused production almost entirely on the Chardonnay and Cabernet. The initial results of this major investment should be apparent with the release of the 1980 and 1981 vintages. In the meantime, most of its offerings range from average to better-than-average quality. The grapes are purchased from Sonoma and Mendocino county vineyards.

The reds are released when fully mature and ready for enjoyment. 130,000 cases per year.

Cabernet Sauvignon: *Varietal, fruity character, medium-bodied* ♥/❈
Chardonnay: *Fruity, light oak, usually balanced* ♥
Chenin Blanc: *Fruity, floral, round, slightly sweet* ♥
Gerwurztraminer: *Spicy, sometimes complex, slightly sweet* ♥/❈
Zinfandel: *Berrylike, light oak and tannin* ♥/❈

SKY VINEYARDS *Sonoma 1979* From high in the mountains east of Glen Ellen, this Zinfandel specialist will release its first wines in 1984. 14 acres have been planted, beginning in 1977, and production is targeted at 3,000 cases per year.

SMITH & HOOK *Monterey 1979* Bucking the current trend in which many Monterey County growers are budding their Cabernet Sauvignon vines over to the production of white varieties, this new winery has declared its intention to make Cabernet exclusively from its 250 acres in the cool Gonzales area. 12,000 cases.

SMITH-MADRONE VINEYARDS *Napa 1977* Quality-oriented winery atop Spring Mountain producing 3,000 cases. 40 acres of vineyards favor Cabernet Sauvignon and Chardonnay with lesser amounts of Johannisberg Riesling and Pinot Noir. The whites have been more appealing than the first reds.

Chardonnay: *Fruity, good acid, oaky* ❈
Johannisberg Riesling: *Slightly sweet, good acid balance, fresh fruity taste* ❈

SMOTHERS *Sonoma 1977* For the 1982 crush, Dick Smothers moved his winery from the historic Vine Hill area in the Santa Cruz Mountains to his brother Tom's property in Glen Ellen, Sonoma Valley. This moves the winery to the grapes, since all but a small quantity of Riesling and Chardonnay has been made from Sonoma County sources. Success has been enjoyed with Gewurztraminer, Chardonnay, and Riesling. 3,700 cases per year.

SOMERSET VINEYARD *El Dorado 1980* After an initial crush of 1,200 cases at other facilities, this winery completed its own plant in time for the 1981 harvest. Zinfandel, Cabernet, and Chenin Blanc are offered, and the near-term goal is 8,000 cases per year, mainly from purchased grapes.

SOMMELIER WINERY *Santa Cruz 1976* This winery makes 3,500 cases per year of red varietals and Chardonnay from different regions. The wines have been marketed at modest prices but have offered little charm.

SONOMA VINEYARDS *Sonoma 1971* Evolved from the Windsor Tiburon Vintners mail-order business. After a shaky beginning due to too-rapid expansion, it has recently settled down. The winery owns or manages 2,600 acres and offers a wide variety of table wines. Its sparkling-wine offerings were discontinued under this label after the winery formed a partnership with Piper-Heidsieck under the name of Piper-Sonoma. The more interesting table wines carry Sonoma County appellations or specific vineyard designations. Those with Northern California appellations are often made from purchased wines or grapes. The overall quality is inconsistent, but vineyard-designated Chardonnays have improved. 3 blended table wines introduced in 1979 brought the production to 600,000 cases.

Cabernet Sauvignon: *Light varietal, thin, tannic* ♥; *"Alexander's Crown": Ripe, harsh, tannic, variable* ♥/✿
Chardonnay: *Vague varietal, clean, crisp* ♥; *the estate-bottled version has more fruit, body, and oak, and after 1976 is* ♥/✿; *"River West": intensely fruity, crisp, oaky* ✿/✿✿
Chenin Blanc: *Varies from fruity to bland, thin to heavy, and slightly sweet to medium sweet* ♥
Pinot Noir: *Medium varietal, spicy, supple, oaky* ♥/✿
Zinfandel: *Varietal fruit, simple, some wood* ♥; *estate-bottled: ripe berry flavors, oaky* ♥/✿
Zinfandel (Old Vines): *Berries and spicy varietal, smooth and rich* ♥/✿

SONOMA-CUTRER VINEYARDS *Sonoma 1981* This large (800-acre), well-known vineyard operation has taken the plunge into winemaking. A facility was completed in time for the 1981 crush and 2,000 cases of barrel-fermented Chardonnay were made. In addition to Chardonnay, the winery is planning to offer small quantities of champagne.

SOTOYOME WINERY *Sonoma 1974* A small (4,000-case) winery that makes 3 red varietals. It has 8 acres near the winery. In the first vintages the quality was not good. Of late the Petite Sirah, which represents most of the annual output, has shown steady improvement. The optimum production is 6,000 cases.

SOUTH COAST CELLAR *Los Angeles 1977* A 1,200-case red wine producer relying on Central Coast and Southern California grapes.

SOUVERAIN CELLARS *Sonoma 1973* This Geyserville winery was built by Pillsbury and is now owned by a limited partnership of 300 growers. They bought the label, but there is no historical link to the early Souverain in Napa. The winery is large and continues to make wines for numerous private labels. Its own wines sport the North Coast appellation. Total cases made number close to 500,000. Recent vintages of red varietals offer good value. The whites are average quality.

🌢 **Cabernet Sauvignon:** *Fruity varietal, moderate intensity, oaky* ♥/❀
  Chardonnay: *Grassy varietal, simple, light oak* ♥
  Chenin Blanc: *Always dry style; sometimes low in fruit* ♥/ᗅ
🌢 **Colombard Blanc:** *Fruity, light, spritzy, slightly sweet* ♥
  Fumé Blanc: *Light, understated, firm, dry* ♥
  Gewurztraminer: *Floral, light spice, fruity, balanced, slightly sweet* ♥/❀
  Zinfandel: *Low varietal, simple, fruity* ♥

SPRING MOUNTAIN VINEYARDS *Napa 1968* Among the first to define a dry, relatively complex style of Sauvignon Blanc, it also made many fine Chardonnays and several good Cabernet Sauvignons. Now drawing from its 125-acre vineyard, it has become less consistent in quality. Recent Sauvignon Blancs and Chardonnays have varied in quality but do not approach the earlier glories exhibited under this label. Rumors of financial difficulty, while seemingly exaggerated, have been prevalent for the last year or so. The prices are above average. Production has reached the 25,000-case level. The winery is reported to have been "for sale" over the last two years.

Cabernet Sauvignon: *Tight, hard wines, medium tannins* ♥/❀
Chardonnay: *Medium intense, balanced, stylish, ages well* ♥/❀❀ *through 1975; thereafter* ♥
Sauvignon Blanc: *Once superb, recently somewhat flawed* ♥

STAGS' LEAP VINEYARD *Napa 1972* A historic winery with 100 acres in the Stag's Leap area, best known for its Petite Sirah. All wines were made elsewhere until 1979, when winery restoration was completed. An attractive Merlot, a promising Cabernet, and a Pinot Noir have been added to the line of estate-grown wines. A dry, sometimes dull, Chenin Blanc is also offered. 10,000-case production.

Petite Sirah: *Ripe, tannic, oaky* ✿

STAG'S LEAP WINE CELLARS *Napa 1972* Cabernet Sauvignon in a supple, refined style is a major success. The 45-acre vineyard is planted to Cabernet and Merlot, and the top-quality varietals bear Stag's Leap Vineyard as an appellation. Wines with Napa Valley appellation are made from purchased grapes and include an attractive Chardonnay and a Johannisberg Riesling. About half of the 20,000-case production is Cabernet. Hawk Crest is a second label.

Cabernet Sauvignon: *Complex, ripe varietal, moderate tannins* ✿/✿✿✿
Chardonnay: *Refined varietal, subtle, light oak* ♥/✿
Johannisberg (White) Riesling: *Delicate varietal, fruity, slightly sweet* ♥/✿
Merlot: *Ripe berries and cedar, good depth, warm* ✿

P. & M. STAIGER *Santa Cruz 1973* Small winery producing several hundred cases a year of unfiltered and unfined wines. Varieties include Cabernet and Chardonnay. The wines are not free of winemaking problems.

ROBERT STEMMLER WINERY *Sonoma 1978* A well-respected, very active wine consultant, Stemmler bottles about 5,000 cases per year under his name. He has 4 acres of Chardonnay, but most wines come from his clients' inventory. The quality of the white varietals varies; Cabernet Sauvignon is the best to date.

STERLING VINEYARDS *Napa 1967* This tourist-alluring winery, majestically perched on a hilltop, was acquired by Coca-Cola of Atlanta in 1977. The line is intended to be trimmed to 4 varietals (Cabernet, Merlot, Chardonnay, and Sauvignon Blanc) as other varieties in the winery's 500 acres of vineyard are replaced. Total production of 65,000 cases is projected to reach a maximum of 100,000 in the near future.

Cabernet Sauvignon: *Ripe varietal, full, flavorful* ♥/✿
Cabernet Reserve: *Big rich varietal, ripe, tannic, oaky* ♥/✿✿✿
Chardonnay: *Good varietal, rich, oaky* ✿/✿✿✿
Merlot: *Complex, herbal, full, warm* ♥/✿
Sauvignon Blanc: *Varietal, oaky* ♥/✿

STEVENOT VINEYARDS *Calaveras 1978* Though one of the first in the county, this winery grew quickly to its current 13,000-case production. It has a 20-acre vineyard and buys grapes from other regions, usually from El Dorado. A line of varietals is offered, headed by a reliably good Chenin Blanc and average-quality reds. Maximum output is targeted at 20,000 cases.

STONE CREEK VINEYARDS Private label owned by a San Francisco–based distributor covering 50,000 cases of inexpensive, drinkable wines. The line regularly includes Cabernet, Chardonnay, Fumé Blanc, and Chenin Blanc, as well as other varietal wines the company discovers while shopping among North Coast wineries.

STONEGATE WINERY *Napa 1973* A 15,000-case winery whose earlier unpredictability is now disappearing as vineyards and winemaking mature. It has a 15-acre vineyard adjacent to the Calistoga-based winery and an additional 30-acre parcel established in the mountain area to the west that is referred to on its labels as Spaulding vineyard. The owned vineyards provide about half of the winery's annual crush. In recent years, the number of varietals offered has been cut back with the expectation that only Cabernet, Chardonnay, Merlot, and Sauvignon Blanc will remain on the list.

Cabernet Sauvignon: *Varietal, rich, sometimes earthy* ♥
Chardonnay: *Fruity, well-balanced oaky, easy to like* ♥/❀
Sauvignon Blanc: *Firm, low varietal, hot, often off character* ♥

STONERIDGE *Amador 1975* From 3.5 acres and grapes from a leased Zinfandel vineyard, this winery makes under 1,000 cases total. Production is predominantly Zinfandel, but includes Blanc de Noirs and Ruby Cabernet.

STONY HILL WINERY *Napa 1953* Small producer (2,000–3,000 cases), located in hills above Napa Valley floor and founded by the late Fred McCrea, a man of incredible energy and vision, and now run by the inestimable Eleanor McCrea. Wines of exceptional quality are sold to the lucky few on its mailing list. One of the first great, small wineries to develop after Prohibition—and still earning bouquets.

Chardonnay: *Intense, fruity, often with high acid, little oak, ages well* ❀/❀❀❀
Gewurztraminer: *Dry, good acid, elegant, spicy* ❀
Johannisberg Riesling: *Slightly sweet, good balance, sometimes intense varietal* ❀/❀❀

STONY RIDGE WINERY *Alameda 1976* Present owners restored the old Ruby Hill Winery and leased the adjacent 120-acre vineyard. Annual 35,000-case output consists of a wide array of wines carrying different appellations and vintages. Red wines have evinced fewer flaws than the whites, though an occasional Chardonnay rises above the crowd.

STORY VINEYARDS *Amador 1973* After making wines as a hobby from his 30 acres of Zinfandel and Mission grapes, Story opened a winery and now produces about 3,500 cases for sale. Production consists predominantly of Zinfandel, but includes a tiny amount of Mission made as a white wine.

STORYBOOK MOUNTAIN VINEYARDS *Napa 1980* The winery site dates back to 1880, and the aging facility for this Calistoga-based winery consists of three tunnels dug into the hills. The 40-acre vineyard is planted entirely to Zinfandel. The current production of 7,500 cases is close to maximum.

RODNEY D. STRONG Another label from the Sonoma/Windsor Vineyards company. Named after the winemaker, this one seems aimed at direct-mail customers and selected retail outlets. The offerings, Sonoma County Cabernet, Chardonnay, and Pinot Noir, mostly sounded better in writing than they tasted in the glass. Prices are not low. Production is about 3,000 cases in all.

SULLIVAN VINEYARDS & WINERY *Napa 1979* Over the first vintages the production of this winery remained small at 1,000 cases. The owner is developing 30 acres on two different parcels in the Rutherford area. Chardonnay, Zinfandel, Cabernet, and Chenin Blanc are the main varietals. With vineyard maturity, the output will increase to a maximum of 6,000 cases.

SUMMERHILL VINEYARDS *Santa Clara 1980* Basically a negociant operation that aims at sales of 54,000 cases in 1982. The old Bertero winery in Hecker Pass has been rebuilt to serve as base of operations for blending and bottling as well as a facility for production of limited amounts of fruit and table wine.

SUMMIT (GEYSER PEAK WINERY) Large (over 1 million-case) line of generics of marginal to low quality. Its success derives from packaging, as most Summit wines come in a wine-in-the-box dispenser for home and restaurant use. Some generics are now sold in aluminum cans by the six-pack.

SUNRISE WINERY *Santa Cruz 1976* This 2,000-case producer splits its production more or less evenly among Chardonnay, Pinot Noir, Zinfandel, and Cabernet Sauvignon. All grapes are purchased from Sonoma County sources except Cabernet from the Arata Vineyard in Saratoga. Quality of recent releases shows improvement.

SUTTER HOME WINERY *Napa 1960* This winery dates back to 1874 and the brand name to 1904, but the present owners didn't assume control until 1960. It made its first Amador Zinfandel in 1968 and a White Zinfandel in 1972; together these account for a lion's share of the 100,000-case annual production. It also offers a medium sweet Muscat Amabile (8,000 cases), and after experimenting with El Dorado Zinfandel in a light simple style, it now makes a fortified Dessert Zinfandel from that appellation. From 1968 to 1973, the Amador Zinfandels were ripe, powerful, and tannic, consistently ✿. Recent vintages have been less intense and also less consistent in quality.

Muscat Amabile: *Varietally assertive, simple, medium sweet* ♥
Zinfandel: *Amador is ripe, slightly tannic, sometimes lacking balanced flavors* ♥/✿

JOSEPH SWAN VINEYARDS *Sonoma 1969* Small (less than 2,000-case) winery now focusing on making Chardonnay and Pinot Noir from its own 10-acre vineyard but more famous for a series of superb Zinfandels produced from 1968 to 1977. The series was interrupted by a loss of the source of the grapes. The search continues for a comparable source. Wine is sold by mailing list to fans of big-styled wines.

Pinot Noir: *Toasty, ripe, concentrated warm, long-aging* ✿/✿✿✿

SYCAMORE CREEK VINEYARDS *Santa Clara 1976* Some old Carignane and Zinfandel vines are included in this Hecker Pass area winery's 13 acres. Other grapes are purchased from Central Coast growers. Production is in the range of 3,000–5,000 cases.

Johannisberg Riesling: *Fresh, flowery, soft* ♥/✿
Petite Sirah: *Light, fruity, rich, easy drinking* ✿
Zinfandel: *Fruity, direct, pleasant* ♥/✿

TAYLOR CALIFORNIA CELLARS Combining the well-known Taylor name of New York with California, Coca-Cola of Atlanta launched a line of generics—Burgundy, Chablis, Rhine, and Rosé—by means of an ad campaign. Most of the wine is purchased and the blends are assembled by the winemaker at the Monterey Vineyard. Aimed at both national and international markets, the line had grown to 10 million cases by 1982. Generics are clean, fresh, and generally have been equal to or better than their major competition at the low-priced end of the market. Several "California" varietals have been added, all nonvintage wines, and some of these—notably Sauvignon Blanc and Chardonnay—are also attractive buys on a price basis.

Burgundy: *Soft, light, a touch of sweetness* 🍷
✓ **Chablis:** *Fruity, balanced, slightly sweet* 🍷
Chardonnay: *Light, slightly grassy, clean* 🍷
✓ **Sauvignon Blanc:** *Light, dry, slightly weedy, crisp* 🍷

THOMAS VINEYARDS (FILIPPI VINTAGE COMPANY) Historic winery claimed to be the state's oldest and now used as a sales and tasting room in Cucamonga. Wines under this label are sold only from the tasting room.

TOBIAS VINEYARDS *San Luis Obispo 1981* Located on a 30-acre mountaintop vineyard between Paso Robles and Templeton, this fledgling operation aspires to 10,000 cases of Zinfandel, Chardonnay, and Petite Sirah only.

TOPOLOS AT RUSSIAN RIVER VINEYARDS *Sonoma 1978* The current owners acquired an old winery, fixed it up a bit, and make about 5,000 cases per year. They have 115 acres (including 85 in Glen Ellen and 25 near Forestville) and sell grapes to other Sonoma wineries. The Topolos line consists of Chardonnay and several red varietals. Quality to date tends to be at the low end. The production goal is 10,000 cases.

TOYON VINEYARDS *Sonoma 1980* After having had other producers make their wines for several years, the owners built a winery in 1980 and are turning out 5,000 cases of varietals. They will need to erase the early history of dismal quality under this label.

TRAULSEN VINEYARDS *Napa 1980* Presently a Zinfandel-only winery making 500 cases over the first few vintages. Owns 2 acres in the Calistoga area. Maximum production goal is 2,000 cases.

TREFETHEN VINEYARDS *Napa 1973* The owners have completely replanted 600 acres to wine varieties in their vineyard adjacent to the winery located north of Napa. Production of table wines has increased slowly to 40,000 cases, although most of their grapes are sold to Chandon, Schramsberg, and several small wineries in the Napa Valley. 4 varietals are produced by Trefethen, plus 2 popular blended wines under the Eshcol logo. Chardonnay is the most successful varietal.

Cabernet Sauvignon: *Ripe, tannic, woody* ♛
Chardonnay: *Crisp, spicy, fairly full, balanced* ❀
Eshcol White: *Fruity, good flavors, especially when the blend is high in Chardonnay* ♛
Johannisberg Riesling: *Light varietal, fruity, fairly dry* ♛
Pinot Noir: *Varietal spice, medium-bodied, lacks intensity* ♛

TRENTADUE WINERY *Sonoma 1969* Primarily a grower whose grapes from the 200-acre vineyard go to Ridge (Geyserville Zinfandel) and many other wineries. Of the 22,000 cases made under its own label, only a heavy Zinfandel and a Petite Sirah attract occasional interest. White wines are generally of poor quality.

TRENTON CELLARS (JOSEPH SWAN VINEYARDS) Second label used for less distinguished offerings from this small winery.

TRINITY VINE Owned by a San Francisco importer, this label includes a typical range of varietal wines, all with NorthCoast appellations. Bottled at Souverain, the wines are generally simple; the reds offer direct varietal character, while the whites are thin. About 20,000 cases are being offered.

TUDAL WINERY *Napa 1979* From its 10-acre Cabernet Sauvignon vineyard north of St. Helena, Tudal makes 1,500 cases as well as another 500 cases of Chardonnay from grapes grown in the Soda Canyon area east of Napa city. Peak production is projected at 4,000 cases split between the two varieties.

TULOCAY WINERY *Napa 1975* Small producer (2,000 cases) specializing in barrel-aged Napa Valley varietals—Cabernet Sauvignon, Chardonnay, Pinot Noir, and Zinfandel. After a promising start, quality has been inconsistent; some wines have succeeded nicely in their full, oaky style, while others have exhibited technical shortcomings.

Cabernet Sauvignon: *Good fruit, tannic* ❀
Pinot Noir: *Ripe-tasting, medium body and tannins* ♛/❀

TURNER WINERY *San Joaquin 1979* Family-owned 560-acre vineyard is located in the Kelseyville area of Lake County. The plantings include Cabernet (245 acres), Zinfandel (80), and Napa Gamay (50), along with six other varieties. An old Lodi winery was acquired relatively cheaply and refurbished by 1979 to put out an assortment of low-priced varietals and generics from Lake County and from Mendocino County. About three-fourths of the 40,000-case output is generics, as the winery slowly works the varietal market with low to average priced versions. Its Lake County Cabernet and Sauvignon Blanc typify the modest quality for the price tags.

TWIN OAKS The private label of a San Francisco–based distributor who thinks the name has a nice "ring" and trots it out from time to time for wines ranging from generics to *méthode champenoise* sparkling wine.

TYLAND VINEYARDS *Mendocino 1979* From a 250-acre vineyard started in 1971, the winery makes 7,000 cases. Most grapes are sold. Major varietals are Chardonnay and Gamay Beaujolais, aged in American oak. Production goal is 14,000 cases.

E. VACHE & CIE (BROOKSIDE CELLARS) A new line of medium-priced, vintage-dated, varietal wines being distributed outside of Brookside tasting rooms. The first releases were fair to poor in quality.

VALLEY OF THE MOON *Sonoma 1944* This winery is best known for its jug generics popular in many California restaurants because of their low prices. An effort to make a few varietals from the 200 acres is under way, leaving room for improvement. Most of its 45,000-case production is in the jug end of the spectrum. Reds have had fewer problems than the whites.

VEEDERCREST VINEYARDS *Alameda 1972* Known primarily as a producer of early-maturing, complex reds, of lightly oaked Chardonnay, and sweet Rieslings and Gewurztraminers, Veedercrest hit hard times in 1981 and reduced its crush by 60% to just 4,000 cases, evenly split into Johannisberg Riesling and the Bordeaux mix of reds, mostly grown on its 50-acre Mt. Veeder ranch. An expected rebound will see the winery committed to its own Cabernet Sauvignon, Merlot, and Malbec and to purchased Chardonnay.

Cabernet Sauvignon: *Fruity varietal, simple, pleasant* ♀/⚘
Chardonnay: *Fruity, light oak, inconsistent* ♀
Johannisberg Riesling: *Lush fruit, rich flavors, sweet* ♀/⚘⚘
Merlot: *Herbal, varietal, soft, supple, some oak* ♀/⚘

VEGA VINEYARDS *Santa Barbara 1978* Small (4,000-case) winery producing Johannisberg Riesling and Gewurztraminer from its own vineyards and Cabernet Sauvignon from the Santa Ynez Valley. Early vintages produced uneven quality results.

VENTANA VINEYARDS *Monterey 1978* A large (300-acre) vineyard and a 30,000-case winery located in Soledad. First releases of limited production varietals were of above-average quality, with Chardonnay, Johannisberg Riesling, and Sauvignon Blanc topping the list. A raft of other varieties are grown and offered; also, sparkling wine has been laid down and will debut in 1983. Ventana Vineyards appears on labels of many wineries buying its grapes.

> **Chardonnay:** *Varietal, full-bodied, oaked* ✪
> **Johannisberg Riesling:** *Sweet-edged, floral and honey style* ✪
> **Sauvignon Blanc:** *Pungent varietal, decent fruit* ❦

CONRAD VIANO WINERY *Contra Costa 1946* Small, family-owned winery north of Oakland making limited quantities of wine from nearby 60-acre vineyard. The heavy-handed style offered seems out of step with improvements in California winemaking but manages to maintain a strong local following.

VICHON WINERY *Napa 1980* Beginning in ambitious fashion, Vichon made 14,000 cases in its first year. All wines are made from Napa Valley grapes. The primary wines are Chardonnay and Cabernet, plus a proprietary blend (Sauvignon Blanc and Semillon) called "Chevrier Blanc." All white wines are barrel-fermented. The Cabernet is a blend of wines from several vineyards. Initial efforts showed good quality but somewhat high prices. A permanent winery is being built west of Oakville. When finished, it will have a capacity of 40,000 cases per year.

VILLA ARMANDO *Alameda 1903* Medium-sized (400,000-case capacity) jug wine producer with a modest line of varietals. The winery is half-owned by the Italian Villa Banfi firm and has reached national distribution through the latter's distribution network. However, the wines tend to be sweetish, often cooked-tasting products of little charm.

VILLA BIANCHI WINERY *Fresno 1974* Substantial (160 acres, 1-million-gallon storage capacity) winery producing wine coolers in pop-top cans, generics under the D'Casa brand, and a half dozen inexpensive varietals.

VILLA MT. EDEN *Napa 1974* Well-financed winery specializing in Cabernet and Chardonnay, with lesser amounts of Pinot Noir, Chenin Blanc, and Gewurztraminer, made from the 87-acre vineyard surrounding the winery. Production is heading toward 15,000 cases annually, 75% of which is dedicated to the two leading varietals. The winery style is decidedly toward ripe grapes and heavy oak character. A "Reserve" Cabernet, established in the 1978 vintage, is grown in a special section of the vineyard. Gamay, offered in early vintages, has been pulled out of the vineyard in favor of Chardonnay.

Cabernet Sauvignon: *Ripe varietal, very oaky, tannic* ♥/❀❀
Chardonnay: *Ripe, rich, yet over-oaked* ♥/❀

VINA VISTA VINEYARDS *Sonoma 1971* This small winery (4,000 cases) began by buying wines and now buys grapes from Sonoma growers. Petite Sirah and Zinfandel head the varietal line offered primarily through a mailing list.

VIN DE BIANE FRES (BROOKSIDE CELLARS) Brand used for top-of-the-line sherries and madeira from this large producer.

VIN MARK (MARKHAM WINERY) This second label is used for limited bottlings of red and white generic wines sold primarily in restaurants.

VOSE VINEYARDS *Napa 1978* Located on Mount Veeder, Vose has 21 acres planted primarily in Chardonnay and Zinfandel with a small section of Cabernet. Production is 5,000 cases, with all grapes from the winery's own vineyard except for occasional purchased lots of Sauvignon Blanc.

Zinfandel: *Fairly tannic, ripe, oaky* ♥/❀

WALKER WINERY *Santa Clara 1979* Small (800-case) winery producing five varietal wines from purchased grapes.

WEIBEL CHAMPAGNE CELLARS *Alameda 1939* 2 production facilities—an aging plant near Fremont (Alameda County) and a new winery in Mendocino County—produce a full array of table wines, champagnes, and dessert wines. Much of the winery's 650,000-case capacity is devoted to private label bottlings of bulk process champagne for wine merchants and restaurants. The winery's transfer process champagnes are often pleasant, but table wines under the Weibel label have shown very poorly over the last decade.

New vintage-dated varietals with specific appellations brought slight improvement in younger wines; aged reds showed no change.

Brut Champagne: *Slightly sweet, floral, very bubbly* ♥
Gamay Beaujolais: *Earthy, tea-like flavors, light fruit* ♥/◌
Green Hungarian: *Sweet, insipid stuff, surpassed in quality by most jug wines* ♥/◌

WENTE BROS *Alameda 1883* Large (750,000-case) family-owned winery with long-standing reputation for white wines; reds have been less well received. Substantial vineyard holdings, 850 acres in Livermore and 600 acres in the Arroyo Seco area of Monterey, provide about half of the winery's grape needs. Another 750 acres recently purchased near the winery will be planted over the next few years. Winemaking for whites stresses cold fermentation in stainless steel to achieve fruity style. In recent years, however, many of the best-selling varieties have been rushed too quickly from fermentation to bottle to retail shelf, leading to a less consistent quality record than in the past. A new *méthode champenoise* sparkling wine, made from Chardonnay, Pinot Blanc, and Pinot Noir, aged two years on the yeast, will debut in 1983. Most prices are eminently reasonable, especially for those varieties where quality has been maintained.

✦ **Blanc de Blancs:** *Chenin Blanc–based, medium sweet, fruity* ♥/✸
   Chardonnay: *Dry, fruity, crisp, medium-bodied, no oak style* ♥/✸; *lately less attractive*
✦ **Grey Riesling:** *Dry, good acid, vinous, well suited for use with fish* ♥
   Johannisberg Riesling: *Slightly sweet, fruity, some grapefruity notes in floral, varietal style* ♥/✸
   Sauvignon Blanc: *Weedy, crisp style, quality has suffered* ◌/✸

MARK WEST VINEYARDS *Sonoma 1976* A family-owned winery located in a cool, sometimes fog-prone region above the Russian River Valley. The 62-acre vineyard is planted to early-maturing wine varieties. Production is in the range of 15,000 cases with half of the total in Chardonnay. A small quantity of champagne is made with first release expected in late 1983.

Chardonnay: *Firm, citrusy, well structured* ♥/✸
Gewurztraminer: *Medium-sweet, floral, citrusy* ♥/✸

WHITEHALL LANE *Napa 1980* Architecturally and oenologically modern facility producing 6,000 cases oriented (80%) to dry whites—Sauvignon Blanc, Chardonnay, Blanc de Noirs—with Cabernet as its only red. 25 acres of replanted vineyard surround the winery.

WILLOW CREEK CELLARS If the place name is Geyserville and the fine print reads "a Robert Haas Selection," the wine under this label, whether varietal or generic, was purchased by an East Coast distributor from Souverain Cellars. The prices are low. The quality varies from average to mediocre.

WILLOW CREEK VINEYARDS *Humboldt 1976* Tiny (200-case) winery has 2.5 acres and buys grapes from Sonoma. 7 varietals are sold to neighbors and through a mailing list. No connection to Willow Creek Cellars.

WILLOWSIDE VINEYARDS *Sonoma 1975* A one-man operation that sells most grapes from its 24-acre vineyard in the Forestville area. The major varieties grown are Zinfandel, Chardonnay, and Pinot Noir. When the mood hits, some 2,500 cases of varietals are made. It doesn't hit when the inventory of wines on hand is large.

WILSON-DANIELS Napa-based marketing and importing wine firm goes whole-hog by selling wines under its own label. Napa grapes are custom-crushed at a client's winery. Offerings so far are Cabernet, Chardonnay, and Sauvignon Blanc, each under 2,000 cases. Prices are not low. Quality is average.

WINDSOR VINEYARDS (SONOMA VINEYARDS) Originally a humble mail-order business known as Tiburon Vintners. Its success led to creation of Sonoma Vineyards, leaving this label to be reworked as a direct-sales line. Sold through a large mailing list (California only), at the winery, or in winery-owned retail outlets, the wines are usually inexpensive and cover a variety of types. Most are of ho-hum quality; sometimes a quality item of limited production is made available. Sales are over 200,000 cases.

WINE AND THE PEOPLE *Alameda 1970* Started as a supplier for home wine- and beer-makers. Now produces limited quantities (about 1,200 cases) of table wines and port from same grapes that it sells to home winemakers under the Berkeley Wine Cellars label. The "Wine and the People" handle is now reserved for wines sold in larger containers, mostly at the winery.

WINE DISCOVERY A label used for ready-made wines bought cheaply and sold at low prices. Offerings vary annually, but have included a Santa Barbara Chardonnay and North Coast Cabernet Sauvignon. Both worth the price, so far.

WINEMASTERS A label belonging to the Guild cooperative wineries. Not long ago, this appeared heading for stardom as Guild's leading name. However, the international cast of European and California wines proved less appealing organoleptically than conceptually. Winemaster wines are now sold primarily to the A & P supermarket chain.

WINERY LAKE VINEYARD (WINE AND THE PEOPLE) The label used by WATP for wines made from grapes grown at Winery Lake Vineyard.

WINES BY WHEELER *Santa Cruz 1959* Pioneer Santa Cruz Mountains winemaker producing 300 cases of wine annually for direct retail sale. Quality has been variable. (Also known as Nicasio Vineyards.)

WITTWER WINERY *Humboldt 1969* Tiny winery (a few hundred cases) in Eureka run as part-time venture by a doctor.

WOLFGANG Private label owned by a San Francisco importer. It has appeared primarily on Petite Sirah made at Sotoyome. Ill-tasting wines to date. The incredibly garish label attracts more attention than the wines.

JAMES WOLNER For the time being, a private label for Chardonnay and Cabernet Sauvignon from the Alexander Valley region. Wolner leases space to make 1,000 cases of Chardonnay, 2,000 cases of Cabernet. He plans to expand to 5,000 cases of each after settling into the Belvedere Wine Company premises in 1982.

WOODBURY WINERY *Marin 1979* This label adds another voice to the port wine revival. Its speciality is Vintage Port, and it debuted with a good 1977 released after 2 years of aging. Grapes are purchased from the North Coast regions, and Woodbury's preference is to blend Petite Sirah with Cabernet and Zinfandel. However, it is experimenting with port made entirely from Pinot Noir. Woodbury also offers limited amounts of high-priced brandy. The port production is 4,000 cases per year. Optimum is set at 5,000.

WOODSIDE VINEYARDS *San Mateo 1960* Among the earliest home winemakers to go commercial, Woodside has maintained its small size (less than 1,000 cases) and commitment to Chardonnay and Cabernet. Recent wines have been clean, well-bred versions.

YORK MOUNTAIN WINERY *San Luis Obispo 1882* Historic winery and vineyards now being refurbished. Chardonnay, Cabernet, and Pinot Noir have been planted. Zinfandel continues to set the pace for the moment. 3,500-case output.

Zinfandel: *Ripe flavor, little refinement, light oak and tannin* ♚

YVERDON VINEYARDS *Napa 1970* A handsome stone winery built by hand. There are 12 acres near the winery and another 80 in the Calistoga area. The early offerings were inconsistent. Some red varietals were made in a fairly full style and succeeded when they were able to avoid an earthy, musty character that occurred all too often. Winemaking ceased in 1974 and 1975. Since then it seems to be a stop-and-go operation. The inconsistent quality may be attributed to frequent changes in winemakers. Cabernet Sauvignon and Chenin Blanc are the 2 primary varietals in the 5,000-case annual output.

ZACA CREEK (ROSS-KELLEREI) Brand used for the first wines produced by this new Santa Ynez Valley winery and expected to be phased out as Ross-Kellerei becomes the winery's major label.

ZACA MESA WINERY *Santa Barbara 1978* A 50,000-case winery supplied by 300 acres owned by or associated with the winery. Slightly more than half of the production is devoted to white varietals—Chardonnay, Sauvignon Blanc, and Johannisberg Riesling. Cabernet Sauvignon is the highest production red, with Zinfandel and Pinot Noir also in the mix. About 4,000 cases of (French) Sirah is made.

Cabernet Sauvignon: *Clean, simple, a little on the light side* ♚; *special lots are aged longer in oak and are richer* ♚/❀
❧ **Chardonnay:** *Balanced, fruity, noticeable oak, good depth* ❀
Johannisberg Riesling: *Floral, citrusy, slightly sweet* ♚/❀
Zinfandel: *Fruity, simple, light tannins* ♚

ZAMPATTI'S CELLARS *Monterey 1978* Located in Carmel and making few hundred cases of *méthode champenoise* champagne. The cuvée is predominantly Pinot Noir purchased from Monterey County. Sales are to neighbors and tourists.

ZD WINES *Napa 1969* Moved from Sonoma to Napa in 1979. Half
of the current production is barrel-fermented Chardonnay
with the remainder made up of Cabernet, Pinot Noir, Zinfandel, and Merlot, almost all from purchased grapes. Some
superb wines have been offered, but the overall record has
been erratic.

Chardonnay: *Medium intense, tart, oaky* ♥/❀
Pinot Noir: *Spicy, sometimes complex,
medium-bodied* ♥/❀

STEPHEN ZELLERBACH VINEYARD *Sonoma 1978* The nephew
of Hanzell's founder, Zellerbach went into the vineyard
business in 1971. He now has 69 acres under vine in the
Alexander Valley—55 acres of Cabernet and 14 of Merlot.
The two varieties are blended to make Cabernet, and until
1982, when a winery was built, winemaking was done at
leased space. Current output is 10,000 cases, close to expected maximum.

Wineries and Wines
Outside California

ADAMS COUNTY WINERY *Orrtanna, Pennsylvania 1975* Makes 5,000 cases of white hybrid and vinifera varietals. The only red is Foch. Owns 2 1/2 acres, so purchases most grapes. Vidal Blanc and occasionally Chardonnay top the list. Also makes Seyval Blanc.

ADELSHEIM VINEYARDS *Willamette Valley, Oregon 1978* A cluster of medals from regional wine competitions is drawing attention to this 7,000-case winery. Chardonnay from its own grapes and Merlot produced from Sagemoor Farms grapes have been its leading varietals. A new winery building was completed in time for the 1982 crush. Its 18-acre vineyard is planted in Chardonnay, Pinot Noir, and White Riesling.

ALPINE VINEYARDS *Willamette Valley, Oregon 1980* Using only the grapes from its 20-acre vineyard, the winery is proud of being one of the few Oregon wineries that has never purchased grapes for wine production. White Riesling, Chardonnay, and Pinot Noir, are the mainstays of its 3,000-case production.

AMITY VINEYARDS *Willamette Valley, Oregon 1976* A 6,000-case winery relying mostly on its own 15-acre vineyards. Pinot Noir, Chardonnay, and White Riesling are the primary varietals. It makes a Pinot Noir Nouveau, and its barrel-fermented Pinot Noir has been among the best produced in Oregon.

Pinot Noir: *Tight, fruity, medium oak, stylish* ♥/❀

ASSOCIATED VINTNERS *Bellevue, Washington 1962* Started by a group of university professors, it became the first Northwest winery to make good-quality vinifera wines. Recent changes include moving to a new winery building, sale of its vineyards in the Yakima Valley, and the tripling of production from 8,000 to 25,000 cases. Its Gewurztraminer remains the most consistently successful wine; Cabernet and Chardonnay are less dependable.

Gewurztraminer: *Spicy aroma and flavor, firm, dry* ♥/✪

ALEXIS BAILLY VINEYARDS *Hastings, Minnesota 1976* Run part-time by lawyer Bailly, who planted 10 acres to French hybrids in 1973. His reds, Leon Millot and Foch, are dark and flavorful, and the Seyval Blanc is pleasant. Production is about 2,000 cases.

BANHOLZER WINECELLARS *New Carlisle, Indiana 1974* Likely the largest in the state with 72 acres planted—including 25 acres of vinifera—this winery makes about 7,000 cases per year. The French hybrids are blended and sold under proprietary names. Of several vinifera varietals, Cabernet and Chardonnay have attracted attention.

BARBOURSVILLE VINEYARD *Barboursville, Virginia 1980* Jointly owned by an Italian wine firm (Zonin Gambellara) and a British investment company, Barboursville is a well-financed winery committed to vinifera wines. Current production is 3,500 cases, and the winery's capacity is 12,000 cases. Ambitious plans call for adding 10 acres per year over the next decade. Cabernet Sauvignon is the favored grape, but the vineyard is planted to a variety of Italian grapes.

BARRY WINE CO. *Conesus, New York 1937* Church-owned winery in the Finger Lakes region using the historic O-Neh-Da Vineyard brand for its dessert and sacramental wines and Barry for its table wines. The emphasis falls on generics and varietal rosés from native American and French hybrid varieties for the often sweet-finished table wines. The winery owns 65 acres, and produces about 50,000 cases per year.

BENMARL VINEYARDS *Marlboro, New York 1971* Launched as a cooperative society of wine lovers, this dynamic Hudson River winery is currently producing around 12,000 cases. From the 72 acres planted, it makes varietal French hybrids and vinifera wines. The most successful have been Seyval Blanc, Baco Noir, and occasionally Chardonnay. Blended Marlboro Village wines are consistently good.

BJELLAND VINEYARDS *Umpqua Valley, Oregon 1968* Annual output of 1,500 cases consists of blackberry wine and small lots of vinifera varietals. The primary emphasis is on dry berry wine.

BOORDY VINEYARDS *Riderwood, Maryland 1942* The owners, Philip and Jocelyn Wagner, began experiments with developing and cultivating French hybrids in 1930. Their success encouraged most wineries east of the Rockies. Today, they make blended table wines in a fresh, youthful style. Production is small. Their influence continues as suppliers of vines to Eastern wineries.

BOSKYDEL VINEYARD *Lake Leelanau, Michigan 1976* Small winery (4,000 cases) founded on mid-1960s plantings that opened up the Grand Traverse region. From an experimental planting of 30 different French hybrids, 6 were chosen and a 26-acre vineyard established. Wines offered are blended generics and varietal hybrids. Best sellers are the De Chaunac Rosé and De Chaunac.

BRIGHT WINE CO. *Niagara Falls, Ontario, Canada 1874* The largest Canadian winery, using 3 facilities and boasting a total storage capacity of over 11 million gallons. Bright established French hybrid vineyards in 1946, and about half of its 1,200 acres are planted to hybrids. It has been moderately successful with making Chardonnay and Gewurztraminer from vineyards located close to Lake Ontario. In its large line, the best sellers are Baco Noir, Foch, rosé, and the Du Barry brand of champagnes. Bright's Brut Champane ranks among the best made from native American grapes.

BRONTE CHAMPAGNES AND WINES *Hartford, Michigan 1933* Now the second largest (around 1-million-gallon capacity) in Michigan, it claims to have been the first to make a Cold Duck and a commercial Baco Noir. It offers numerous types of wine, ranging from hybrid table wines to Charmat champagne. The most interesting wines are the nonvintage Baco Noir, Foch, and Hartford Port. Champagnes under the Bronte and Jean Doreau labels are popular items, enjoying annual sales of over 20,000 cases.

BROTHERHOOD WINERY *Washingtonville, New York 1839* Possibly the oldest ongoing U.S. winery, it attracts thousands of tourists to its vast aging caves. Offering a large array of table and dessert wines, it enjoys more success with ports and cream sherry. Storage capacity is 500,000 gallons.

BUCKINGHAM VALLEY VINEYARDS *Buckingham, Pennsylvania 1966* A well-regarded French hybrid producer. From its 14-acre vineyard and purchased grapes, it makes 7,000 cases annually.

BUCKS COUNTY VINEYARDS *New Hope, Pennsylvania 1973* Operating a wine museum and winery, the owners offer close to 20,000 cases per year. In addition to several French hybrid varietals, it makes Chardonnay and Johannisberg Riesling. The wines are made from purchased grapes, except for those from its own 4 acres. Inconsistent quality.

BULLY HILL VINEYARDS *Hammondsport, New York 1970* Run by Walter S. Taylor, who left the family wine business after a tiff, it makes close to 25,000 cases of varietal hybrids, regional blends, and small amounts of champagne in the Finger Lakes area. The consistently good wines are the vintage-dated red and white, along with a Seyval Blanc—fruity, light, and dry.

BYRD VINEYARDS *Meyersville, Maryland 1977* After planting 15 acres to vinifera and hybrid varieties, the owners built a winery and made their first wines in 1977. The 5,000-case output is primarily white varietals under the Byrd label. Blended table wines are labeled Church Hill Manor.

CASA LARGA VINEYARDS *Fairport, New York 1980* A small (2,000-case) winery located in the Finger Lakes area. Vinifera varietals represent 90% of its output, led by Chardonnay. Most grapes come from the owner's 12-acre vineyard.

CEDAR RIDGE VINTNERS *Snohomish, Washington 1978* Encouraged by his uncle, famed winemaker André Tchelitscheff, Alex Golitzin has edged into annual production of approximately 250 cases of Cabernet Sauvignon from grapes grown in the Yakima Valley.

CENTURY HOME WINE *Willamette Valley, Oregon 1977* Housed in a historic 1860 structure, the winery makes 1,000 cases of berry and grape wines. It uses 2 acres of vinifera and also makes Concord and Niagara wines, all for direct sale.

CHALET DEBONNE VINEYARDS *Madison, Ohio 1971* Its 40-acre vineyard is planted to labrusca and French hybrid varieties. 8,000-case production is sold at the winery. The most popular wines are blended labrusca and hybrid wines.

CHATEAU BENOIT *Willamette Valley, Oregon 1979* A 22-acre vineyard was planted in the Eugene area in 1976. Winemaking operations were moved north to Carlton in 1980 and an additional 15 acres have been planted. 5,000 cases were made in 1981 of 5 varietals. The winery's goal is 20,000 cases, with emphasis on white varietals. The first releases were of average quality.

CHÂTEAU GAI WINES *Niagara Falls, Ontario, Canada 1890* Located near Niagara Falls, this 5-million-gallon capacity winery produces a full line. The table wines are primarily from French hybrids. Some red vinifera, notably Pinot Noir and a Cabernet-Merlot blend, have been moderately successful. Its champagnes, particularly Spumante, are popular sellers.

CHÂTEAU GRAND TRAVERS *Traverse City, Michigan 1974* An ultramodern, multimillion-dollar winery in the Grand Traverse region that represents a major commitment to vinifera wines. The first varietals—Chardonnay and Johannisberg Riesling—coming from its 100-acre vineyard won several high awards in Michigan. A well-balanced late harvest Chardonnay shows excellent winemaking ability. The annual production of 15,000 cases includes generic bottlings and fruit wines.

CHÂTEAU LAGNIAPPE *Cleveland Heights, Ohio 1974* Produces annually about 2,500 cases of blended hybrids, a few hybrid varietals, and about 300 cases of vinifera varietals. Careful winemaking is evident in all wines; the Seyval Blanc and Vidal Blanc are quite successful.

CHÂTEAU LUCIENNE The primary champagne label for the Monarch Wine Co., which, under numerous brands, produces close to 250,000 cases per year. The champagnes are transfer process, made from New York–grown labrusca varieties, and priced inexpensively. Other labels include Chateau Laurent, Pol d'Argent, and Le Premier Cru.

CHÂTEAU STE. MICHELLE *Woodinville, Washington 1934* Until the 1960s the winery produced fruit and berry wines and dessert and Concord-based wines. Then it established vinifera vineyards in the Yakima Valley and made a major commitment to vinifera wines. It now has around 3,000 acres planted, and its production averages close to 300,000 cases. The parent company, U.S. Tobacco Company, built a handsome winery in a suburban area of Seattle, where most of its premium white wines are produced. Another facility in the Yakima Valley is used for red wines, and a new facility was built in 1982 in the Patterson area, designed for white wine production.

Though its early reputation rested on successful Johannisberg Riesling and Grenache Rosé, Ste. Michelle began making good Fumé Blanc in 1977 and occasionally offers good vintages of Gewurztraminer, Chardonnay, and Cabernet Sauvignon. A limited amount of Johannisberg Riesling Ice Wine (exceptional!) debuted in 1980, and approximately 2,000 cases of champagne are produced each year. Annual production could reach 1 million cases by the late 1980s.

Cabernet Sauvignon: *Medium varietal, variable, oaky* ☙
Fumé Blanc: *Medium varietal, flavorful, balanced, dry* ☙/☙
Grenache Rosé: *Cranberry color and flavors, fruity, medium sweet* ☙/☙
Johannisberg Riesling: *Floral, sometimes austere, sometimes medium sweet with Botrytis complexity* ☙/☙

CHEHALEM MOUNTAIN WINERY *Willamette Valley, Oregon 1979*
A 4,000-case winery producing Pinot Noir, Chardonnay, and White Riesling from grapes grown in its own 20-acre vineyard.

CHICAMA VINEYARDS *Vineyard Haven, Massachusetts 1971*
Located on Martha's Vineyard, its wines are popular among the vacationing set. There are 35 acres planted to vinifera, and annual production is close to 6,000 cases. The quality record is uneven, and prices are on the high side. Small amounts of Brut Champagne by the *méthode champenoise* are the most expensive.

CLINTON VINEYARDS *Clinton Corners, New York 1977* A Seyval Blanc specialist whose first vintage won many awards. About 15 acres are planted to Seyval Blanc in the Hudson Valley region, and 4,500 cases are viewed as the maximum production. A few acres were planted recently to Chardonnay and Johannisberg Riesling.

COLORADO MOUNTAIN VINEYARDS *Golden, Colorado 1978*
After the only Colorado winery folded, the partners in a 20-acre vineyard opened their own winery. It has made Colorado-grown Johannisberg Riesling and Pinot Noir Blanc. Chardonnay and Gewurztraminer are also planted. Its 3,000-case output is filled out by Napa Valley Cabernet and Zinfandel and by Monterey County Chenin Blanc.

COMMONWEALTH WINERY *Plymouth, Massachusetts 1978*
Small, new winery expecting to make wine from local grapes when they mature; both vinifera and hybrids are

planted. For the time being, wines are made from hybrids purchased in neighboring states. Results to date have been clean and pleasant.

COTE DES COLOMBES *Willamette Valley, Oregon 1977* Current production of 4,000 cases is divided among 5 vinifera wines, including Pinot Noirs made from two separate clones. The winery has a 10-acre vineyard and its production goal is set at 10,000 cases.

DOMAINE DE LA VENNE *Hume, Virginia 1980* A large, 50-acre vineyard known as the Oasis Vineyard uses the Domaine de la Venne as its brand. The plantings are largely vinifera with lesser amounts of Chelois and Chancellor. All wines are 100% varietal, except for a blend of white hybrids. Early output was under 1,000 cases, but a winery is being built with a capacity of 35,000 cases annually.

DUPLIN WINE CELLARS *Rose Hill, North Carolina 1975* 9 growers with about 75 acres scattered throughout the county became partners in this winery. 3 varietal wines are offered: Noble, Carlos, and Scuppernong. All are sweet-finished. Total production is about 14,000 cases.

ELK COVE VINEYARDS *Willamette Valley, Oregon 1977* This 7,000-case winery has 22 acres planted to early-ripening vinifera and is planting additional acreage with the intent of focusing on Pinot Noir.

Chardonnay: *Appley, clean, crisp* ♥/✸
White Riesling: *Flowery, flavorful, slightly sweet* ♥/✸

EYRIE VINEYARD *Willamette Valley, Oregon 1966* After experimenting with a number of varieties, this 5,000-case winery has focused half its production on Pinot Gris, a varietal winemaker David Lett believes goes particularly well with fish. The rest of the production from 27 acres of vines and purchased grapes is barrel-fermented Chardonnay, Pinot Noir, and Muscat Ottonel.

Pinot Noir: *Medium body, spicy, fruity, varietal* ♥/✸

LOU FACELLI VINEYARDS *Caldwell, Idaho 1981* Idaho's second new winery venture began with a 700-case crush, two-thirds in Chardonnay and Johannisberg Riesling with the remainder in dry-styled fruit and berry wines. 6 acres have been planted, with the focus on Riesling.

FARRON RIDGE (CHATEAU STE. MICHELLE) Second label used for a line of generic wines.

FENN VALLEY VINEYARDS *Fennsville, Michigan 1973* While offering over 20 different wines, this producer has gained a reputation for solid quality. It has 70 acres planted to hybrids and some vinifera; production totals just over 15,000 cases annually. The most consistent wines are Vidal and Seyval Blanc for whites and de Chaunac and Chancellor for reds. Gewurztraminers have been made from West Coast grapes. Hybrids are used to produce small amounts of champagne by the *méthode champenoise.*

E B FOOTE WINERY *Seattle, Washington 1978* Six varietals are produced from purchased grapes by this small (2,000-case) winery. The emphasis is on Chardonnay and Johannisberg Riesling.

FORGERON VINEYARD *Willamette Valley, Oregon 1977* Located in an untried, cold-climate area west of Eugene, this winery has 20 acres planted to several vinifera and a few French hybrids. The first releases totaled 1,200 cases and included an attractive White Riesling, finished medium sweet to balance an unusually high acidity. The winery's goal is an annual production of 12,000 cases by the mid-1980s, all from grapes grown in its immediate vicinity. Pinot Noir, White Riesling, and Chardonnay are the heart of the line.

DR. KONSTANTIN D. FRANK & SONS *Hammondsport, New York 1962* The winery's legal name, Vinifera Wine Cellars, reveals Frank's preference for vinifera wines. In his 100-acre Finger Lakes vineyard, 70 are planted to commercial varieties, the remainder going to ongoing experiments with new varieties. On occasion, the winery makes exceptional late harvest Johannisberg Rieslings and ripe Chardonnays. Annual production comes close to 6,000 cases.

FRONTENAC VINEYARDS *Paw Paw, Michigan 1933* Offers 40 different wines in every imaginable type made from grapes, fruits, and berries. The grape wines produced by this 500,000-gallon-capacity winery are usually labrusca generics, often sweet-finished.

GLENORA WINE CELLARS *Dundee, New York 1977* A quality-conscious, innovative, and very successful Finger Lakes winery with 375 acres planted. Its major emphasis is on vintage-dated varietals, primarily French hybrids. Small amounts of Chardonnay and Johannisberg Riesling have met with success. Unusual wines include an excellent Cayuga White and a Foch Nouveau. Present 20,000-case production will expand with vineyard maturity. Rapidly gaining a fine reputation.

GOLD SEAL VINEYARDS *Hammondsport, New York 1865* Now owned by Seagram's, this large (over 1.5-million-case) winery in the Finger Lakes region is best known for its bottle-fermented champagnes. They are offered under Gold Seal or Henri Marchant or with the Charles Fournier signature, honoring the firm's longtime winemaker. Fournier Blanc de Blancs may be the state's best champagne. The table wines cover all types, but emphasize blended hybrids and sweet-finished generics, which are labrusca-based. New plantings of about 100 acres of vinifera in the 600-acre vineyard consist of Chardonnay, Johannisberg Riesling, and Pinot Noir. Initial bottlings of the vinifera varietals were favorably received.

GOLDEN RAIN TREE WINERY *Wadesville, Indiana 1975* Started by a consortium of growers in southwestern Indiana, this winery makes hybrid wines. Most are blends, with the best given a Director's Choice title. Production is over 20,000 cases. Sales are from the winery or in neighboring states.

GOOD HARBOR VINEYARDS *Good Harbor, Michigan 1981* Situated on the Leelanau Peninsula, Good Harbor has a present capacity of 4,000 cases. Its 15-acre vineyard of hybrids is planted primarily to Seyval Blanc, de Chaunac, and Foch. The offerings include varietals and blended red, white, and rosé wines. Good Harbor is gradually expanding to 40 acres, and has an optimum production of 14,000 cases in mind.

GRAND RIVER WINERY *Madison, Ohio 1971* For several years, grapes from the 32-acre vineyard went to other wineries. The winery is now completed, and production capacity is about 10,000 cases. Wines offered include Pinot Noir and blended French hybrids. Chardonnay and Gamay Beaujolais are planted.

GREAT RIVER WINERY *Marlboro, New York 1944* Formerly known as Marlboro Champagne Cellars, the winery now concentrates on French hybrid table wines grown in its 100-acre Hudson River Valley vineyard. It offers 4 varietals and blended red and white table wines. All champagnes are *méthode champenoise* and are marketed under the Marlboro or Chaumont brands. The winery is now owned by the Renfield Corporation, which also owns Sonoma Vineyards in California.

GREAT WESTERN VINEYARDS *Hammondsport, New York 1860*
Made at the Pleasant Valley Wine Company, the first winery in the Finger Lakes, Great Western wines are now part of Coca-Cola of Atlanta's wine division. While maintaining Great Western's reputation for good-quality champagnes, solera-aged sherries, and reliable ports, the new owners have added life to the varietal wines. Most varietals are made from hybrids, led by Seyval Blanc, de Chaunac, Cayuga White, and Baco Noir. A line of Special Selection wines has been added, which includes a clean, balanced Verdelet and a crisp Aurora Blanc. The current offerings of popular generic wines are less sweet, less labrusca-tasting than in the past. All champagnes are made by the transfer method. The Brut remains reliable in quality, and a Naturel is the top-of-the-line item. A Vidal Blanc Ice Wine was made in 1980, a Catawba Ice Wine in 1981.

GROSS HIGHLAND WINERY *Absecon, New Jersey 1934* Best known for its Charmat champagnes under Gross Highland and Bernard d'Arcy labels, which together represent close to a third of its 40,000-case output. Also offers a small amount of cream sherry and table wines with a labrusca personality.

HAIGHT VINEYARDS *Litchfield, Connecticut 1978* The state's first winery. It has 20 acres planted to Chardonnay, Johannisberg Riesling, and Foch. Production of the 3 varietals totals 2,000 cases. The early vintages were well-received.

HAMMONDSPORT WINE CO. *Hammondsport, New York 1840* This old winery in the Finger Lakes was acquired by the large Canandaigua Wine Co., which uses the name as a label for its champagnes and varietal French hybrids. Made by both the bulk and transfer processes, the champagnes represent close to 200,000 cases per year. The best are of average quality.

HARGRAVE VINEYARD *Cutchogue, New York 1973* With 55 acres of vinifera on Long Island's North Fork, Hargrave has been most consistent with Cabernet Sauvignon and has also made a good vintage or two of Chardonnay, Pinot Noir, and Sauvignon Blanc. Production is about 8,000 cases.

HENRY'S ESTATE *Umpqua Valley, Oregon 1978* 31 acres have been planted to early-ripening vinifera varieties since 1972, and the first wines were made in 1979. Both Chardonnay and Pinot Noir are barrel fermented; Gewurztraminer conventionally fermented. Present production is 7,000 cases. Vineyards could expand to 50 acres, and production would increase to 10,000 cases.

HERON HILL VINEYARDS *Hammondsport, New York 1977* 37 acres planted in 1970 in the Finger Lakes district; a 9,000-case winery completed in 1977. Its 2 vinifera, Chardonnay and Johannisberg Riesling, so far have ranked among New York's best. The dry-finished hybrids and native American varietals have also won awards. The Seyval Blanc has been consistently good.

HIDDEN SPRINGS WINERY *Willamette Valley, Oregon 1980* Produces Chardonnay, Pinot Noir, and White Riesling primarily from its own 20-acre vineyard. The near-term goal is a 4,000-case production by 1984.

HILLCREST VINEYARD *Roseburg, Oregon 1963* In the Umpqua Valley. One of the state's pioneers with vinifera plantings, beginning in 1961. Most of its current 8,000-case output consists of White Riesling, which represents two-thirds of its 30-acre total. Erratic quality to date.

HINMAN VINEYARDS *Willamette Valley, Oregon 1979* The southernmost winery in the Willamette Valley, its current production is 4,000 cases, made mostly from purchased grapes. 19 acres are planted in Pinot Noir, White Riesling, and Gewurztraminer.

HINZERLING VINEYARDS *Prosser, Washington 1971* Planted 17 acres in the Yakima Valley to vinifera in 1971 and 1972, and produced its first wines in 1976. It has since added 4 acres and is currently making 5,000 cases per year. The winery has been noteworthy for attractive late harvest Gewurztraminer and Johannisberg Riesling bottlings. Its Chardonnays and Cabernets have not attracted as much attention. Recent emphasis has been on Bordeaux-style blends of Cabernet Sauvignon with Merlot, Cabernet Franc, and Malbec.

Johannisberg Riesling: *Fruity, citrusy, medium sweet* ♥/❀

HONEYWOOD WINERY *Salem, Oregon 1934* The state's oldest operating winery offers a line of fruit and berry wines. It also makes Concord wines. Since adding a White Riesling in 1979, it has converted almost half of its 15,000-case production to grape wines.

HOODSPORT WINERY *Hoodsport, Washington 1980* Chenin

Blanc and Johannisberg Riesling are produced by this 3,000-case winery, along with fruit and berry wines.

HUDSON VALLEY WINES *Highland, New York 1907* Old-timer turning out an array of generic wines, mostly sweet-finished, labrusca-flavored. It has 200 acres and is directing attention toward a hybrid varietal program, led by Foch and Chelois. Also sells about 5,000 cases of champagne.

IMPERATOR The primary label used by a large (2.5-million-gallon capacity) company, Robin Fils & Cie, out of New York. Production of its inexpensive bottle-fermented champagne is close to 500,000 cases.

INNISKILLIN WINES *Niagara-on-the-Lake, Ontario, Canada 1975* This new winery, finished in 1979, is located on the Niagara peninsula. Built mostly underground, it produces 40,000 cases today; 100,000 cases eventually. There are 50 acres planted to French hybrids and some vinifera varieties. Purchased grapes are used for blended wines. Foch is its most successful varietal wine.

JEFFERSON STATE (VALLEY VIEW VINEYARDS) A label used for generic wines as well as varietals produced from grapes purchased from vineyards away from the winery's immediate area.

JOHNSON ESTATE *Westfield, New York 1962* This winery offers a range of varietals and generics from French hybrids and native American grapes. Seyval Blanc and Chancellor Noir are the better hybrids; a Dry Delaware is the most popular wine. Production is over 15,000 cases per year. Vineyards total 125 acres located near Lake Erie.

JONICOLE VINEYARDS *Umpqua Valley, Oregon 1973* From its own 5-acre vineyard and purchased grapes, this small-scale (2,500-case) winery offers Cabernet Sauvignon and other vinifera varietals. The present facility was completed in time for the 1976 crush.

KIONA VINEYARDS *Richland, Washington 1980* Located in a warm microclimate at the southeastern end of the Yakima Valley, this winery is emphasizing Cabernet Sauvignon and Chenin Blanc. Additional plantings will expand its 27-acre vineyard to 75 acres. Production will continue in the 6,000-case range until the new vineyards reach maturity.

KNUDSEN-ERATH WINERY *Willamette Valley, Oregon 1967*
Current production of 20,000 cases consists of several vinifera varietals, headed by Chardonnay, Pinot Noir, and White Riesling. About 60% of its production comes from the partners' 96-acre vineyards (an additional 40 acres have recently been planted). Chardonnay is its most consistent wine. Approximately 700 cases of champagne were made in 1981, and a new facility for sparkling-wine production is planned.

Chardonnay: *Citrusy, subtle varietal and oak flavors, crisp* ♥/❋

F. W. LANGGUTH WINERY *Mattawa, Washington 1982.* An overseas investment for a large volume (8 million cases) German wine producer, the initial target of this new winery is 260,000 cases annually. All grapes are purchased, although 220 acres have been planted contiguous to the winery by a separate investor. The goal is a blended white from some combination of Johannisberg Riesling, Gewurztraminer, Chardonnay, Muscat, and Müller-Thurgau.

LEELANAU WINE CELLARS *Traverse City, Michigan 1975* A modern, well-designed winery making fruit and berry wines and a growing line of hybrids and viniferas in the Grand Traverse region. It has about 20 acres of hybrids and 6 of vinifera, with plans for another 35 vinifera acres in a few years. First wines, from purchased hybrids and Washington State vinifera, were uneven in quality. Winery could grow to 40,000 cases annually. Leelanau currently sells over 15,000 cases, part of which is grape wine. Most popular are the Leelanau Red, White, and Rosé. Chardonnay and Pinot Noir come from its own acreage, and Cabernet and Merlot are made from Washington State grapes. The winery has a capacity of 40,000 cases.

LEONETTI CELLARS *Walla Walla, Washington 1977* A little (500-case) winery with 3 acres planted primarily to Cabernet Sauvignon and Merlot.

MARKKO VINEYARD *Conneaut, Ohio 1968* From 10 acres planted in 1968, it makes a little under 2,000 cases annually. 2 main varieties are offered—Chardonnay and Johannisberg Riesling—both in a dry style with some oak aging. The quality from this northeastern Ohio winery has been uneven. Cabernet has been added.

L. MAWBY VINEYARDS *Sutton Bay, Michigan 1978* Proud of being Michigan's smallest winery (500 cases), L. Mawby operates out of a home basement. Only three blended wines are offered—red, white, and rosé. The red is 100% Foch, finished dry. The two others are medium-sweet. All are made from hybrids, but Mawby has established trial plantings of vinifera.

MAZZA VINEYARDS *North East, Pennsylvania 1972* Offering a line of hybrid and vinifera table wines, bottle-fermented champagnes, and a Catawba Rosé. Most of the 12,000-case output is made from purchased grapes. Also makes fruit and berry wines.

MEIER'S WINE CELLARS *Cincinnati, Ohio 1895* A large (2.5-million-gallon capacity) winery best known for its inexpensive champagnes and dessert wines. Close to 100,000 cases of Charmat champagne are produced, and port and sherry sales are close to that mark. Labrusca grapes are used for the line of table wines, but French hybrids are increasing in Meier's vineyards located on Isle St. George. Vinifera varieties were established in 1977. Best item remains the cream sherry.

MEREDYTH VINEYARD *Middleburg, Virginia 1975* A family-run, small (7,000-case) winery. Its 40-acre vineyard is planted predominantly to hybrids, led by Maréchal Foch and Seyval Blanc. From a test plot it made Virginia's first Johannisberg Riesling in 1978. A rich de Chaunac is emerging as the most consistently successful wine.

MOGEN DAVID WINES *Chicago, Illinois 1932* The largest producer of kosher, sweet Concord wines in the United States. It is owned by Coca-Cola of New York and has vineyards in several states; the largest acreage is in New York, where both French hybrids and vinifera varieties have been planted. A trio of Mogen David Light wines, blends of labrusca and California wines, has been added.

MON AMI CHAMPAGNE Used by Ohio's Catawba Island Wine Co. for its line of *méthode champenoise* champagnes. The same company owns Meier's Wine Cellars. The label is used for about 5,000 cases of champagne made predominantly from labrusca varieties. The quality is good for those who enjoy the labrusca flavor.

MONTBRAY WINE CELLARS *Westminster, Maryland 1966* After offering the first U.S. Seyval Blanc in 1966, this quality-minded, small (2,000-case) winery scored other firsts. It made Maryland's first Johannisberg Riesling, Chardonnay, and Cabernet and, in 1974, a rare ice wine. The 20 acres are mostly hybrids. Vinifera plantings are being increased.

MOUNT ELISE VINEYARDS *Bingen, Washington 1975* Formerly known as Bingen Wine Cellars, this winery has 35 acres of vinifera varieties planted on a mountainous site overlooking the Columbia River Gorge. Production will reach 7,000 cases when the present vineyards all come into bearing. Emphasis is on Gewurtzraminer, Pinot Noir, and Beaujolais, of which the Gewurtztraminer has been the most successful.

MOUNT HOPE WINERY *Cornwall, Pennsylvania 1980* A new small winery located on a historic 87-acre estate. 10 acres of French hybrids were planted in 1980. The initial 5 wines were produced off-site from purchased grapes.

MOUNT PLEASANT VINEYARDS *Augusta, Missouri 1968* A leader of the state's wine revival. Makes table wines from both French hybrids and American varieties. The best are the Seyval Blanc and a Missouri Riesling. 3 blended wines carry the *Emigré* proprietary name. Production is currently at 10,000 cases. The winery owns 25 acres and leases another 20 nearby.

NEHALEM BAY WINE CO. *Nehalem, Oregon 1974* Using a converted cheese factory, the winery began by producing fruit and berry wines. Today, about half of the 4,000-case total consists of vinifera varietals. Virtually all of the wines are sold at the winery, located in the Tillamook cheese area.

NEUHARTH WINERY *Sequim, Washington 1979* Small (1,800-case) winery offering over half a dozen table wines made from grapes purchased in Washington and California.

NISSLEY VINEYARDS *Bainbridge, Pennsylvania 1976* Using a century-old barn as the winery, the owners produce close to 8,000 cases annually. Their 27 acres are planted to French hybrids. The best wines to date are the de Chaunac and Aurora.

OAK KNOLL WINERY *Willamette Valley, Oregon 1970* Known first for its numerous fruit and berry wines, it began making vinifera table wines in 1975. About 5,000 cases of vinifera varietals are produced each year, all from purchased grapes. It is still best known for fruit and berry wines.

OLIVER WINE CO. *Bloomington, Indiana 1972* One of the first
small Indiana wineries, it now makes over 10,000 cases. The
vineyards, planted to French hybrids, have been expanded to 40 acres. The biggest seller from the tasting
room is a Camelot Mead.

PEACEFUL BEND VINEYARDS *Steelville, Missouri 1972* Tiny,
family-run winery making small amounts of 2 blended hybrid wines. Each is of good quality.

PENN-SHORE VINEYARDS *North East, Pennsylvania 1969* Most
of the 20,000-case output consists of labrusca-flavored
wines. New plantings in the 125-acre vineyards have been
to Seyval Blanc, Chardonnay, and Johannisberg Riesling. It
produces about 5,000 cases of champagnes and has recently offered a *méthode champenoise* Seyval Blanc. Catawba wines are Penn-Shore's best sellers.

PIEDMONT WINERY *Middleburg, Virginia 1978* One of the leading vinifera growers in the state, Piedmont makes about
1,000 cases of varietals. Its 26-acre vineyard consists mostly
of vinifera varieties with Seyval Blanc as the major hybrid.
Production is building slowly toward target of 2,500 cases.

PLANE'S CAYUGA VINEYARD *Ovid, New York 1980* Another
new family-owned winery in the Finger Lakes area. The
owners established a 45-acre vineyard emphasizing hybrids, particular Cayuga and Chancellor. Small amounts of
Chardonnay and Johannisberg Riesling are planted. The
current output is about 1,000 cases, with 10,000 cases as the
target when the vineyards reach maturity.

PONZI VINEYARDS *Willamette Valley, Oregon 1970* From 10
acres of vinifera planted in 1970, and 30 additional acres
under contract, it currently offers 4,000 cases per year. The
most consistent quality has been with its White Riesling. It
was the first Oregon winery to offer Pinot Gris, a varietal
that is becoming an increasing proportion of its output.

POSSUM TROT VINEYARDS *Unionville, Indiana 1978* Tiny (700-
case) winery making French hybrid wines. 6 acres are
planted to Foch and Ravat, both made as varietals. The
Foch is richly flavored.

PRESQUE ISLE WINE CELLARS *North East, Pennsylvania 1964* A
small (4,000-case) winery whose founders were active in
launching the state's wine industry. They have 20 acres, 16
of hybrids and 4 of vinifera, and have made small lots of

palatable Chardonnay and Cabernet. The winery sells grapes and winemaking equipment to home winemakers.

PRESTON WINE CELLARS *Pasco, Washington 1976* A quality-minded winery that is the third largest (60,000 cases) in the Pacific Northwest. It has 180 acres of vinifera varieties planted; 75% of the total consists of white grapes. Recently it has won awards for both Chardonnay and Fumé Blanc. Other major varietals include Chenin Blanc, Johannisberg Riesling, Merlot, Muscat Blanc, and Pinot Blanc.

Chardonnay: *Fruity, balanced, firm, crisp* ♥/❁
Fumé Blanc: *Spicy, floral, firm, some depth and oak* ♥/❁

RED HILLS VINEYARD *Willamette Valley, Oregon 1979* Label used by the Arterberry Ciderworks for its line of bottle-fermented champagnes. The champagne is made of Chardonnay and Pinot Noir and production is targeted at 900 cases. Moved to a larger facility in 1982, the winery will add table wines of the same varieties.

RENAULT WINERY *Egg Harbor City, New Jersey 1864* The state's oldest winery. With a storage capacity of 500,000 gallons, it offers a vast assortment of table wines, champagnes, and vermouth. The winery attracts thousands of tourists.

ROSATI WINERY *St. James, Missouri 1934* Offers 11 different wines consisting of Concord-based generics and a few French hybrid varietals. Uses Rosati for its transfer method champagne and Sparkling Burgundy; Ashby Vineyards for table wines. Annual 20,000-case output.

ST. JAMES WINERY *St. James, Missouri 1970* A new, relatively modern, broad-line winery. The 35-acre vineyard is planted to native American varieties and French hybrids. Most popular wines are sweet generics and Pink Champagne. Production at 20,000 cases.

ST. JULIEN WINE CO. *Paw Paw, Michigan 1921* A large (1.5-million-gallon capacity) winery offering a vast array of wines and attracting many tourists to its Paw Paw facility. It produces a line of popular Charmat champagnes under the Chateau St. Julien label. A new facility located in Frankenmuth houses the sherry solera where its award-winning Solera Cream Sherry is made. St. Julien is now making small quantities of bottle-fermented champagne and is beginning to produce table wines from hybrids.

STE. CHAPELLE VINEYARDS *Caldwell, Idaho 1976* Located 25 miles northwest of Boise, this modern winery, completed in 1979, is aiming toward a 60,000-case production by the mid-1980s. It currently makes 35,000 cases of vinifera varietals from its own 90-acre vineyards and from local growers. Its output is almost entirely Chardonnay and Johannisberg Riesling, which has been of surprisingly good quality since the beginning. The style for Chardonnay was changed in 1980 toward a high-acid, moderate-alcohol, and low-oak wine that the winemaker believes will better complement food.

Johannisberg Riesling: *Flowery, fruity flavors, medium sweet* ♥/❊

SAKONNET VINEYARDS *Little Compton, Rhode Island 1975* From 40 acres planted to 12 varieties, the winery makes varietal hybrids and limited amounts of vinifera wines. Production is over 6,000 cases, half of its future maximum. Aurora and Vidal Blanc share honors as best wines. Pinot Noir and Chardonnay show promise among the vinifera wines.

SALISHAN VINEYARDS *La Center, Washington 1976* Its small (1,500-case) crushes occurred elsewhere until the winery was built in 1982. Pinot Noir is the predominant vinifera grape in its 12-acre vineyard.

SISKIYOU VINEYARDS *Cave Junction, Oregon 1978* In 1982, a new facility was completed, production nearly tripled to 7,000 cases, and its 12 acres of vines began bearing. The first winery in the southwestern part of Oregon, the initial success of this operation has stimulated the planting of additional vineyards in this area. The focus is on red varietals, almost uniquely among Oregon wineries.

SOKOL BLOSSER VINEYARDS *Willamette Valley, Oregon 1977* Its 45-acre vinifera vineyard was started in 1971, and the winery crushed its first vintage in 1977. With a 25,000-case capacity its handsome winery is already Oregon's largest. 10 varietals are offered, but the major emphasis falls on Chardonnay, White Riesling, and Pinot Noir. Many of its releases have recently won awards in regional competition.

Sauvignon Blanc: *Grassy, refined fruity flavors, crisp* ♥/❊

STONE HILL WINE CO. *Hermann, Missouri 1965* The second largest U.S. winery in 1900. Now owns 55 acres planted mostly to native American grapes. The nonvintage generics and champagne rank among the state's best efforts.

Production, including fruit and berry wines, is close to 15,000 cases.

SWISS VALLEY VINEYARDS *Vevay, Indiana 1974* Tiny (500-case) winery. Its 3 acres of French hybrids were sufficient to revive winemaking in historically important Switzerland County.

TABOR HILL VINEYARD *Buchanan, Michigan 1970* After experimenting with 45 varieties, the winery settled on several French hybrids, Johannisberg Riesling, and Chardonnay. Greatest success has been with white varietals—Seyval Blanc, Vidal Blanc, and Johannisberg Riesling—with all three occasionally made in a late harvest style. Baco Noir is the best red. Blended generics account for a large part of the 36,000-case output. New owners appeared in 1979 to steady a shaky financial situation created by overexpansion.

TAYLOR WINE CO. *Hammondsport, New York 1880* The seventh largest U.S. winery (33-million-gallon capacity). It was acquired in 1977 by Coca-Cola of Atlanta. Owns 1,200 acres in the Finger Lakes area, planted to hybrids and native American varieties. Best known for its inexpensive, bottle-fermented champagnes and its Lake Country blended table wines. Under the Taylor label the table wines are mostly sweet-finished generics. A new line of soft wines is being introduced.

TEDESCHI VINEYARD *Maui, Hawaii 1977* A 20-acre vineyard was planted primarily to Carnelian on the basis of successful trials. Since the first vinifera varietal will not appear until 1982, the winemaker is making a dry pineapple wine called Maui Blanc and plans a sparkling pineapple wine.

PAUL THOMAS WINES *Bellevue, Washington 1979* The main emphasis of this 10,000-case winery is dry fruit wines, although small quantities of Sauvignon Blanc, Johannisberg Riesling, and Cabernet Sauvignon have been produced from purchased grapes.

THOMPSON WINERY *Monee, Illinois 1964* From 30-acre vineyard it produces bottle-fermented champagnes sold under the Père Marquette and Père Hennepin labels. Production is just under 5,000 cases, including blended table wines.

TRULUCK VINEYARDS *Lake City, South Carolina 1978* The only small, family-owned winery in the state, Truluck has 70 acres planted predominantly to hybrids, from which it produces both varietals and generics. The most popular offering to date is the Carolina Rosé. Current production of 6,000 cases will gradually build to the maximum of 25,000. A tiny percentage consists of vinifera wines, the first to be made in South Carolina.

TUALATIN VINEYARDS *Willamette Valley, Oregon 1973* The first few vintages offered were made from Washington- and Idaho-grown vinifera grapes, but the winery expects 70% of its production by 1983 to come from its own 65-acre vineyard. Current production of 14,000 cases is about half of its projected maximum output. To date, most of the varietals have been early-maturing whites. The winery emphasizes both White Riesling and Gewurztraminer, which have varied widely in quality through 1979.

White Riesling: *Perfumed and spicy at best, medium sweet* ♥/✿
Muscat of Alexandria: *Fragrant, sometimes fresh, sometimes flat* ♥

VALLEY VIEW VINEYARDS *Jacksonville, Oregon 1976* Located in a historic gold mining region, this winery has 26 acres of vinifera, and an additional 80 acres have been planted in the vicinity. It crushed in its own facility in 1978, after its first 2 vintages were made elsewhere. Cabernet and Chardonnay are the dominant varieties; others are planted for experimental purposes. The quality of the 9,000-case output has been erratic.

VENDRAMINO VINEYARDS *Paw Paw, Michigan 1976* A supplier of home winemaking equipment planted 10 acres to French hybrids in 1973 and now makes about 2,000 cases annually. The best wines are the blended table wines—red and white. In the works are varietal Aurora and Seyval Blanc. The winery has gained some attention for its onion wine.

MANFRED VIERTHALER WINERY *Pierce, Washington 1976* A restaurant-winery combination, its 20 acres represent the first commercial vineyards in the Puget Sound area during the current era. About 30% of its 6,000 cases is made from its own grapes, and the emphasis is on Johannisberg Riesling, Gewurztraminer, and Müller-Thurgau varietals. Quality to date has been spotty.

VILLA MEDEO VINEYARDS *Madison, Indiana 1974* Produces around 2,500 cases of blended hybrid table wines and native American varietals. The hybrids are grown in the winery's 11-acre vineyard.

WAGNER VINEYARDS *Lodi, New York 1978* Overlooking Seneca Lake in the Finger Lakes area, Wagner produces 20 wines. Its varietals and proprietary-named blends come from the family-owned, 120-acre vineyard. De Chaunac accounts for 40 acres, and is followed in importance by Seyval Blanc and Aurore. Vinifera plantings include Johannisberg Riesling and Chardonnay which is made in a rich, oak-aged style and has earned high critical praise. Current production is about 10,000 cases.

WARNER VINEYARDS *Paw Paw, Michigan 1939* The state's biggest winery, having 2 facilities and a combined capacity of 3 million gallons. Among its large line the best items are the solera-aged sherries and ports and bottle-fermented champagnes. The table wines offered are ordinary at best. Recent experiments with vinifera varieties suggest future improvement is possible. The winery's 225-acre vineyard is planted mostly to French hybrids.

WHITE MOUNTAIN VINEYARDS *Laconia, New Hampshire 1969* 25 acres planted to cold-tolerant French hybrids. The early vintages were blended with California wines. The first home-grown varietal appeared in 1975. Capable of making about 10,000 cases annually.

WIDMER'S WINE CELLARS *Naples, New York 1888* This large (4-million-gallon capacity) winery in the Finger Lakes region is owned by the R. T. French Co. of mustard fame. Its large line of wines carry New York State and American appellations. The finest are the Solera Sherries, both the Pale Dry and Cream, and a Special Selection Port. Whereas most table wines are sweet-finished generics, Widmer has succeeded with both a dry Cayuga White and Moore's Diamond. Charmat-process champagnes total close to 20,000 cases annually. Lake Niagara is used as a proprietary name on champagnes and generic table wines.

WIEDERKEHR WINE CELLARS *Altus, Arkansas 1880* Located in the northwestern part of the state, this large (1.8-million-gallon capacity) winery owns 575 acres of vineyards planted mainly to labrusca and French hybrids. It offers a wide range of table, dessert, and sparkling wines. Several popular table wines carry proprietary names, and its Dry Cocktail Sherry heads the dessert wine sales. Its ambitious efforts with vinifera varietals, notably Johannisberg Riesling and Chardonnay, have yet to produce wines beyond the neutral, simple level. Best known today for inexpensive champagnes. On occasion, however, it has made interesting Johannisberg Riesling in a late harvest style. Otherwise, it is best known for its slightly sweet to medium sweet proprietary table wines.

HERMANN J. WIEMER VINEYARD *Dundee, New York 1979* Wiemer is a well-known winemaker formerly associated with the Taylor Wine Co. He established a 20-acre vineyard in the Finger Lakes region and favors vinifera varieties. Of the 3,000-case output, he has fared best with a dry Johannisberg Riesling and slightly sweet Gewurztraminer.

THE WINERY RUSHING *Merigold, Mississippi 1977* The first "ole Miss" winery since Prohibition now has 32 acres planted to muscadine grapes. Grapes from North Carolina were used for first products—blended table wines. This modern winery has a capacity for 15,000 cases annually. Its current production is 7,000 cases.

WOLLERSHEIM WINERY *Prairie du Sac, Wisconsin 1976* An old property, founded in 1857, was purchased in 1973. 20 acres were planted to French hybrids and a few to Chardonnay and Johannisberg Riesling. Vinifera grapes have experienced problems, but good wines have been made from Seyval Blanc and Foch. The annual production, including fruit and berry wines, is 5,000 cases.

WORDEN'S WASHINGTON WINERY *Spokane, Washington 1980* Johannisberg Riesling and Fumé Blanc are the focus at this 22,000-case capacity winery. All grapes are purchased and the initial wines have been well-received in regional competitions.

YAKIMA RIVER WINERY *Yakima Valley, Washington 1978* Moved to a new facility in 1982. Production is expected to double to 10,000 cases of six varietals. All grapes are purchased.

Wine Language

ACETIC All wines contain acetic acid—vinegar. Usually the amount is quite small, being less than 0.06% and ranging as low as 0.03%. When table wines reach 0.07% or above, tasters begin to notice a sweet, slightly sour and vinegary smell and taste in the wine. Such wines are acetic and are also said to have ascescence. At low levels, ascescence often enhances the attractiveness of a well-made wine. At higher levels (over 0.10%), the acetic qualities can become the dominant character of the wine and are considered a major fault. A related substance, ethyl acetate, contributes the smell associated with the presence of acetic acid.

ACIDIC Describes wines whose total acid is so high that they taste tart or sour and have a sharp feel in the mouth.

ACIDITY Labels mentioning acidity express it in terms of total acid, a measure of the several most common acids. These are tartaric, malic, lactic, and citric. The acidity of balanced dry table wine falls in the range between 0.6% and 0.75% of the wine's volume. However, for sweet wines, 0.70% total acidity or less is considered low because the wine usually tastes flat or unbalanced. For balance, generally, the sweeter the wine, the higher the acidity should be. It is legal in California to correct deficient acidity by adding malic, tartaric, or citric acid to achieve a balanced wine.

AFTERTASTE The taste left in the mouth after the wine is swallowed. Both the character and the length of the aftertaste are considered. Finish is a related term.

ALCOHOL BY VOLUME Wineries are required by law to state the alcohol level on their labels—usually expressed as a numerical percentage of the volume. For table wines the law allows a 1.5% variation in either direction from the stated percentage as long as the alcohol does not exceed 14%. An alternative taken by a few producers is to describe the wine as a table wine or light wine, omitting the percentage notation. By definition, sherry ranges from 17%–20% alcohol by volume; other dessert wines fall into the 18–21% range.

ANGULAR The combination of hard, often tart-edged flavors and tactile impressions given by many young dry wines. Angular wines are the opposite of round, soft, or supple.

APERITIF A legal classification for wines having not less than 15% alcohol by volume; vermouth is the best example. However, current fashion also uses the term generically to describe any wine likely to be enjoyed before a meal, regardless of alcohol level.

APPLEY This term often carries additional modifiers. "Ripe apples" suggests a full, fruity, open smell characteristic of some Chardonnays. "Fresh apple" aromas are occasionally associated with Rieslings, whereas "green apple" aromas come from wines made from barely ripe or underripe grapes. And, should you encounter a wine with the aromas of "stale apples," you are probably smelling a flawed wine exhibiting the first stages of oxidation.

AROMA Traditionally defined as the smell that wine acquires from the grapes and from fermentation. Now, more commonly means the wine's smell, including changes that occurred in the bottle. One assesses the intensity of aroma and also describes its character with virtually any adjective that fits, ranging, for example, from appley to raisiny and from fresh to tired. Bouquet has a similar meaning in common usage.

ASCESCENCE The sweet and sour, sometimes vinegary smell and taste that, along with a sharp feeling in the mouth, mark the presence of acetic acid and ethyl acetate.

ASTRINGENT Many red wines and a few whites have a rough, harsh, puckery feel in the mouth, usually from tannin. When the harshness stands out, the wine is astringent. Tannic astringency is reduced with age, but sometimes a wine will fail to outlive the tannin.

AUSTERE Used to describe wines, usually dry, relatively hard, and high in acid, that lack depth and roundness. Young Cabernet Sauvignon and Chardonnay are often austere when grown in cool climates or harvested early. Such wines may soften somewhat with age.

BALANCE A wine has balance when its elements are harmonious —no one part dominates. Acid balances against sweetness; fruit balances against oak and tannin; alcohol balances against acid and flavor. Wine not in balance may be acidic, cloying, flat, or harsh, among other things.

BARREL FERMENTED The practice of fermenting wine in small casks (usually 55-gallon oak barrels) instead of in large tanks. Advocates believe that it contributes better harmony between the oak and the wine and increases body. Its liabilities are that more labor is required and greater risks involved. It is being used increasingly with California Chardonnay and for a few of the dry Sauvignon Blancs, Pinot Blancs, and Chenin Blancs.

BERRYLIKE The expected aroma and taste of Zinfandel. Berrylike is equated with the ripe, sweet, fruity qualities of blackberries, raspberries, cranberries, and cherries. Other red grapes may also produce wines with berrylike character.

BIG A wine, either red or white, possessing rich, full flavors and fairly full body. Big red wines are usually tannic. Big whites often are high in alcohol and glycerine.

BITTER 1 of the 4 basic tastes (along with sour, salty, and sweet). Some grapes—notably Gewurztraminer and muscat— often have noticeable bitterness in their flavors. Another major source of bitterness is tannin. If the bitter quality dominates the wine's flavor or aftertaste, it is considered a fault. In sweet wines a trace of bitterness may complement the flavors and make the wine more enjoyable.

BODY The tactile impression of weight or fullness on the palate usually experienced from a combination of glycerine, alcohol, and sugar.

BOTRYTIS CINEREA A mold or fungus that attacks grapes under certain climatic conditions. Botrytis requires high humidity and/or some moisture. When it commences just before the grapes reach maturity, it causes them to shrivel, concentrating both sugar and acid. It is beneficial and highly desirable for some white varieties, especially Johannisberg Riesling. The resulting wines are uniquely aromatic and flavored, sweet and luscious, if the Botrytis is widespread. Lacking official definition, wines said to have Botrytis vary both in flavor intensity and in sweetness.

BOTTLE FERMENTED Generally indicates the champagne was not produced by the bulk process. It could apply to either the *méthode champenoise* or the transfer process. However, since producers following the former method usually say so on their labels, champagne bearing this description is more likely made by the transfer method.

BOTTLED BY When it appears by itself without the "produced" or "made," the indication is that the named winery played a very minor role in the wine's production. The wine could have been purchased ready-made and simply bottled; or it could have been made under contract by another winery only to be transferred, aged, and then bottled by the designated producer.

BOUQUET Technically, that part of a wine's smell that develops after it is put in the bottle. Since most of the smell develops before bottling and bouquet comes mostly with years of cellar aging, the term aroma is almost always more appropriate when discussing a wine's smell.

BRAWNY Wines that are full of muscles and low on elegance. The term is used mainly for younger reds with high tannin and alcohol levels—thus referring both to body and to texture. Petite Sirahs with Napa, Sonoma, and Mendocino appellations are more likely than not to be brawny. Most reds from Amador are brawny.

BREED Used for the loveliest, most harmonious, and refined wines, those whose charms reach classical expectations of varietal character, balance, and structure. The term is usually reserved for wines from the best varieties and is rarely associated with common grapes like French Colombard or Ruby Cabernet.

BRIARY Like the thicket of thorns from which the wine term is derived, a briary wine gives a prickly, aggressive tactile impression on the palate not unlike flecks of black pepper. The term is most often applied to young, dry red wines with noticeable tannin and alcohol.

BRILLIANT The appearance of very clear wines: absolutely no visible suspended or particulate matter in evidence. Brilliant wines are often the product of heavy filtration, a process that may remove the flavor along with the solids. See also Clear, Unfiltered, Cloudy, and Hazy.

BRIX Name of a system used by American winemakers to measure the sugar content of grapes, must, and wine. On labels Brix normally refers to the degree of ripeness (meaning the sugar level at harvest) and occasionally is used to indicate the sugar in the finished wine. For most table wines the usual range at the harvest is 20° to 25° Brix. By multiplying the stated Brix at harvest by .55, one obtains the approximate alcohol by volume possible if the wine were fermented to dryness.

BROWNING The normal tints of young table wines contain no brown. Browning is a sure sign that wine is beginning to age. Wines with good depth and character can be quite enjoyable even though a good deal of browning shows. For lesser wines the onset of browning usually signals the downside of the hill.

BRUT An exclusive champagne modifier widely used to designate a relatively dry-finished wine, often the driest champagne made by the producer. In the absence of a legal definition, *brut* does not guarantee, however, that the champagne will be dry. Wineries in the United States use the term as they see fit.

BULK PROCESS A speedy, large-volume, and inexpensive method of making champagnes. The secondary fermentation that provides the bubbles takes place in a large, closed container, as opposed to a bottle. Wineries have the option of putting either "bulk process" or "Charmat" (a synonymous term) on their labels.

CANDYLIKE Modern technology enables winemakers to capture the perfumed fresh fruit aromas and flavors of the grape. This candylike fruitiness can be attractive in wines intended for early consumption, such as *nouveau*-style wines and slightly sweet whites and rosés. It is out of place in longer-aging reds and in the better white varieties.

CARBONIC MACERATION A technical procedure in which grapes are placed whole into a fermenter. Their weight breaks the skins, beginning an intracellular fermentation. The resulting wines (usually red) are intensely fruity, light-bodied, and meant for early consumption. Some wines labeled *"nouveau"* are made this way. Occasionally a winery may blend some carbonic maceration wine with conventionally fermented wine for added fruitiness and freshness.

CASK # Sometimes attached to very special wines; sometimes used as a gimmick. It is meant to imply that the wine spent its entire cellar life in one cask and that it was produced in small amounts. Neither condition need be met for the term to be used.

CELLARED BY Technically means the wine was not produced at the winery where it was bottled. Usually indicates that the wine was purchased from someone else and aged or cellar treated by the bottling winery, but there is no minimum time requirement for aging. This lack of precision makes "cellared by" highly suspect, even though it occasionally appears on wines that received long aging and personal attention from the bottling winery.

CHARMAT Same as the bulk process of champagne making. The second fermentation occurs in large tanks, not individual bottles. It is a large-volume method involving fewer hand procedures. Since the champagne can be made quickly and the costs are lower, it is the usual method for all inexpensive champagnes. Many wineries prefer this label term since it sounds better than "bulk process."

CHEWY Rich, heavy, tannic wines are said to be chewy because, figuratively, one could not swallow them without chewing first.

CITRUSY A wine with aroma and flavor constituents reminiscent of citrus fruits. Such wines need not be high in acid since citrusy refers to taste sensations that go beyond the basic qualities of sour, sweet, salty, and bitter. Many white wines from colder climates, especially Monterey County, have a citrusy quality that recalls grapefruit.

CLASSIC An overworked word that is meaningless in the context of a label.

CLONE A group of vines originating from a single, individual plant whose descendants have been propagated asexually, usually by means of cuttings or grafts. A clone is selected for its special viticultural and wine merits (productivity, adaptability to particular growing conditions, and wine quality). Clonal selection studies have improved California Chardonnay and could lead to improved Pinot Noir.

CLOSED-IN Wines that are presently low in intensity, but high in concentrated, correct character, and that are expected to develop greater intensity with age.

CLOUDY An obvious lack of clarity in wines is undesirable. With the exception of old wines not decanted properly, cloudy wines are usually the result of winemaking error. They are caused by a variety of unwanted occurrences, such as protein instability, yeast spoilage, and refermentation in the bottle. Cloudy wines usually taste unpleasant.

CLOYING When the sweetness annoys by dominating flavors and aftertaste, a wine is said to be cloying. Such excessively sugary wines lack the balance provided by acid, alcohol, bitterness, or intense flavor.

COLD STABILIZATION A clarification technique involving lowering the temperature to 32° F. for 1 to 3 weeks. The cold encourages the tartrates and other insoluble solids to precipitate, rendering the wine clear. The tartrates cast by the wine are actually tasteless and harmless and are removed for appearance only.

COMPLEX A wine of beauty and balance harmoniously combining many aroma and flavor elements is considered complex. This is the elusive quality that separates a great wine from a very good one.

COOPERAGE Those who build wooden barrels are called coopers. In present usage cooperage refers to any container for holding or aging wine. Collectively, it covers containers of all sizes and of all materials, from oak to stainless steel.

CRACKLING A wine with less effervescence than champagne, but with sufficient amounts of carbon dioxide in solution to remain bubbly after being poured into glasses. If produced by the bulk process, the labels must so state. If the label reads only "crackling," its bubbles were likely added by artificial carbonation during bottling. Taxed at a lower rate than champagnes, crackling wines are normally low-priced.

CREAM Loosely used term for a style of sherry that is very sweet and is intended for enjoyment with desserts.

CROSS A grape created by mating 2 members of the same vine species. For example, the mating of 2 *Vitis vinifera* grapes, Cabernet Sauvignon and Carignane, produced Ruby Cabernet. Other notable crosses are Emerald Riesling, Flora, and Carnelian.

CRUSH Popularly used in the United States for the harvest season or the vintage. It also refers more specifically to the breaking (or crushing) of grape skins, which begins the winemaking process.

CUVÉE Commonly used in the United States to identify a specific batch or lot of wine (as in Cuvée 8). In general, it refers to a blend of wines. Seen on both champagnes and table wines as a substitute for a vintage date.

DECANTING Procedure by which wine is poured slowly and carefully from the bottle into another container before serving. The purpose is to leave the sediment behind. Many old red wines and a few young ones made with a minimum of clarification tend to throw a deposit or sediment in the bottle.

DELICATE Any wine of light to medium-light body and of lower-intensity flavors can be described as delicate. The term is usually, but not always, applied to attractive wines.

DEMI-SEC For reasons now forgotten, the language of champagne relating to sweetness is misleading when interpreted literally. Although this word means half-dry, *demi-sec* champagnes are usually slightly sweet to medium sweet. The term is occasionally applied also to still wines.

DEPTH A wine with flavors of good intensity that seem to fill the mouth from front to back. It is a characteristic that one should expect of most premium wines, save for youthful, lighter-bodied whites. See also Lingering.

DESSERT WINE A term with 2 meanings. The first is a legal classification of wines whose alcohol content is at least 17%, but not higher than 24% by volume, and whose higher alcohol was obtained by adding either brandy or neutral spirits. Such wines are also known legally as fortified wines. The second use is general, covering sweet and very sweet wines of any alcohol level that are customarily enjoyed with dessert or by themselves after a meal.

DIRTY This term covers a multitude of vinous sins. All of the foul, rank smells that can show up in wine—from the musty cachet of unclean barrels to the cabbage and garlic odors of undesirable fermentation by-products—render a wine dirty.

DOSAGE In bottle-fermented champagne, the yeast sediment collected is eventually removed. Along with it a little wine is lost. To replace the wine and to adjust the sweetness level of the final product, winemakers add a dosage, usually a mixture of sweet syrup and wine.

DRY A wine with no perceptible taste of sugar in its makeup. Wines fermented to dryness have 0.2% residual sugar or less. Most wine tasters begin to perceive the presence of sugar at levels of 0.5% to 0.7%. For our purposes, we use *dry* for any wine with residual sugar up to 0.5%. The term is used more loosely on wine labels.

DUMB A young wine with undeveloped aromas and flavors is often called dumb because it seems unable to speak. Closed-in is a similar term. Both words are reserved for wines expected to improve.

EARTHY Wine tasters use this term to cover characteristics that range from the pleasant, rich earthiness of loamy topsoil to the unpleasant, rotting-grass earthiness of the compost heap. Earth may be dirt, but an earthy wine is not necessarily dirty.

ELEGANT Wines of grace, balance, and beauty are called elegant. The term is applied more often to white wines than to reds, although a few medium-bodied Cabernet Sauvignons of breed and complexity may also be called elegant.

ESSENCE Used for a time by wineries to describe a late harvest, sweet red wine. It appeared on several Zinfandels made from grapes picked at 35° Brix or higher.

ESTATE BOTTLED Once used by producers for those wines made from vineyards that they owned and could see from the winery. More recently, its definition has been stretched beyond recognition. Currently, no regulations govern its use in this country. The government has proposed to tighten its definition and restrict its application after 1983.

ETHYL ACETATE The sweet, vinegary smell that often accompanies acetic acid is ethyl acetate. It exists to some degree in all wines and can complement other elements in the aroma and taste, especially those of sweet, rich wines. In most wines, however, noticeable ethyl acetate is considered a flaw.

EXTRA DRY In keeping with the French champagne tradition, wines labeled extra dry are not. They usually possess residual sugar in the 2–6% range and bridge the gap between the drier brut-styled wines and those still sweeter.

FAT The combination of medium to full body and slightly low acid gives wine a fat impression on the palate. The wine feels and tastes a bit more obvious and often lacks a touch of elegance. In fuller-flavored wines the fat quality is highly prized by some tasters. A fat, oily Riesling would be less so, unless made in a late harvest style.

FERMENTATION A complex chemical reaction by which yeasts through their enzymes transform the grapes' sugar into equal parts of alcohol and carbon dioxide. The process generates heat, so most winemakers control the temperature nowadays by circulating cooling agents within the jackets of their stainless steel fermentation tanks.

FIELD BLEND This was once a widespread practice in California. Vineyards were planted to several different varieties, and the grapes were harvested together to produce a single wine. Thus, the wine was blended in the field. A few such vineyards, mainly of red varieties, remain in California.

FIELD CRUSHING Generally used in concert with mechanical harvesters. The grapes are picked and immediately crushed in the vineyards or field, the fresh juice must being ultimately transferred to the winery for fermentation. The advantages are that the juice avoids oxidation and, since a blanket of carbon dioxide surrounds it, the juice will not ferment too early. Still experimental and somewhat controversial with regard to wine character.

FILTERED A mechanical process of removing yeast cells and other particles from wine after fermentation. Sometimes used before fermentation to clarify press juice. Most wines (except those labeled unfiltered) are filtered for both clarity and stability.

FINED Technique of clarifying wine by introducing various agents. The most common fining agents are bentonite (powdered clay) and gelatin; the most traditional is egg whites. Such agents precipitate to the bottom of the tank or barrel, carrying suspended particles with them.

FINISH The tactile and flavor impressions left in the mouth when wine is swallowed. The tactile sensations of the finish may be hot, harsh, tannic, smooth, or soft and lingering, short, or nonexistent.

FLAT Caused by lack of balance or lack of flavor. Flat means the absence of vigor and liveliness and is caused by very low acidity. Flat flavors are insipid or old.

FLOR A specific yeast that imbues *flor* or *fino* sherries from Spain with their unique aroma and flavor. This *flor* yeast (Saccharomyces fermentati) does not occur naturally in the United States or in other wine regions outside Spain. However, several Canadian and California researchers have developed a *flor* yeast culture that can be introduced to the would-be sherry and imparts a similar character. The technique is called the submerged *flor* or cultured *flor* process.

FLORAL (also Flowery) Literally the characteristic aromas of flowers. Floral is employed without modifier to describe pleasant, often delicate aromas found in white wines. In particular, Johannisberg Riesling often displays such attributes, as do Chenin Blanc, Muscat, and Gewurztraminer to a lesser degree. Very few red wines are floral.

FORTIFIED A wine whose alcohol content has been increased by the addition of brandy or neutral spirits. In the United States sherries are fortified to a minimum of 17% alcohol by volume; other fortified wines have an 18% alcohol minimum. Dessert wine is a synonymous term when used to describe a wine that has been fortified.

FOXY Poorly chosen word traditionally used to describe the unique musky and grapey characters of many native American labrusca varieties and many French-American hybrids.

FREE-RUN JUICE The juice that flows freely after the grape skins are crushed and before the stems and pulp are pressed for the remaining yield. About 60–70% of the total juice yield is free-run; it is generally smoother, less bitter, and less tannic than press wine. A few special bottling wines are fermented entirely from free-run. However, most winemakers choose to blend the two in some proportion.

FRESH The lively, youthful, uncomplicated qualities sought in lighter reds, rosés, and most whites. Such wines are usually fruity and clean and have ample acidity.

FRUITY The distinctive aroma and taste of fruit, found mostly in young wines. A fruity wine usually has intensity, freshness, and distinctive character; for example, it is berrylike, apply, or herbaceous. Young wines lacking fruitiness, especially whites, are often sweetened to fill the holes in their flavor profiles.

GASSY Said of table wines containing carbonation (gas) usually from unwanted fermentation in the bottle. The term spritzy also describes carbonation in wine, but does not carry the negative connotation of gassy.

GENERIC WINE Any wine whose name is part of a general category or type, as opposed both to varietal wines (which are derived from a grape variety such as Cabernet Sauvignon) and to specially coined proprietary names (Masson's Rubion, Phelps's Insignia). The best-known generic designations are those with European place-names (Burgundy, Chablis, Chianti, Champagne, and Rhine) as well as the type categories (Blanc de Blancs, Blanc de Noirs, Claret, Rosé, Sherry, and Table Wine).

GLYCERINE This by-product of fermentation is found to some extent in all wines. It is most noticeable in higher-alcohol and late harvest wines, in which high levels of glycerine give the wine a slippery, smooth tactile impression and contribute fullness to the wine's body. Glycerine has a sweet taste on the tip of the tongue.

GRAPEFRUITY Cold-climate white wines often exhibit a distinct grapefruity character. Such wines also may contain floral qualities that blend nicely with the more citrusy grapefruit notes. The young white wines of Monterey County frequently possess this intriguing, fresh quality.

GRAPEY Simple flavors and aromas more like fresh table grapes than fine wine. Many of the native American varieties and French-American hybrids produce grapey wines.

GRASSY A light fresh grassiness can enhance some wines (especially Sauvignon Blanc). However, the more grassy a wine is, the more likely it is to be unappealing. In the extreme, grassiness can take over a wine and render it unattractive.

GREEN Wines made from unripe fruit have a green taste. The flavors are usually monochromatic, somewhat sour and angular, and often grassy. The color green (light tints in a straw/pale yellow color) is not unusual in many young white wines, especially Johannisberg Riesling, and does not necessarily signal a green wine.

GROWN, PRODUCED, AND BOTTLED BY Used by a few producers to declare explicitly that they performed all functions, from growing the grapes to bottling the wine. Much more precise and reliable than "estate bottled."

HARD Tactile firmness taken one step further by high acidity or tannin yields a hard wine. The quality is appropriate in young red wines suitable for aging and can also enhance dry white wines that are served with shellfish.

HARSH Highly astringent wines, often relatively high in alcohol, may give this nasty, rough tactile sensation. With age, some of the nastiness goes away, but the relevant question is whether the wine is worth the wait. Rough and hard are related terms.

HAZY Wines with moderate amounts of visible particulate matter. If you see a slight haze in wine, especially if it carries the words unfined or unfiltered, there is probably no cause for alarm. But if the wine is so hazy that the suspended matter causes it to lose clarity, it may be flawed.

HEARTY Generally used to describe the full, warm qualities found in red wines with high alcohol, especially those made in straightforward styles such as the heavier red jugs, some Zinfandels, and Petite Sirahs.

HERBACEOUS Literally, the taste and smells of herbs (undefined as to species). Herbaceous is often said to be a varietal character of Cabernet Sauvignon and, to a lesser extent, of Merlot and Sauvignon Blanc.

HOT Wines high in alcohol that tend to burn or prickle the palate and nose are called hot. This character is accepted in dessert offerings like port, sherry, and late harvest Zinfandel. It is noticeable but less appreciated in Cabernet Sauvignon and Chardonnay and actually undesirable in light, fruity wines like Johannisberg Riesling.

HYBRIDS Varieties developed by geneticists through crossing (and often recrossing) grapes from 2 or more different species. Full-scale efforts began in the search for resistance to the phylloxera disease. Grapes resulting from the cross-pollination experiments of vinifera with a native American variety became known as French hybrids or as French-American hybrids. Those hybrids presently cultivated in the United States were chosen for their ability to survive cold winters and to yield balanced wines in short growing seasons. Among the best known hybrids are Baco Noir, de Chaunac, Foch, Seyval Blanc, and Vidal Blanc.

JAMMY, JAMLIKE The combination of ripe, concentrated fruitiness and the natural grapey or berrylike character of certain red varieties yields wines that have jamlike aromas and flavors. Zinfandel from Amador County is frequently jammy.

JUG WINES Inexpensive wines generally sold in large containers. The term originates in the tradition of consumers' bringing their own containers, jug bottles, to wineries for their purchases. Most wines so described are generics, but a few varietals also appear in jug containers. Jug wine quality describes wines low in character and palatable at best.

LABRUSCA Shorthand for the native American grape species, *Vitis labrusca,* whose wines have a heavy, grapey character of the sort typified by Concord grape juice.

LATE HARVEST On labels, a signal that the wine was made from grapes picked at a higher Brix than normal. The term describes the condition of the fruit, not the calendar date. It is possible, though not requisite, that the high sugar levels were achieved through the influence of Botrytis cinerea. The general implication for late harvest white wines is that the wine is finished sweet to some degree; for red wines it means they may be either high in alcohol or finished sweet. Most late harvest wines are enjoyed after the main course as unfortified dessert wines.

LEAFY Some wines, including attractive wines, exhibit a slightly herbaceous, vegetative quality analogous to the smell of leaves. When a wine is leafy, it is not necessarily flawed and may actually be more interesting if the leafy quality adds a note of complexity.

LEES The sediment falling to the bottom of a wine container. When mentioned on labels, it usually refers to the sediment precipitated during fermentation, most of which consists of dead yeast cells. Wine is normally removed from the lees as soon as possible, since they often contribute inappropriate and unappealing odors and flavors.

LEMONY White wine with fairly high acid often takes on a lemony quality. Such wines are not necessarily tart or sour; the acid may be balanced by intense flavors or sweetness.

LIGHT WINE Through the confluence of high technology and Madison Avenue marketing techniques, Light Wine was spawned in 1981. By legal definition, a Light Wine should contain fewer calories per comparable serving than a regular glass of table wine. In order to make a claim of "fewer calories" on the label, the producer must authenticate and document that statement. Wines can be made Light by decreasing either one or both sources of calories—alcohol and sugar. Most commonly, the calories are reduced by picking the grapes very early, before full maturity, or by removing the alcohol in a finished wine through a vacuum distillation process. Used as a tasting term, "light" indicates the wine's viscosity is hard to distinguish from water.

LIMITED BOTTLING In the absence of legal definition, this high-sounding phrase is used on bottlings that run the gamut from small lots of special wine to every drop of the designated wine that the producer has to offer.

LINGERING Both flavor and tactile impressions may remain in the mouth after the wine is swallowed. When the aftertaste or finish remains in the mouth for more than a few seconds, it is said to be lingering. One would hope that the character is also clean, balanced, and attractive.

LIVELY Wines that are fruity and fresh in character, usually with ample acidity, are called lively because of their vigor. Such wines may occasionally be spritzy and usually are relatively low in sweetness and alcohol. The term is applied more often to white wines, but sometimes to reds.

LOT # Used in several different ways. The most legitimate is to differentiate wines of the same type from the same vintage that were bottled at different times. It also can suggest that the wine is a blend of 2 or more different vintages or different growing regions. A very few use it to indicate that the same wine was aged in different kinds of barrels. However, the term has no legal definition and, therefore, means as little or as much as the winery wishes it to mean.

LUSH Wines with the soft, viscous tactile impression created by high levels of residual sugar (usually in the sweet and very sweet ranges) are called lush.

MADE AND BOTTLED BY Though sounding the same as "produced and bottled by," this term has an entirely different meaning. The only requirement is that the named producer fermented a minimum of 10% of the wine in the bottle. That is hardly an intimate personal involvement with the wine.

MADERIZED This term originates in the brownish color and slightly sweet, slightly appley, sometimes nutty character found in the wines of Madeira. However, it is not intended as a compliment when used in conjunction with table wines. Maderized wines have been exposed to air and have lost their freshness. Sherrified is a similar term, but oxidized is the most common synonym.

MALOLACTIC FERMENTATION A secondary fermentation oc-curing in some wines, this natural process converts malic acid into softer lactic acid and carbon dioxide, thus reducing the wine's total acidity. It is also accompanied by fairly unpleasant odors that blow off as the gas escapes into the air. If it is not complete before bottling, the gas and undesirable odors remain trapped in the wine, usually spoiling its appeal. Malolactic fermentation is said to add complexity as well as softness to red wines, but, with the exception of high-acid Chardonnay, is considered undesirable in whites.

MATCHSTICK An unpleasant smell coming from high levels of sulfur dioxide (a widely used chemical preservative); similar to the smell of burnt matches. A cardboard or chemically grassy note often comes across as well. Fairly common in newly bottled white wines. It should dissipate with airing.

MEDIUM SWEET We use medium sweet to describe wines with residual sugar levels in the range of 1.5–2.9%. Such wines are perceptibly sweet to the taste, yet are not so sweet as to be limited to use with dessert. However, wines labeled medium sweet may be much sweeter than our range, because there is no industry agreement on how the term should be applied. See also Sweet.

MÉTHODE CHAMPENOISE The most labor-intensive and costly way to make champagne. Once the wine is placed in the bottle to begin its second fermentation, it never leaves that bottle until it is poured into a glass for drinking. When expertly done, the champagne achieves a persistent effervescence of extremely tiny bubbles. It is the only permitted method for all French champagnes. On U.S. labels, producers normally state that their wine was made by the *méthode champenoise* and often add "fermented in this bottle." However, if the label reads "fermented in the bottle" or "bottle fermented," chances are that the wine was made by the transfer process.

MOUNTAIN Labels carrying this term are often attached to wines of lowly jug wine quality. Most come from grapes grown in the flattest and hottest areas of California, where the mountains are seen only on clear days.

MOUTH-FILLING Wines with intense round flavors, often in combination with glycerine or slightly low acidity. They seem to have character and tactile presence everywhere in the mouth.

MUSCATTY The character of muscat grapes shows up from time to time in the wines of other varieties—most notably Flora and Gewurztraminer. (See Muscat Blanc for a more complete description of muscatty character.)

MUST The unfermented juice of grapes produced by crushing or pressing.

MUSTY A wine with dank, moldy, or mildewy smells, the result of being stored in improperly cleaned tanks and barrels, being made from moldy grapes, or victimized by a poor cork.

NATURAL A champagne term indicating that the wine is either totally dry or the driest made by the producer. Variants occasionally seen are *naturel, natur,* and *au naturel.* The term lacks strict definition.

NOSE The character of a wine ascertained through the olfactory senses is called its nose. This can also be called the aroma and includes the bouquet.

NOUVEAU A style of light, fruity, youthful red wine often presented as harbinger of the new vintage. In the United States some are produced by carbonic maceration, and others are simply bottled as soon as possible. *Nuevo* and *premier* are synonyms. All indicate a wine that is best when young.

NUTTY Table wines exposed to air will often take on a nutty smell similar to some sherries. The wine is usually oxidized and, thus, flawed.

OAKY Having aroma or taste elements contributed by the oak barrels or casks in which the wine was aged. Both vanillin, which comes from the oak itself, and toasty or roasted qualities, derived from the char contributed by the open flame used to heat the staves during barrel-making, are common characteristics of oaky wines.

OFF-DRY On our scale of describing and measuring sweetness in wine, we equate off-dry with slightly sweet and mean that the residual sugar in the wine is barely perceptible (0.6–1.4% residual sugar). In wine-labeling the term has no agreed-on definition and is used by wineries indiscriminately to indicate levels of sweetness from slight to overbearing. (See Sweet for a more complete discussion.)

OILY The fat, round, slightly slippery tactile impression on the palate created by the combination of high glycerine and slightly low acid. It is a characteristic found and enjoyed in many of the best Chardonnays and also in other big wines, as well as in sweet, late harvest wines.

OVERRIPE Grapes left on the vine beyond normal maturity develop a concentrated, often dried-out, sometimes raisiny character. Zinfandel can yield very attractive overripe-tasting wines; Chardonnay and Cabernet are generally not enhanced by overripe qualities.

OXIDIZED Wine exposed too long to air takes on a brownish color, loses its freshness, and often begins to smell and taste like sherry or old apples. Oxidized wines are also called maderized or sherrified.

PERFUMED The strong, usually sweet and floral aromas of some white wines, notably Johannisberg Riesling, Gewurztraminer, and Muscat.

pH A chemical measurement (hydrogen ions in solution) used by wineries—along with grape ripeness and acid levels—as a possible determinant of grape and wine quality. pH in general affects a wine's color, taste, textural feel on the palate, and long-term stability. The desirable pH range for table wines is 2.9–3.5. For most dessert wines a range of 3.4–3.8 is normal.

PHYLLOXERA A vine disease brought about by tiny aphids or root lice that attack *Vitis vinifera* roots. It was widespread in both Europe and California during the late 19th century. Eventually, growers discovered a solution, which entailed grafting vinifera onto native American root stocks that were naturally resistant to phylloxera. Most vines today are grafted, except in the new vineyards of California's Central and South coasts and the Pacific Northwest.

POMACE The mass of grape skins, seeds, and stems left after a wine has been pressed.

PONDEROUS Wines that are full in body and low in acid or tannin are ponderous. They have weight on the palate, but nothing to give them balance and structure.

POWERFUL Wines high in alcohol (and tannin for reds), often with big flavors, are said to have power. Brawny is a similar concept. The term is applied most often to red wines, but may also be useful to describe big, dry white wines.

PRESS WINE Juice extracted under pressure after pressing for white wines and after fermenting for reds. It is the opposite of free-run juice. Press wine has more flavor and aroma, deeper color, and often more tannins—all resulting from longer contact with grape skins. Wineries usually handle it separately and later blend all or part back into the free-run and bottle what is left under second labels, using generic or proprietary names; some may sell it off in bulk to other producers.

PRIVATE RESERVE This high-minded phrase may once have had meaning for special, long-aged wines. Lacking external regulation, it is now used inconsistently. It should apply to wines deemed worthy of special attention. Often it does, but not often enough to serve as a reliable guide.

PRODUCED AND BOTTLED BY Indicates that the named winery crushed, fermented, and bottled at least 75% of the wine in the bottle. Quite different from the similar-sounding "made and bottled by."

PROPRIETOR'S RESERVE A variant of "private reserve."

PRUNEY Very overripe, dried-out grapes give a pruney, pungent quality that is undesirable in fine wines.

PUCKERY Used to describe wines high in tannin, which tend to dry out the mouth and cause one's teeth and cheeks to feel as though they were stuck together.

RACKING The most traditional way of clarifying a wine: transferring it from one container to another, leaving the precipitated matter behind. This labor-intensive practice has been augmented (and often replaced) by filtration, fining, and centrifugation.

RAISINY Somewhat rich, almost caramel, concentrated, dried-grape taste. Some wines, such as late harvest Zinfandel and port, can be pleasant with a little raisiny character, but most other wines are not. Some wines made from Central Valley–grown grapes taste raisiny because the excessive heat of the area dries out the grapes even as they are ripening on the vine.

REFINED Said of wines that are in balance, have distinct varietal character, and are not brawny nor out of proportion. The term is almost always used in a highly favorable context with varieties that tend to be powerful if left unchecked.

REGIONS I–V A classification of grape-growing regions according to the amount of heat to which the vines are exposed during the growing season. Its basis is the "degree day" system, using 50° F. as the base line. (There is almost no shoot growth below 50° F.) The mean temperature above 50° F. each day during the period of vine growth is multiplied by the number of days in the period, giving the total of degree days.

Using the degree-day system California is divided into five climatic categories. Region I is the coolest (fewer than 2,500 degree days) and is comparable to European areas where Johannisberg Riesling and Gewurztraminer thrive. Region II is warmer (2,501–3,000 degree days) and is comparable to Bordeaux. Region III (3,001–3,500) is comparable to the Rhone region in France and to Tuscany in Italy. Region IV (3,501–4,000) compares with the Midi of France, and Region V (4,000+) experiences conditions comparable to Mediterranean growing areas.

RESIDUAL SUGAR A statement of the unfermented grape sugar in a finished wine expressed either as the percentage by volume or the percentage by weight. Thus, residual sugar either of 2.6% or of 2.6 gm/100 ml is exactly the same. Such information helps determine how the wine should be enjoyed and is most often found on sweet-finished white wines. For a detailed breakdown, see Sweet.

RICH Wines with generous, full, pleasant flavors, usually sweet and round in nature, are described as rich. In dry wines, richness may be supplied by high alcohol and glycerine, by complex flavors, and by vanilla, oaky character. Decidedly sweet wines are also described as rich when the sweetness is backed up by fruity, often ripe flavors.

RIPE The desirable elements within each grape's own special varietal character come out when the grapes reach optimum maturity in the vineyard. Ripe-tasting wine usually has round flavors, tends toward being rich, and is more sweetly fruity than other wines possessing the same levels of scientifically measurable sweetness.

ROTTEN EGG The smell of hydrogen sulfide (H_2S) in wine, a flaw that ranges from mildly bothersome at low levels to malevolent at very high levels.

ROUGH The grainy, somewhat puckery tactile sensation of young, tannic red wines. A related term, astringent, refers to more noticeable levels of harsh tannins.

ROUND Used to describe both flavors and tactile sensations. In both contexts, round connotes completeness, the absence of angularity or any dominating characteristic. Round flavors are balanced and tend toward richness and ripeness. On the palate, round wines usually are slightly low in acid, often have glycerine or residual sugar to fill in the angles or cover any roughness, and are low in tannin.

SEC Literally means dry. However, tradition is that a champagne labeled *sec* falls in the sweet to very sweet range.

SELECT Implies that the wine has special qualities. Lacking legal definition and consistent application, it most often means nothing.

SELECT HARVEST Absolutely inconsistent usage and, therefore, meaningless.

SELECTED LATE HARVEST Seen on white wines, primarily Johannisberg Rieslings, but lacking consistent usage. A few producers use it to indicate that the grapes were riper and the wine finished sweeter than a late harvest style. However, the phrase has different meanings from winery to winery.

SHARP The slightly biting tactile sensation of excess acidity, or high acetic acid, and the accompanying bite in the taste.

SHERRIFIED When table wines are exposed to air over long periods, they become oxidized. One of the signs of oxidation is a nutty aroma and taste reminiscent of sherry. Maderized is a comparable term.

SIMPLE Wines with very straightforward character—immediately accessible with no nuances or complex notes. Most of the world's wines are simple when compared to the highly praised château and estate bottlings, yet can be delightful if clean, fruity, and fairly well balanced.

SLIGHTLY SWEET Most appropriately used to describe the levels of sweetness lying just above the threshold of perception (in the range of 0.6–1.4% sugar). Off-dry is a similar term. See Sweet.

SOFT Describes wines low in acid or tannin (sometimes both) that are, therefore, not firm and hard on the palate. Also used for wines with reduced alcohol levels and less of the consequent hot impact of higher alcohol.

SOLERA A blending system used for both sherries and ports. A *solera* consists of barrels stacked in tiers with the oldest wine on the bottom tier and the youngest on top. As wine is drawn from the oldest barrel for bottling, younger wine from each tier is moved forward a stage. The objective is to blend for uniformity and consistency. About 10 California wineries and several in New York and Michigan maintain *soleras.*

SOUR When wine is so high in acid that it is out of balance, it tastes sour or very tart. As a tasting term, it is used for a wine high in acetic acid and volatile acidity.

SPICY Somewhat pungent, often attractive aromas and flavors suggestive of cloves, cinnamon, anise, caraway, and similar substances. The most typically spicy grape is Gewurztraminer; other varieties that may show lesser degrees of spiciness are Zinfandel and Chardonnay.

SPRITZY Wines with fairly modest degrees of pinpoint carbonation are described as spritzy. In slightly sweet and medium sweet white wines, a little spritz can give a lively impression that enhances the wine's balance. Most dry wines are not enhanced by spritziness.

STALE Wines that have lost their fresh, youthful qualities and have taken on dull, tired, sometimes stagnant qualities— often from being stored too long at the winery in large containers before bottling. Tanky is a related term.

STRUCTURE A wine's structure is determined by the interplay of those elements that create tactile impressions in the mouth: acid, tannin, glycerine, alcohol, body. It is a term that needs a modifier like firm, sturdy, or weak to be meaningful.

SUPPLE Used most often to describe the tactile impression of red wines possessing general amiability and underlying softness in spite of fairly firm structure, ample acid, and noticeable tannin. Young, hard wines are often allowed to age until they achieve more agreeable, supple qualities.

SWEET One of the 4 basic tastes perceived by the tongue, as opposed to the hundreds of flavors that we actually experience with our olfactory senses. The presence of sugar (or occasionally of glycerine) is required to taste sweetness, according to the wine scientist.

A few wine writers, ourselves included, have attempted to define sweetness levels in terms that can be applied consistently. The gradations of sweetness appearing in *Connoisseurs' Guide to California Wine* and adopted in this book are:

Less than 0.5% residual sugar	Dry
0.6–1.4% residual sugar	Slightly Sweet
1.5–2.9% residual sugar	Medium Sweet
3.0–5.9% residual sugar	Sweet
More than 5.9% residual sugar	Very Sweet

The scents of intense fruitiness, of ripe or overripe grapes, and of vanilla oakiness often seem to be sweet, especially when found in conjunction with each other. For that reason, when we use sweet to describe a wine's aroma, we add other descriptive terms to indicate the probable source of the sweet scents. The sweet taste of wine may be similarly modified when describing a nonsugary sweetness. Varying levels of acid, alcohol, and tannin and the inherent bitterness of some grape varieties balance against sugar and affect the level of sweetness that is perceived in wine.

TANKY The tired, somewhat dank qualities that show up in wines aged too long in large tanks.

TANNIN The puckery substance in red wines and a few whites is tannin. It is derived primarily from grape skins, grape seeds and stems, and the barrels in which wine is aged. Brawny, young red wines usually have substantial tannin that requires years of cellar aging to soften. Tannin serves as a natural preservative that helps the wine develop, but must be kept in balance with depth and potential. Excessively tannic wines can remain tannic long after the flavors have peaked. Tannin can dry out the aftertaste and can taste bitter if not kept in balance. Astringent is a related term.

TART The sharp taste of acidity in wine is described as tart or sour.

THIN Wines lacking body and depth are known as thin. Such wines tend to feel and taste watery. The French describe such wines as meager—a very apt word.

TIGHT Young wines with angular flavors and a hard tactile impression in the mouth. Closed-in and dumb are related terms.

TOPPING Winery practice of adding wine to barrels and tanks to replace what was lost by evaporation. It minimizes contact with air and, thus, oxidation.

TRANSFER PROCESS A modern method of making bottle fermented champagne. At the end of its second fermentation, the wine is poured out of the bottle into pressurized tanks where it is filtered to remove the sediment prior to being rebottled. Such champagnes may be labeled "bottled fermented" or "transfer process," often accompanied by "fermented in the bottle."

UNDERRIPE When grapes fail to reach maturity on the vine, their wines usually lack round flavors and tactile impression. Typically, their varietal character remains undeveloped, they possess high acidity, and they display green flavors.

UNFILTERED Indicates that the wine achieved its state of clarification and stabilization without being filtered. However, this does not mean that other cellar treatments, such as fining, centrifugation, and cold-stabilization were necessarily also avoided.

UNFINED Seen on many Cabernets and Zinfandels to suggest the wine received minimal treatment. It means the wine was not fined, though it could well have been filtered or clarified by other methods.

VARIETAL A wine named after the predominant grape variety in its composition. Current regulations, enacted in the 1930s, require a wine to have only 51% of a given grape in its makeup to qualify as a varietal. This antiquated ruling is now under deserved attack, and in 1983 the limit will probably be raised to 75%. The varietal system took hold in California in the 1960s, and today most of the finest wines produced are varietals.

VARIETAL CHARACTER The unique combination of smells, tastes, and tactile impressions typically offered by a grape when ripened to maturity. The most highly prized wine grapes have distinctive and attractive varietal character. Lesser grapes have less distinct varietal character. And some grapes, including such familiar names as Green Hungarian and Grey Riesling, have virtually no uniquely identifiable character. In Zinfandel the berrylike taste is the typical varietal character; in Cabernet it is black currants; and in Chardonnay it is a round, oily texture and generous, round, fruity flavors. Breed is a related concept.

VEGETAL The smell and taste of some wines contain elements reminiscent of plants and vegetables. In Cabernet Sauvignon a small amount of this vegetal quality is said to be part of varietal character. However, when the vegetal element takes over the wine or when it shows up in wines in which it does not belong, those wines are considered to be flawed. Wine scientists have been able to identify the chemical constituent that makes wines smell like asparagus and bell peppers, but are not sure why it occurs more often in Central Coast vineyards than in others.

VERY SWEET In our system of differentiation, wines that possess 6.0% or more residual sugar are described as very sweet. Their obvious, inescapable sweetness leads generally to enjoyment with dessert or by themselves after the meal. Some of California's most exciting (and expensive) wines fall into this category, including late harvest Rieslings and Gewurztraminers.

VINOUS Literally meaning winelike, vinous is usually applied to dull wines lacking enough character to be described in more vivid terms. Vinous, and its noun, vinosity, are used with relatively clean wines.

VINTAGE DATE To give a wine a vintage date, the winery must have made at least 95% of the wine from grapes harvested in the stated calendar year. Such dates provide useful information about a wine's freshness or its aging requirements. However, a vintage-dated wine is not necessarily a "vintage" wine, even though most high-quality wines carry vintage dates.

VINTED BY A pleasant-sounding but meaningless phrase that may be used on wine labels even when the named winery had no more involvement with the wine than purchasing it in bulk from another winery and bottling it upon arrival.

VITICULTURAL AREA This is now a legal entity, representing an effort by the federal government to upgrade the use of place names and grape-growing regions on wine labels when the area is smaller than a state and does not conform to county boundaries. Interested parties must petition the government and make a case for the uniqueness of the particular region on the basis of climate, soil, elevation, history, and definable boundaries. Beginning in 1983, only those areas approved and established may be used on labels and in advertising. The federal requirement is that 85% of the wine in question is made from grapes grown within that specified viticultural area. If the wine is a varietal bottling, a minimum of 75% of that wine must be made from the designated grape variety.

VITIS LABRUSCA A species of wild grape vine believed to be native to North America. Few of the grapes used to make wine are pure labrusca because most have been accidentally cross-pollinated with other species, including vinifera. All labrusca-type wines share, to varying degrees, a characteristic aroma and flavor traditionally and inexplicably described as foxy. This is another way of saying that they smell like Concord grape juice and have a strong grapey personality. The best-known wine varieties are Concord, Catawba, Delaware, and Niagara.

VITIS VINIFERA The species of grape vine responsible for the world's best wines. It probably originated in the Mediterranean basin and subsequently was cultivated throughout Europe. Today, the species is often referred to as the Old World or European vine. The vinifera (wine-bearer) family may have close to 5,000 members, but fewer than 100 are considered important as wine grapes. As a family, vinifera vines require sufficient heat to bring the grapes to ripeness and are not at all hardy to freezing winter spells. They are also vulnerable to numerous parasites and to many fungus diseases. Vinifera vines also interbreed easily and do not breed true when propagated from seeds.
Freezing winter temperatures have stymied their cultivation in many parts of the United States; high summer humidity encouraging various molds has eliminated their cultivation in many Southern states as well. With its mild, rainy winter and long, dry, warm summer, California offers a climate generally favorable to vinifera vines. Parts of Washington, Oregon, Michigan, and New York and several mid-Atlantic states have also been successful in cultivating the European vine.

VOLATILE Aromas that come out of the glass aggressively, almost fiercely. They are usually caused by high levels of volatile acidity and alcohol or by chemical faults.

VOLATILE ACID The smell of ethyl acetate and the palate sharpness of acetic acid (they almost always occur simultaneously) is often referenced collectively as volatile acid or volatile acidity. Occasionally wine labels will tell the level of volatile acidity (VA) in the wine. In general the lower, the better. The threshold at which most tasters notice VA in wine is just under 0.1%—more than most wines contain. The legal limit of volatile acidity is just over 0.1%.

WARM Some red wines—Cabernet, Merlot, Petite Sirah, and Zinfandel—possess both flavor intensity and balance to offset their high alcohol. Such wines are described as warm. This is a positive attribute, unlike the term hot, which refers to excessive alcohol.

WEIGHTY Wines with a heavy, full-bodied sense of presence on the palate.

WOODY The smell or taste of the wooden containers in which wines are aged—usually strongest for wines aged in new barrels. The aromas and flavors of some wines are substantially benefited by the extra dimension garnered from the wood. However, wines that stay too long in the barrel become excessively woody and lose their interest. Oaky is a closely related term.

Touring

A visit to California's wine country can begin anywhere within its borders, for virtually every large city is within range of some vintner. Flourishing vineyards dot the landscape in most parts of the state and encompass over 1,000 square miles—an area larger than the entire state of Rhode Island. Although some are more obvious about it than others, most premium wineries love to have visitors. In the continuing boom-and-bust history of the wine industry, they have never been able to take their customers for granted. In fact, you can probably count on your fingers the number of wineries complacent about their position in the market over the next couple of years. The tasting room, therefore, becomes a valuable means of promoting the winery's reputation and output.

Casual dress is appropriate for visiting wineries. In the North and Central Coast areas during summer, you can usually expect morning temperatures in the sixties and overcast skies until 10 or 11 a.m. The mid-afternoons are warm. Occasionally a summer hot spell will take temperatures over 100° for a few days, but that is unusual; and evenings are generally cool. The humidity stays low all year.

Spring and the fall harvest season are filled with beautiful days, some of them cool. In winter it is important to wear warm shoes (thick soles are best) because winery floors are often cold and damp. Rain is concentrated in the months between November and March, but an occasional shower comes in April. From May through September, expect no more than a freak rainstorm.

We have divided our discussion of touring into six main segments by geography. This was done to facilitate a more compact look at the options. If you live in San Jose and have never visited a winery, you need look no farther than your doorstep. If you are in San Francisco, your choices are wider, but some decisions must be made. Napa's concentration of well-known wineries is hard to top. But do not overlook the charms of the Sonoma Valley if you want a relaxing, easy day, and the Redwood Highway's winery area approaches Napa in beauty and touring facilities. The choices south of San Francisco, although fewer and farther between, stretch all the way to Southern California. Each of the areas has its own unique set of virtues, and it is up to you to match them with your interests.

NAPA VALLEY Napa's 100 or more establishments cover every premium winemaking and marketing style and approach. Full-line, million-gallon wineries exist side by side with tiny "boutique" properties. Champagne makers share the land with Burgundians and seekers of the "California Lafite." For every venerable Inglenook and Charles Krug, there are two, three, four fledgling Shafers, Duckhorns, and Buehlers. Here are our impressions of the pluses and minuses of Napa's major taste-and-tour wineries.

Visiting the Major Wineries The comparative tastings made by *Connoisseurs' Guide* often find Inglenook or Krug, Mondavi or Beaulieu wines rating on a par with and often surpassing the offerings from less-established vintners. Clearly, large size, diversity, and "Fortune 500" corporate ownership have not disqualified the major wineries as producers of fine wines and as solid objects of interest for visitors.

Beringer Vineyards Beringer's Rhine House is perhaps the most impressive example of European architecture in the wine country. Its richly decorative style and stained glass make it an attraction in itself; a tour here is as much for a view of the facilities as for a look at winemaking. Inside the winery's limestone caves, beautifully crafted wood barrels date back to the earliest days of the Napa Valley's vinous history. At tour's end, in a wood-paneled room in the Rhine House, the tour group is allowed to sample several wines. Beringer presents an air of civility missing to some extent at other taste-and-tour wineries.

Beaulieu Vineyards The visitor center is something of a shrine to the grape. The magnificent vineyard photography lining the walls is in itself easily worth the stop. So, for that matter, is the fifteen-minute film-and-slide extravaganza devoted to the grape-growing side of winemaking. While you examine the photography or wait for a tour to begin, Beaulieu will quietly ply you with a glass or two of their wine choices for that day. Tours are quite informative, especially when combined with the movie.

Chandon Hidden from view by a tiny knoll, this multi-million-dollar complex comes complete with a visitor's center and restaurant. It now ranks among the most popular tourist stops, both for what it offers and the fact that it is the first major facility to visit as one travels the valley from south to north.

The grounds are quite attractive, and the general design manages to conceal the considerable magnitude of the winery. The well-informed tour guides try to blend history with modern technology. The history of champagne making comes through the exhibit on display in the large waiting room. The actual tour commences with a look at numerous large-scale fermenting tanks, moves on to the riddling room where vibrating machines are replacing hand-riddling, proceeds to the aging area, and concludes with the bottling lines.

Neither quaint nor personal, the tour provides an adequate understanding of champagne making at one of California's best. We suggest you avoid the busy summer weekends because of the crowds and because nothing much in the way of winemaking is going on. One civilized touch at Chandon is that the visitor can enjoy a glass (or bottle) of its wines in the foyer or the adjoining patio. That is a pleasant way to begin, or better yet to end, a day of touring the wine country.

Christian Brothers The Christian Brothers' St. Helena

wine-aging facility (no winemaking here) is an alternative to visiting Beringer. Greystone, as it is called, also offers a glimpse of limestone caves. Their tour is lengthy, but not always as informative as we like. In addition, Brother Timothy's much heralded corkscrew collection is on display. The tasting portion is conducted at tour's end.

If you are looking for a ride off the valley floor, Christian Brothers also offers taste and tour at their winemaking facility, Mont La Salle. You will need a map to get there. In fact, getting there is the prime reason for taking the trip. The tour is informative and fairly comprehensive, but no more so than others in the valley.

Inglenook Vineyards The pleasures of dropping in at Inglenook are familiar to the frequent Napa Valley visitor. On a crowded Saturday afternoon, when cars line the highway bumper to bumper and the parking lots are filled at Mondavi, Christian Brothers, and Beringer, the scene at Inglenook retains a degree of calm.

The probable reason is that Inglenook tours rate among the least attractive in the Napa Valley. Winemaking activities are not carried out at the visitor facility, so the short walk-around becomes a history lesson and another look at cask and tank aging in a dark room. Nevertheless, the main Inglenook building, erected circa 1880, is worth seeing, and the intimate half-mile drive through the vineyards— from Highway 29 to Inglenook's front door—is pleasant enough.

You will not be disappointed by tastings at Inglenook. The setting is a museumlike gallery just inside the winery's main door, and tasting is available whether or not you take the tour.

Hanns Kornell One of Napa's three champagne-only houses. The plant, an old winery converted by proprietor Kornell in 1958 to his special purposes, is anything but spectacular. The tour, however, is of value not for the plant but for what goes on within it. Tour guides, sometimes members of the Kornell family, lead visitors through a step-by-step explanation of how the classic and expensive *méthode champenoise* champagnes are produced. On weekdays the whole dramatic disgorging process is on display. Tasting generally occurs at the end of the tour.

Charles Krug Winery Virtually across the street from Beringer and Christian Brothers, the Charles Krug Winery is another of the Napa Valley's historic sites. Krug offers a generally informative, comprehensive, and helpful tour much like those of Christian Brothers and Martini. The rambling length is required to explain Krug's methods and to show off the winemaking and storage facilities. Tasting is available at tour's end, although persistence may enable you to slip into the tasting room without going through the tour. However, tour groups have priority. Typically, three lower-priced wines are offered. Compared to Mondavi's ultramodern setup (see below), a visit to Krug offers a view of a more traditional winemaking approach.

Louis M. Martini Winery This winery is as unpretentious as any in the valley. The plant, office, and visitor facilities are totally functional. So is the tour and the attitude toward visitors. If there is a saving grace about visiting Martini, it lies in the availability of wine to taste. All of its regular wines are poured at a long bar by generally knowledgeable hosts. The glasses are fairly small, to be sure, but interested, serious tasters can sample their way through a number of Martini wines. We frequently take a quick swing through the Martini tasting room when we are buying wines just to check their latest offerings. Incidentally, no other winery offers a broader and more reasonably priced collection of aged wines.

Robert Mondavi Winery We often suggest that first-time visitors to the Napa Valley take the Robert Mondavi tour. It is one of the few tours that starts with the vines. We find the tour informative, well planned, and able to present a good view of how a modern winery operates. The better guides at Mondavi can answer specific questions about the uses of the winery's sophisticated equipment. (Not all tour leaders here—or anywhere—are as knowledgeable as they might be.) Be sure to press your guide about Mondavi's choice of stainless steel versus wood fermentation and aging, about their use of the centrifuge to clarify some wines and not others, and about changes in styles of their wines.

Wine tasting at Mondavi, however, is *not* one of our favorite experiences. It is provided only at the end of a tour and is generally not available unless you take the tour. Your tour group is ushered into a cubicle of a room for the pouring of three wines. While you stand around elbow to elbow, the tour guide passes among the group, filling glasses and explaining the wine.

Still, if you want to see how a modern, full-line winery operates and to learn a little in the process, a stop at Mondavi rates very high.

Sterling Vineyards "Stark, monastic, and lonely" or "rich and alive"—it all depends on one's point of view. From our perspective, Sterling's rugged, starkly modernistic architecture is a thing of beauty made doubly exciting by the premium winery within its confines. It is almost a model winery. But, in our opinion, Sterling is a place to be visited only by those with a basic understanding of what winemaking is all about. (Tours at one or two other wineries should suffice as preparation.) At Sterling the walk-around is strictly a do-it-yourself operation, from viewing galleries with signboards explaining what is unfolding before you. Sterling's hilltop location is accessible only by tramway from the winery's valley-floor parking lot. A fee is charged —a practice that some find annoying. However, it restricts the visitor flow to manageable numbers, thereby making Sterling an excellent choice on those crowded summer and harvest weekends.

After Beringer . . . What? When you have had your fill of the bigger wineries, there are still another 100 or more in and around the valley. Some are more accessible than others, but each has its virtues for dyed-in-the-wool fans. A couple seem to bring us back frequently.

Sutter Home Winery This is a frequent stop on our travels. Its recent fame is based not on a Napa Valley wine, but on Amador County Zinfandel, now the major item in the Sutter Home line. You will find the Zinfandel and their attractive White Zinfandel and Moscato Amabile available for tasting.

Pope Valley Winery If you want to try something different in a Napa Valley winery, venture off the valley floor to the Pope Valley Winery. It is a genuine, down-home treat. You will need a map to find it and a healthy respect for old-time winemaking. This is a winery in a barn with tasting on the premises. Pope Valley is in the beginning of a new era under owner-manager Jim Devitt, who is quite willing to talk about his plans, the unique problems and successes of his winery, and most other things vinous.

Franciscan Vineyards A spacious tasting room and a tour-optional attitude make this an inviting way to conclude a day in Napa Valley. Several wines are offered.

Chateau Montelena When we first began traveling from winery to winery, Montelena was a remote outpost north of Calistoga visited by those who happened to be in the area to watch the famous geyser perform. The geyser still is active, but now plays second fiddle to the winery. The handsome stone building has a fascinating history, comes with a man-made lake and picnic facilities, and a reputation for excellent wines. The result is that the picnic facilities should be reserved weeks in advance during the summer and the tasting room is congested most of the time. The tasting room is small, but usually newly released wines are offered to visitors. Also, there is occasionally an opportunity to purchase some older vintages no longer available elsewhere.

V. Sattui Before you come to either Louis Martini or Sutter Home Winery, you may wonder about the crowd of people enjoying a picnic on the right as you journey north. V. Sattui has become a popular place to stop and understandably so, since the winery also has one of the best selections of cheeses and gourmet foods available for winery visitors. The staff is ready to provide full picnic fare, including plastic wine glasses with which to enjoy a bottle of wine. The picnic area is large. Ernie's Wine Warehouse, offering a wide selection of wine, is located right across the street.

Markham Winery As you move up the valley making your way toward Calistoga or Sterling Vineyards, Markham is open for tasting every day. The tasting room is large and seldom crowded. Three or four wines are offered on a regular basis, consisting of new releases and the least expensive items.

Tastings Only Several new wineries have tasting rooms open to the public on a regular basis. Rutherford Vintners due north of Rutherford is open daily and offers a full range of wines. Napa Wine Cellars is the only winery constructed as a geodesic dome. The tasting room provides a pleasant, casual atmosphere that we appreciate. Whitehall Lane Winery is one of the newest and most attractive additions along Napa's winery road, and visitors are cordially received and allowed to linger over samples of its new wines. Heitz Cellars presents us with a bit of a dilemma. As much as we admire its wines, the separate tasting and sales-room facility just south of St. Helena is a bit on the seedy side. Do not expect to be offered a sample of its vineyard-designated Cabernet Sauvignons. But those wines can usually be purchased there. So if you want to taste one of Heitz Cellars' wines or buy some of the top-notch Cabernets, a special stop is in order.

By Appointment Only Many of Napa's smaller establishments are working wineries with limited production operated by a very few people. They have no visitor centers, tour guides, audio-visual aids, or oak-paneled, wall-to-wall-carpeted tasting rooms. When a visitor arrives and engages the attention of owner, winemaker, or cellarman (sometimes one person is all three), the actual operation of the winery stops. For that reason, most unannounced calls result in an "I'm sorry. We're in the middle of bottling (or pumping, fixing, cleaning, racking, filtering). I won't be able to see you."

The solution, of course, is a prearranged visit. The requirements are simple enough: an honest, knowledgeable interest in the small winery you care to visit. Familiarity with its wines, history, ownership, and objectives is also important. A letter to the winery is the first step. With luck, you will get a favorable response. After all, winery owners are just like everybody else: They enjoy meeting their friends. Among our favorites in this category are Caymus Vineyards, the ultimate in winemaking simplicity; Trefethen

Vineyards, a refurbished old estate that retains much of the original charm; Joseph Phelps, an elegant, striking winery; and Flora Springs, with its beautiful setting. For those who enjoy panoramic views of the entire valley as much as we do, Smith-Madrone along Spring Mountain Road in the western hills and Burgess Cellars sitting above the Silverado Trail in the east are both hard to find, and hard to beat for views.

SONOMA VALLEY Sonoma Valley houses a baker's dozen wineries. Only one of these, Sebastiani, has achieved the general distribution and size of Napa's larger concerns. For this reason alone, a visit to the rustic Sonoma Valley is a much more relaxed, almost casual affair. The flow of visitors is smaller, and the strings of tourist buses, so common in the Napa Valley, less bothersome.

Sebastiani Vineyards Sebastiani offers the only genuine taste-and-tour opportunity in the Sonoma Valley. Wood carvings are not new to the wine business, but no West Coast winery has so formidable a collection of new carvings as Sebastiani.

An outdoor perch for tour groups overlooks the grape-receiving area. The tours come and go, but true aficionados are welcome to stay on during harvest times to watch the winery weigh in and inspect ton after ton of freshly harvested grapes. Sebastiani is also a good tasting stop (no tour necessary), since their wood-paneled tasting room offers a fairly complete line to sample.

Buena Vista Winery An ideal alternate to Sebastiani from the standpoint of historic interest is Buena Vista Winery. Within its hoary walls, you can practically feel the presence of the fabled Agoston Haraszthy. The informal tour is, in fact, no tour at all, but a series of pictures and drawings attached to walls and barrels. They depict scenes going back some hundred years to the founding of Buena Vista by Haraszthy and of the California wine industry. We consider it one of the highlights for any visitor to the Sonoma Valley.

Buena Vista also possesses the most elaborate picnic grounds in the wine country. Towering eucalyptus and formal plantings provide travelers with refreshing relief from the day's heat. Buena Vista's new owners have greatly improved and enlarged the facility. The old building adjacent to the winery is now a large, very attractive tasting room complete with fireplace. It also houses a historical display—photos, sketches, wine artifacts—and a rotating art exhibit featuring Sonoma County artists. Buena Vista's picnic grounds are well used even on weekdays, so we recommend an early arrival. A series of concerts during the summer weekends are popular, but be forewarned that ticket-holders tend to make a whole day of it.

Hacienda Wine Cellars This is one of the most idyllic stops anywhere in the region and is rarely crowded. Lolling under the trees at Hacienda with a bottle of Claire de Lune Chardonnay suits perfectly our predilections for a day in the country. Just right for relaxing and feeling yourself a part of the wine country.

Grand Cru Vineyards A visit often brings you face to face with one of the principals, Al Ferrara, who runs the place, or with Bob Magnani, who makes the wine. The deck of their A-frame tasting facility and office sits on a knoll overlooking the valley. You can picnic there or retreat to the picnic tables under nearby trees when the sun gets too hot.

Kenwood Vineyards Up Highway 12 from Grand Cru is the inviting Kenwood winery. This is one of the wine country's most relaxed places. You can get all the conversation you would ever need and an opportunity to taste some of winemaker Bob Kozlowski's latest creations. Just drive up to the barn and walk inside: There is the winery and tasting room. Then, glass in hand, walk back out the door and enjoy the sun, vineyards, and tree-lined vistas. You will find most of the wines available for tasting, the tour nonexistent, and the people friendly.

Chateau St. Jean Not much farther up the road is Chateau St. Jean, new and spectacularly successful. Tasting occurs in the stately villa that dominates the sloping hillside. The tasting room is tiny, and few of the top wines are poured. The grounds are attractive, and picnic tables are available.

St. Francis Vineyards Directly across the highway from Chateau St. Jean, St. Francis offers tastings only. Open every day during the summer and on weekends only in the winter, its tasting room is attractive inside and the visitor can sample all five of the wines made. This is a good opportunity to try the complete line of this up-and-coming winery.

NORTHERN SONOMA If you miss the Napa turnoff while heading north on Highway 101, do not despair. Simply continue another 40 miles to the Alexander, Dry Creek, and Russian River valleys. Many wineries there welcome visitors, and this includes one of the most visited of all California wineries, Italian Swiss Colony. Here also are four of the most handsome, visitor-oriented wineries in existence: Sonoma Vineyards, Simi Winery, Korbel, and Souverain.

Souverain Nestled into the hills near Highway 101, Souverain's stunning winery was inspired by old Sonoma County hop kilns. You will find it a rich architectural experience throughout. Besides architecture and marvelous scenic views, there is an art show, a restaurant, an elegant picnic site, and an informative winery tour. Adjacent to the dining room, a terrace surrounding a large fountain has been set aside for picnicking. No blanket-on-the-grass operation here. The winery provides chairs and tables and awnings. For picnics without hardships, this is your best choice.

Sonoma Vineyards The other spectacular, relatively new winery building in this area belongs to Sonoma Vineyards. In the midst of a cluster of purely functional buildings is a structure in the shape of a cross. Each of the four wings contains the various types of vessels used in winemaking. In the middle of the building is the heart of the operation, containing pumps and filters and centrifuges and all the apparatus of modern winemaking. Floating on a platform above all of this unromantic hardware is a tasting room comfortably provided with tables and chairs and viewing decks from which the winery's operations can be watched at your leisure. A formal tour is available.

Simi Winery This thoroughly modern winemaking operation is housed in a huge stone building of the historic Montepulciano Winery (parts of which date back to 1876). The tour is particularly informative. The guides have organized a master reference work containing all there is to know about Simi, and they are able to respond to most any question. Tasting is independent of touring, and most Simi wines are available to taste. A pleasant area has been set aside for picnicking.

Korbel Winery This winery receives a lot of visitors each year—for good reason. We have tagged along on the Korbel tour and regard it as one of the best places to see champagne-making. Across from the winery, a nicely finished, one-story California ranch-style tasting room offers tastes of Korbel's wide range of wines.

Italian Swiss Colony It may not be historically accurate to say that Italian Swiss Colony was a tourist facility before it was a winery, but its many owners have always taken advantage of the area's substantial tourist traffic. This popular rest stop along Highway 101 sees close to 400,000 visitors each year. The grounds are well landscaped, and there is a large grassy area for picnicking. Visitors sometimes line up to take photographs of their children, whose smiling faces appear above boards painted with Swiss costumes. If this does not suit your taste, avoid this winery completely.

Dry Creek Vineyards You can meet the president of the winery, the winemaker, and the national sales director—simultaneously—by stopping at Dry Creek and introducing yourself to David Stare. Dry Creek Vineyards is the same kind of "bare basics" premium winemaking setup you can see only by appointment in the Napa Valley, but no appointment is needed here. The winery is surrounded by its own young grape vines. Most wines can be tasted.

Most other wineries in Northern Sonoma County are generally very informal in their approach to visitors and tend to offer tastings only. Tourists are allowed to drop in, taste whatever is available, and leave. The atmosphere is both friendly and casual, and at many, the sales pitches are non-existent. Instead of bending your ear, the tasting room personnel often are more likely to rub elbows, share a glass of wine, and tell you some anecdotes about the good old days. The only problem is that getting away is sometimes difficult.

Pedroncelli Winery This winery is off the main road, but typifies the Sonoma County ambience. The tasting room is quite spacious, and several wines are offered to taste at leisure.

Trentadue Winery At the opposite direction of the highway from Souverain, this winery ranks as one of the most unusual of all. Its tasting room is also a gift shop crammed full of items from cheeses to jewelry and every imaginable gift. Every wine made here is available to taste in this delightful, if a bit funky atmosphere.

Geyser Peak Winery Here are attractive picnic possibilities and attractive grounds. But the tasting room is small, and the atmosphere is a bit hurried and less than congenial for those not interested in purchasing wines.

Johnson's Alexander Valley A real delight for those seeking informality and down-home hospitality, Johnson's is located along Highway 128. The owners are just as proud of their restored theater pipe organ as their wines. All wines are offered; the organ plays only on a few weekends. If novelty appeals to you, then you might want to stop by.

Foppiano Vineyards If you should arrive at a quiet moment, you might end up tasting wines in a restored railroad caboose.

Landmark Vineyards Just off the Windsor exit, Landmark Vineyards is much more traditional. Its tasting room was once the dining area in a stately old mansion. Unfortunately, the winery receives visitors only on weekends. If your schedule allows, Landmark is well worth a visit.

SOUTHERN SONOMA After Korbel, what? Before returning to the main wine route, a side trip to several small wineries in the Russian River Valley area is now possible. On Westside Road, you could well begin with Mark West Vineyards, which has a compact tasting room and more peacocks on the grounds than you'd probably care to hear from. Farther up the road is Davis Bynum, offering several wines to taste in a room that looks makeshift, but is not. The most interesting winery is the Hop Kiln Winery because it is a restored historic, hops-drying kiln. It is by itself reward for going on this side excursion, and several wines are available to sample in the spacious tasting room.

BY APPOINTMENT ONLY In Sonoma County this should be interpreted in a slightly different way than usual. It is not that those wineries refuse visitors unless by advance notice so much as it is that they don't expect anyone to want to visit them. In most instances, the wineries will go out of their way to accommodate your request. The lone exception is Jordan Vineyards, open only to V.I.P.s and celebrities.

MENDOCINO COUNTY Because Mendocino County is 120 miles from San Francisco, its wineries have not seen many visitors. Weibel is betting all this will change and has invested a considerable sum in a rather slick visitors' center—shaped like an upside-down champagne glass—at their new Ukiah winery.

Parducci Wine Cellars Capital has gone into equipment, a building for case goods and bottling, new vineyards, and a handsome new tasting room and gift shop. One of the pleasures we find in visiting this winery is in talking with John Parducci and Joe Montessori, who seem to share responsibility as winemakers.

Fetzer Vineyards An operation that began as a home-winemaking venture, Fetzer has now grown substantially. Tours are by appointment only; tasting is available in nearby Hopland at the winery's sales room.

LIVERMORE VALLEY

Concannon Vineyards Concannon has recently catapulted itself into contemporary winemaking techniques through a large investment in new equipment. Yet the winery retains its homeyness. The tour proceeds from a discussion of how the family got into winemaking to an inspection of the vines; finally it leads past the bottling line to an informal tasting in the shipping area. Concannon is a fine blend of winery tradition and contemporary winemaking.

Wente Bros. This family-run operation is much larger than Concannon. Its tours, given only on weekdays, are a good opportunity to see contemporary winemaking techniques. The tasting room is independent of the tour and open daily. Most of the line is available. The winery is surrounded by 800 acres of vineyards.

Mirassou Vineyards Set alone in the eastern foothills of the Santa Clara Valley, Mirassou enjoys a country setting and is surrounded by new vineyards. The tasting room was converted from a concrete fermentation tank and a fireplace was added, so the room is cool on hot summer days and warmed by a real log fire in the winter. All of the regular line is available for tasting. Periodically the tasting room is used to test consumer response to new wines. Mirassou also gives a good tour.

Paul Masson Vineyards Paul Masson's modern pink and cream-colored facility in Saratoga can be visited only on weekdays and should be toured only if you can tolerate being processed like the thousands of bottles that are run through each of their multiple bottling lines. Since no wine is made at this plant, the tour's best feature is a demonstration of the transfer method of champagne making. The many wines of Paul Masson are also available for tasting.

Bargetto Winery This winery always seems like an anomaly to us. It is in the town of Soquel, and there is not a sign of vine around. But Bargetto has achieved a particularly nice ambience in its tasting room. Just about everything is available for tasting. The tour is interesting and offers a unique opportunity to see fruit wine being made.

Ridge Vineyards Considering its limited visiting hours, the difficulty of reaching the site, and the lack of a tour, Ridge hardly appears to have a visitor's program. Open only on Saturdays for most of the year, this winery offers its fans the opportunity to talk with Dave Bennion or Paul Draper about winemaking and to pick up odd lots and limited-quantity wines that never reach retailers. The site is marvelous for a picnic.

Monterey Vineyard Nicely designed tours take visitors throughout the winery, an architecturally impressive structure in Gonzales. The guides will point out the many special touches that have been designed into the facility. Wine tasting is an integral part of the visit.

Firestone Vineyard Located on a bluff overlooking vineyards and mountains, this modern Santa Ynez Valley winery is well set up to welcome visitors. The compact, cathedral-like building allows an easy view of Firestone's equipment and winemaking. Tasting takes place in a gem of a room with views both inside and outside of the winery.

Zaca Mesa Winery Betting that the Santa Barbara area will become well-trafficked soon, this winery completed a full visitor's center recently. A new wing was added to the winery and now serves as the reception center. It is a spacious room decorated with stained glass windows. Most wines are available for tasting, and a formal tour given by tour guides is part of the package.

Santa Ynez Valley Winery and Vega Vineyards These two wineries are now ready to receive visitors, but on weekends only. Santa Ynez Valley is a converted old dairy, fairly typical for the area, and Vega Vineyards offers large picnic grounds. Both offer tours and tastings, so the wise suggestion is to plan a visit on the weekend. Stopping by all four wineries will provide a good look at what is going on in this new but important wine region.

REFERENCES Many guidebooks and winery commentaries are available to help you get the most out of touring the wine country. In our opinion, the following are the most useful.

Sunset's California Wine Country This 9-by-12-inch softcover book from Sunset is the most widely distributed touring guide. Updated several times since its original publication, the work has recently undergone a total revision. It is the best general-purpose touring guide available.

Wines of America Leon Adams's excellent book is not a touring guide nor a substitute for one. It is highly recommended because Adams has assembled an authoritative biographical compendium of United States wineries, past and present. A thorough look at the pertinent chapters is a great primer for enhancing the pleasure of your trip before heading out to visit vintners.

Vintage Image Wine Tours At $4.95 each for editions on the Napa Valley, Sonoma-Mendocino, and the Central Coast, these books give generalized background information and specific touring guidance, including advice on restaurants, lodgings, and side attractions.

California's Wine Wonderland In 30 pages this free pamphlet provides basic maps and visiting information for most wineries in California. Write to the *Wine Institute*, 165 Post Street, San Francisco, California 94108. This is well worth the stamp.

Largest U.S. Wine Producers Offering Branded Table Wines

Producers and Brands *(In California, Except as Noted)*	*Storage Capacity in Gallons (000s)*
E. & J. GALLO Gallo, André, Paisano, Carlo Rossi	253,000
HEUBLEIN Beaulieu, Inglenook, Colony, Jacaré	133,000
NATIONAL DISTILLERS Almadén, C. Le Franc, Le Domaine	88,000
GUILD Cresta Blanca, Winemasters, Cribari	59,000
SIERRA Phillip Posson Sherry, Perelli-Minetti	54,000
COCA-COLA OF NEW YORK Franzia, Mogen David, Tribuno	42,800
COCA-COLA OF ATLANTA Sterling, Monterey Taylor, Great Western	39,300
MONT LA SALLE Christian Brothers	39,200
LA MONT M. La Mont, Mtn. Gold, Mtn. Peak	36,000
JOSEPH E. SEAGRAM Paul Masson	32,500
JFJ BRONCO JFJ Bronco, CC Vineyards	29,800
CANANDAIGUA *New York* Richards, Virginia Dare	22,500
DELICATO Delicato	22,000
CA GROWERS Setrakian, Growers, Le Blanc	19,100
GIUMARRA Giumarra, Breckenridge	12,500
GIBSON Gibson, Chateau Moreau	8,800
ROBERT MONDAVI Robert Mondavi	7,300
EAST-SIDE Conti-Royale, Royal Host	7,300
CHARLES KRUG Charles Krug, C. K. Mondavi	6,500
BEATRICE FOODS Assumption Abbey, Brookside	6,400
SEBASTIANI, Sebastiani	6,000
FREDONIA *New York* Old Waldorf, Star Brothers	4,800
WIDMER'S *New York* Widmer's, Lake Niagara	4,000
TURNER Turner	3,800
PAPAGNI Papagni, Yerba Buena	3,600
MONARCH *New York* Manischewitz	3,500
SONOMA Sonoma, Windsor, Tiburon	3,400
SOUVERAIN Souverain	3,300
WENTE Wente Bros.	3,200
GOLD SEAL *New York* Gold Seal, Henri Marchant	3,000
NORTON SIMON San Martin	3,000
WARNER *Michigan* Cask, Warner, Pol Pereaux	3,000
PARAMOUNT DISTILLERS *Ohio* Meier's	2,900
LOUIS MARTINI Louis Martini	2,700
CUCAMONGA CA Bonded Winery #1, Pierre Biane	2,500
J. SCHLITZ BREWING Geyser Peak, Summit	2,5000
MARTINI & PRATI Fountain Grove, Martini & Prati	2,500
MIRASSOU Mirassou	2,500
ROBIN FILS CIE *New York* Capri, Imperator	2500
WEIBEL Weibel, Leland Stanford	2,400
U.S. TOBACCO *Washington* Chateau Ste. Michelle	2,000
F. KORBEL Korbel	2,000
MONARCH *Georgia* Bojangles, King Cotton	2,000
LOST HILLS Barengo, Lost Hills	2,000
LAIRD CO *New Jersey* Sly Fox, Laird's	2,000
BERINGER Beringer, Los Hermanos	1,800
WIEDERKEHR *Arkansas* Wiederkehr, Granata	1,800

Acreage Planted in Principal Grape Varieties

		Alameda	Amador	Mendocino	Monterey	Napa
Barbera	1960	12	0	0	0	4
	1981	14	5	26	0	
Cabernet Sauvignon	1960	4	0	0	0	4
	1981	39	50	925	4,489	5,56
Chardonnay	1960	95	0	40	6	
	1981	129	1	901	3,140	4,2
Chenin Blanc	1960	6	0	0	19	2,
	1981	170	0	507	3,572	2,2
French Colombard	1960	75	0	219	0	3
	1981	67	0	1,102	804	4
Gamay Beaujolais	1960	26	0	1	0	
	1981	36	0	634	1,039	4
Gewurztraminer	1960	0	0	0	0	
	1981	7	0	228	990	5
Grey Riesling	1960	79	0	20	0	
	1981	421	0	197	678	3
Johannisberg Riesling	1960	20	0	0	0	1
	1981	17	0	377	3,350	1,5
Merlot	1960	0	0	0	0	
	1981	2	6	102	632	6
Muscat Blanc	1960	6	6	0	0	
	1981	30	5	3	140	
Napa Gamay	1960	14	0	24	0	4
	1981	71	0	110	964	1,
Petite Sirah	1960	86	0	155	0	1,7
	1981	110	0	541	2,205	8
Pinot Blanc	1960	45	0	0	15	
	1981	75	0	32	1,098	1
Pinot Noir	1960	29	0	17	3	1
	1981	76	0	323	1,971	2,3
Sauvignon Blanc	1960	67	0	23	0	2
	1981	161	54	462	1,212	1,
Semillon	1960	550	0	2	0	
	1981	298	1	23	624	
Sylvaner	1960	15	0	10	0	
	1981	58	0	26	656	
Zinfandel	1960	358	404	1,062	0	9
	1981	74	898	1,336	2,415	2,
All Other Grapes	1960	1,304	163	3,530	4	3,9
	1981	213	84	2,442	2,258	1,4
Totals	1960	2,791	573	5,103	47	9,
	1981	2,068	1,104	10,297	32,237	26,

California (by County), 1960, 1981 (as of January 1)

San Benito	San Luis Obispo	Santa Barbara	Santa Clara	Sonoma	Central Valley	All Others	Totals
0	0	0	16	38	37	78	229
0	47	0	0	66	18,892	243	19,305
75	0	0	26	84	0	11	615
508	942	1,092	184	4,480	2,651	1,952	22,881
43	0	0	10	16	9	6	295
979	506	1,514	53	4,504	577	460	17,033
59	0	0	10	54	0	0	402
97	524	331	38	833	22,839	1,113	32,279
0	0	0	162	341	578	7	1,700
0	58	0	98	1,217	39,919	543	44,252
20	0	0	0	0	0	0	61
501	60	355	85	606	130	83	3,994
52	0	0	0	23	0	0	117
262	93	325	5	1,153	18	42	3,645
0	0	0	0	0	40	2	164
85	90	0	10	124	369	146	2,424
58	0	0	0	20	0	0	201
327	185	1,749	31	1,464	371	811	10,186
0	0	0	0	0	0	0	2
0	166	275	0	517	211	63	2,667
40	0	0	0	0	42	12	106
0	40	21	25	64	889	49	1,397
0	0	0	35	31	0	31	630
0	91	0	1	397	1,022	945	4,751
0	0	0	203	1,493	581	174	4,440
0	112	63	101	1,072	5,499	727	11,254
145	0	0	69	40	0	0	336
170	0	30	65	168	76	20	1,930
142	0	0	40	105	0	26	531
764	96	724	94	2,839	55	67	9,402
25	0	0	34	261	73	28	788
15	522	261	8	919	1,324	610	7,269
9	0	0	95	155	244	0	1,276
24	24	12	67	173	1,445	15	2,848
127	0	0	177	78	34	23	596
122	20	169	26	49	171	4	1,411
158	472	0	469	3,964	7,380	8,300	23,516
204	1,008	75	123	4,664	12,657	3,558	29,148
771	22	0	1,880	3,896	45,100	19,838	80,484
501	125	23	560	2,513	97,777	6,791	108,765
1,684	494	0	3,226	10,599	54,118	28,536	116,489
4,559	4,709	7,019	1,574	27,822	200,892	18,242	336,841

Shipments of California Wine to All Markets, 1938–1979

(In Thousands of Gallons by Types of Wine)

Year	Table Wines	Over 14% Alcohol	Sparkling	Total
1938	16,299	38,591	89	54,979
1940	19,350	56,146	177	75,673
1945	20,537	59,821	552	80,910
1950	22,650	96,960	423	120,033
1955	26,440	90,770	789	118,000
1960	35,989	91,751	1,706	129,355
1961	38,639	94,270	1,931	143,840
1962	39,770	85,914	1,972	127,656
1963	43,820	88,323	2,151	134,294
1964	48,719	92,025	2,740	143,483
1965	52,657	87,461	3,216	143,334
1966	55,230	85,619	3,857	144,706
1967	61,590	82,603	4,779	148,972
1968	71,038	79,619	6,034	156,690
1969	87,581	75,900	8,906	172,386
1970	111,084	70,469	14,563	196,116
1971	138,043	70,938	16,694	225,657
1972	155,294	67,100	15,696	238,090
1973	164,338	63,273	15,010	242,622
1974	177,249	57,312	14,556	249,116
1975	197,173	59,915	15,439	272,527
1976	200,758	55,358	15,909	272,025
1977	216,162	53,655	17,954	287,771
1978	230,460	49,272	18,843	298,575
1979	250,892	43,397	19,881	314,170
1980	276,879	39,935	21,850	338,664
1981	297,039	36,922	23,971	357,932

Grape Production and Number of Bonded Wineries, by State

State	Tons Crushed (000s)*		Bonded Wineries†	
	1970	1980	1970	1980
California	1,506	2,891	240	470
New York	150	171	39	54
Washington	54	145	10	18
Pennsylvania	43	54	5	28
Michigan	58	48	12	20
Ohio	10	12	28	41
Arkansas	7	7	10	9
North Carolina	na	4	4	4
Missouri	na	4	20	19
Other States	-	3	67	159
Total United States	1,838	3,338	435	822

*Grapes crushed for all purposes. From 50% to 96% of the grapes crushed in Michigan, Pennsylvania, New York, and Washington are used for fruit juice and jelly, not for wine.
†Bonded wineries in other states in 1980: Colorado 1; Connecticut 4; Delaware 1; Florida 5; Georgia 4; Hawaii 1; Idaho 2; Illinois 5; Indiana 9; Iowa 14; Kentucky 3; Maryland 11; Massachusetts 3; Minnesota 2; Mississippi 4; New Hampshire 1; New Mexico 4; Oklahoma 4; Rhode Island 5; South Carolina 3; Texas 5; Vermont 1; Virginia 10; West Virginia 1; Wisconsin 9.

California Vintages

This vintage chart summarizes information presented and discussed in more detail on pages 29 through 33. The five wines covered are those whose aging characteristics and general quality levels vary the most according by vintage in California.

	'70	'71	'72	'73	'74
Cabernet Sauvignon					
Chardonnay					
Pinot Noir					
Zinfandel					
Amador County Zinfandel					

Good to great year

Average to slightly above average year

Below average year

Virtual loss